Nicole and Natalie Appleton were members of All Saints, who sold in excess of six million albums across the globe. They released their own album at the beginning of the year. Nicole and Natalie both live in London with their respective partners, Liam Gallagher and Liam Howlett, and their children, Gene and Rachel.

TOGETHER

NICOLE AND NATALIE APPLETON

PENGUIN BOOKS

PENGUIN BOOKS

Published by the Penguin Group
Penguin Books Ltd, 80 Strand, London WC2R ORL, England
Penguin Putnam Inc., 375 Hudson Street, New York, New York 10014, USA
Penguin Books Australia Ltd, 250 Camberwell Road,
Camberwell, Victoria 3124, Australia
Penguin Books Canada Ltd, 10 Alcorn Avenue, Toronto, Ontario, Canada M4V 3B2
Penguin Books India (P) Ltd, 11 Community Centre,
Panchsheel Park, New Delhi – 110 017, India
Penguin Books (NZ) Ltd, Cnr Rosedale and Airborne Roads,
Albany, Auckland, New Zealand
Penguin Books (South Africa) (Pty) Ltd, 24 Sturdee Avenue,
Rosebank 2196, South Africa

Penguin Books Ltd, Registered Offices: 80 Strand, London WC2R ORL, England

www.penguin.com

First published by Michael Joseph 2002
Published in Penguin Books 2003
1

Grateful acknowledgement is given for kind permission to reproduce lyrics from the following:
'The Wind Beneath My Wings', lyrics by Henley/Silbar, published by Warner/Chappell Music
Ltd. 'I Need You', lyrics by All Saints, published by Universal Music Publishing Ltd. 'Never
Ever', lyrics by Shaznay Lewis, Sean Mather and Robert Jaza Yeri, published by Universal
Music Publishing Ltd and BMG Music Publishing Ltd. 'I Know Where It's At', lyrics by
Shaznay Lewis and Melanie Blatt, published by Perfect Songs. 'Grace', lyrics by Robbie
Williams, published by Universal Music Publishing Ltd and EMI Music Publishing. 'Love Is
Where I'm From', lyrics by Robbie Williams and Nicole Appleton, published by Universal
Music Publishing Ltd, BMG Music Publishing Ltd and EMI Music Publishing.

Set in 11/13 pt Monotype Bembo
Typeset by Rowland Phototypesetting Ltd, Bury St Edmunds, Suffolk
Printed in Great Britain by Clays Ltd, St Ives plc

We dedicate this book to our sisters: Lee and Lori

CONTENTS

ACKNOWLEDGEMENTS

We would like to thank our family for all the love and support they have always given us.

Special thank you to Tara Joseph.

Thank you to Liam Howlett for strength, serenity and love.

Thank you to Liam Gallagher for giving me pure confidence again.

Gusi com in here.

Thank you to Rachel for keeping me smiling. I love you more than anything.

Thank you to Gene for being the most amazing light in my life. I love you.

Thank you to Roz for helping us remember the good times and heal the bad times.

ACKNOWLEDGEMENTS

1 - ICEBERG

NATALIE NICOLE

Something awful is going to happen in Rio.

Out of the window of the aeroplane I saw a flash of lightning tear the sky. I started to shake.

The PR from the record company came to sit beside me.

'Robbie Williams is such a lovely guy,' she said. 'You're so lucky to be engaged to him.'

'Yes,' I said. 'I'm going to be very happy.'

But even as I said the words, I did not believe them.

When we got to the hotel, I went straight to my room. The light on my telephone was flashing. I had a message. I knew it was from Rob. I was scared to play it. I walked around the room, unpacked, picked up the telephone and dialled for my message.

'It's me,' Rob said. 'Call me.'

I could hear in his voice that something wasn't right. He had been fine when I had left him six days earlier, and fine last night on the telephone, but now –

I dialled Rob's number in England.

'What's going on?' I asked him.

'We don't see each other enough,' Rob said. 'I think we should end our relationship.'

'We're engaged,' I said. 'Doesn't that mean anything to you?'

'Yes,' Rob said. 'It does. But I'm confused.'

'I knew something was going to happen.' It was all I could say. 'I knew it.'

I was very calm. I did not shout. Rob had made up his mind, there was nothing for us to talk about.

'Is that it then?' I asked him.

His voice was very small. 'Yes it is.'

I put the phone down, and I started to cry, to howl. I had five days in Brazil before I could go home. How could he do this when I was so far away and I had so much work to do? Why did he do it over the telephone? Why couldn't he wait until he saw me? What on earth had happened in the last few hours? I was crying so loudly, the others heard me and came to the door.

'Nic, are you all right?'

'Let us in.'

'What's going on in there?'

I didn't want to tell them, I didn't want anyone to know. They loved Rob and our relationship was seen as something really positive. I couldn't bear for everyone to know that it was over. I refused to let anyone in. I wouldn't speak or open the door.

NATALIE NICOLE

I was sunbathing by the pool. All Saints were doing a circuit of South America and this was our only chance to get a bit of sun. But upstairs in her hotel bedroom, my little sister was crying her heart out. I couldn't just sit there. I went back upstairs.

'Let me in, let me in,' I kept begging her.

I was in pain with her. When Nic's heart breaks, my heart breaks too.

Eventually, the storm subsided a little and I unlocked the door. When Nat, Mel and Shaznay hugged me, I just cried more. I was jet-lagged and shocked. Shaznay went to the mini bar and got me a drink. No one knew what to do. It took an hour for them to pull the ragged parts of me together. I kept thinking: I have to work, I have to work, when all I wanted was to be at home and hidden under my duvet. It was 2 p.m., we were not working until the next day.

'Can we go to the bar in the hotel?' I asked. 'I want to get hammered.'

I took my engagement ring off. I had a tan and the ring left a white band around my finger. I couldn't take that off. It stared clearly back at me: you were engaged to Rob and now you are not.

The bar was closed so we ended up in the sandwich centre. Melanie was six months pregnant so she was not drinking but, together with Nat, our assistant Shiara Juthan and our tour manager, Johnny Buckland, I got plastered on tequila – shot after shot after shot. I had twenty shots in two hours. I was loud and careless and totally unlike myself. I was trying to obliterate myself.

I was so angry with Rob, so filled with despair and so panicked at the thought that I had to give interviews and perform the next day – so many people were counting on me. I wanted to numb out totally. I wanted everything to disappear.

'I want to go for a walk on the beach,' I said.

It was 4 p.m. The sun was shining, the beach was deserted. We started walking but I fell behind. They were all up ahead. I was such a puppet, never doing what

I wanted. I had totally blurred the line between my personal life and the band. It is all my fault, it is all my fault. The words were running around in my head. I turned towards the water and started walking into the ocean. I wondered what it would be like to immerse myself completely. I could just walk and walk and walk.

'Nicole,' Shiara screamed at me.

She ran into the sea and pulled me out. 'What are you doing?' she asked.

'I'm going to keep walking.'

It seemed so simple. Just one foot in front of the other. Walking away from it all. Then the tears, again. I was far from home, far from anything that might comfort me. I had no answers to anything, my life was a mess.

Shiara steered me back to the hotel. My clothes were soaking, so I went to my room. There were no messages from Rob – not on the hotel telephone and not on my mobile. I couldn't stay there, waiting for him not to call me. My heart was shattering.

I went back to the bar and had a few more drinks. Shaznay and I played a game with our hands. I laughed. I was out of it. I didn't care.

When Shaznay and Melanie went to bed, I stayed up with the others. I was still hard at it at 7 a.m. and the first interviews were due to start at 2 p.m. I went back to my room. I felt like a zombie but couldn't sleep. My heart was going to explode.

At 2 p.m., Shiara knocked on the door.

'Are you all right?' she asked.

'I haven't slept.'

'You've got to eat something,' she said. 'You have interviews to do down by the pool.'

4

Food? The thought of it turned my stomach.

'Tomato soup,' I said. 'I might be able to eat that.'

Shiara brought me the soup and I tried to get some down, but the mixture of alcohol and pain had twisted my stomach into a knot.

'Let me sit it out a bit longer,' I said. 'I'll meet you all down by the pool.'

Rob, hangover, guilt – it was a deadly concoction. I put on a pair of dungarees and looked at myself in the mirror. I looked like a child in a clown's outfit. My face was gaunt, my eyes were sunken in. I tied my hair back. I always take care with how I look, but that day I looked so awful I didn't care. I put on a big pair of black sunglasses and went down to the pool.

I had the sensation that it was not me walking out into the hallway and going down in the lift. My body was doing it, but I wasn't there. The girls and ten Brazilian journalists were all seated around a big white plastic table.

'Hi,' I said. 'I'm sorry I'm late but I've been feeling unwell.'

I sat down. I looked around the table at each of the journalists' faces, then I burst into tears and ran from the pool and back to my room.

Look what Rob's done to me, that was all I could think, sitting alone in my room and howling. He had turned me into a freak. I had been his shoulder to cry on, much as he had been mine.

I rang Rob. I told him I hated him.

'You've lost the best thing that ever happened to you,' I yelled.

Rob was very quiet. He hates confrontation. I got off the telephone feeling slightly better. In the mirror my eyes were swollen and red. I felt ugly and rejected. I had a show to do.

I went to the TV studio in the same unflattering dungarees. As we got out of the car, we were swarmed by fans. Beautiful suntanned girls in skimpy clothes. I felt hideous.

'Nicole,' one of the girls called out in broken English. 'I just want you to know you're so lucky to be with Robbie.'

The contrast couldn't have been sharper – the mess that was my life and the way the world saw me. To them I seemed to have everything – everything that would make their lives glamorous and full. In reality I had nothing: a band I hated and, now, rejected by the man I loved.

Backstage, each of us had a different make-up artist. I sat there like a doll, as a woman with orange hair worked away at my face. Dirty make-up sponge, big apple-red Aunt Sally cheeks, orange eye shadow. She painted my eyebrows light brown and smeared blue eye liner around my eyes. No mascara.

Melanie came in, looked at me and burst out laughing. Then everyone came in to see.

'Do you want to change it?' Shiara asked.

'No,' I said, 'I don't care.'

I wanted to go in front of the cameras looking as awful as I felt inside. In the midst of this crazy machine that went on around us, it was a way I could be real. Look, my grotesquely painted face said to the world, I am in pain.

2 - STAR WARS

NATALIE NICOLE

I always wanted a brother. When Nicole turned out to be a girl I was disappointed. I was a tomboy. I liked to be out of doors, making things, imagining. I wanted a playmate – not a tag-along girl.

My favourite game was *Star Wars*. I used to turn the kitchen table upside down and put a sheet over it, then I tipped the chairs up with their legs in the air – and I had a marvellous ship. I was Han Solo, a space pirate, rebellious and cool; Nic was Luke Skywalker. There was only one problem. Her hair was too long. It ruined the effect.

'I'm going to cut your hair so you look like Luke,' I announced.

I got Dad's gardening scissors and took them back to Nic.

'If you don't let me cut your hair,' I threatened, 'then you're not coming to my birthday party.'

Nic was five years old. My birthday was months away, but she was a gullible, easy-going playmate. When I had finished with her, Nic looked more like a brother than a sister. Success. I was delighted. Nic was not so sure.

Neither were our parents when they saw what I had done.

'We were in *Star Wars*,' I tried to explain. 'I was

Han Solo and Nic needed to look like Luke Skywalker.'

I was severely told off. It was a small price to pay.

NATALIE NICOLE

When we look back at old pictures, it is always me and Nat together, like bookends. But if we weren't sisters, I don't know if we would be friends. We are totally unalike. As children we played together, but I never got to choose the games. Nat's always been in charge.

Eating sweets on the bus, Nat would make me share mine with her. Then, when we got home, she would eat all of hers by herself. (How delighted I was when, one day, she left her sweets on the bus.) Nat nicknamed us Butch and Boss when we were small – naturally she was Boss – and the bottom line was that I had to do whatever she said or I couldn't go to her birthday parties.

NATALIE NICOLE

I called her Butch because it sounded important. I wore hats all the time. I had a beret, a bowler hat, a woolly hat and a turban. Whenever I put on my favourite hat (a bell-shaped fisherman's hat in bright red and blue) it turned me into the Boss – it gave me absolute power.

When I was seven – and Nic was five – our parents separated. They had moved together from Britain to Canada during the sixties; now they had to decide where to live and what to do with their four daughters. They split us between them. Dad moved back to England with Nic and Lori, who was nine. I stayed in Canada with Mum and Lee, then fifteen.

The family was split. It was terrible. Everything felt wrong. My parents were separated – Nic and I were separated. I coped by shutting off and focussing all my adoration on my mum.

Mum met Dr Stanley at the hospital where she worked. He arrived at our house soon after Dad left with a puzzle, a teddy bear and an ice-cream sandwich, called a Klondike Bar. Mum was never romantic or happy with Dad, but with Stanley she became a different woman.

I watched Mum become a person, not just a wife, not just a mother. A vivid, shining woman. She thrived on Stanley's love, becoming calmer and more composed. Mum had long auburn hair and – in her cowboy hat, dark jeans and rodeo shirt – she looked, to me, like Sue Ellen from *Dallas*. She was beautiful.

We lived in a huge new condominium. Two semi-circular buildings, thirty storeys high with underground parking. We used to ride the lift every day and I would stretch and stretch to reach the PH button – I always wanted to go there, to the Penthouse, but I was never tall enough.

NATALIE NICOLE

Lori and I were taken to London. Dad did his best, he went out of his way to make sure we were entertained. He took us to all the sights – to the Tate Gallery, and Trafalgar Square to feed the pigeons. We climbed trees on Hampstead Heath and watched the Christmas lights come on in Oxford Street. We went to Butlin's and Brighton and to the fair. He tried to make up for the fact that he and Mum no longer lived together; that our family was torn in two.

Dad resented Mum, bitterly. We were not allowed to talk about her; it was too painful for him. He insisted Lori and I cut off from her and, if we were unable to, we had to keep our feelings (all that missing) to ourselves. It was hard. One day I was watching television and there was a woman on the screen who reminded me of Mum.

'The woman on TV looks like Mum,' I said.

Dad sent me straight to my room.

NATALIE NICOLE

Separated from my sisters and living in Canada, I went to so many different schools. It was never easy for me. I didn't want to go to school because the other children were so hard on me. I never felt accepted. I used to ask them:

'Can I please go to lunch with you?'

But no one wanted to hang out with me. I was the new kid and kids can be cruel. I used to take ornaments from home – china figures of Snow White and the seven dwarves – and give them to girls in my class to try to befriend them. I drew pictures for them too.

NATALIE NICOLE

Mum's relationship with Stanley lasted, on and off, for two years, but the strain of separating the family was too much for her. She came back to England to live with us. It was the best thing in the world. Around her, I could relax and be a child. I basked in her attention. Mum loved us equally, unconditionally. She made me feel special and deeply loved.

Soon after Mum got back, I kissed a boy for the first time. His name was Billy. We were in the maze outside school. My best friend Athena challenged me to a dare.

'Kiss him.'

'No, you kiss him.'

Billy stood there.

'I'll kiss him if you do.'

'Okay, you do it first,' I said, 'then me.'

Athena kissed Billy on the mouth, then I did. He had brown hair. I thought he was fantastic. I wanted him to really like me. I thought and thought of what I could do. The idea – when it came to me – seemed brilliant. I stole Mum's favourite silk scarf, wrapped it up in one of my sister Lee's empty hair-dye boxes and gave it to Billy.

'This is for you to give to your mum,' I said.

Mum had just come back to live with us. She was amazing. I thought Billy would feel the same way about his mum – that giving a present to his mum would be his favourite thing too. Billy looked embarrassed and uncomfortable. Then he opened the little square box, found the scarf and waved it around and around for all his friends to see.

NATALIE NICOLE

We were all living together again – Mum, Dad, Lee, Lori, Nic and I. I had my playmate back. Nic and I created our own world. We left the house together in the morning and didn't come back until it was dark. We didn't need anyone else.

We used to line up my Matchbox cars and count

them. Twenty cars. I loved my cars; I used to clean them all the time and practise parallel parking. Then Nic and I would pick our favourites in turn – a maroon Rolls-Royce was usually Nic's first choice, and I went for the green Cortina. We would form the cars into gangs. The red cars were girls and the blue cars were boys. When we played with the cars, they lived like they were people. We used to hold them by their back wheels and make them talk to each other. My cars were always the leaders.

Now that I was back under Dad's roof, he lavished his attention on me. I was his favourite child, the apple of his eye – a fact he didn't try to conceal. I looked like Mum – I had the same colouring – and I think that is why he always favoured me. He used to call me Fat Cat.

When we all lived in Canada, although Nic was smaller and more in need of carrying than I was, it was always me he carried – no matter how far we had to walk. Now if Dad saw something in a shop he thought I would like, he would buy it for me and bring it home. He only did this for me. He didn't care that the others would feel left out.

Mum was the centre of my world. I adored her. Dad singling me out made me uncomfortable. I wished he would stop.

'You're Dad's favourite,' my sister Lori said, over and over. 'It's not fair. You know you are.'

Lori hated the inequality. Worse, she blamed me for being Dad's favourite. One evening, just before dinner, Nic and I ran after the ice-cream van and came home clutching cones. Dad was furious. He told us we were not allowed to wander off. He snatched the ice creams away and spanked Nic. He didn't hit me.

I felt guilty. Separated and set apart. Dad thought that by spoiling me I would feel secure and loved. But it was the opposite; it created a rift and made Lori hate me.

Lori became increasingly spiteful about the way I looked. If I went to sit next to her, she would walk away saying:

'You're too skinny to sit with.'

I looked at my thin arms with their blue veins and I thought she was right. I was disgusting.

'I'm not walking down the street with her,' she would complain to Mum. 'She's a freak, look how skinny she is, it's embarrassing.'

Alone with me, she would taunt: 'How can anyone like you? You're too ugly to like.'

Then she would point at the bright blue vein in my left arm.

'You're so skinny you're going to die.'

I lifted Matchbox cars as weights to try to create a muscle in my arm. I hoped it would make the hated vein go away. I found Lee's cover-up stick and, from then on, I used it to plaster the vein with make-up. I couldn't bear the sight of it. It seemed monstrous.

Lori was constantly drawing attention to my big bottom lip so I was always biting on it, sucking it into my mouth, trying to hide it. Sitting in front of the TV, I would become absorbed in a programme and forget to hold my lip in; it would hang down and then, suddenly, I would hear Lori:

'Look, everyone. Look at Natalie's lip.'

I didn't know what to do with myself. I was convinced I was a freak.

'You're fat,' I would retort.

I wouldn't go out of my way to call attention to Lori's weight but, when she goaded me, there it was. The hatred sat between us.

'I want surgery,' I begged Mum. 'I want my lip cut in half.'

I used to go to bed thinking of ways to make Lori stop. I used to pray to God at night: please make Lori love me.

Lori's tormenting made me embarrassed about my weight and the way I looked – a hang-up that has lingered. When, years later with All Saints, the media portrayed me as a beautiful woman, it felt weird. Inside I felt like the same insecure, unattractive young Nat. The outer and inner did not match.

I never fought back against Lori. Instead I was mean to Nic. I thought that was what big sisters were supposed to do. I would punch Nic to make her cry, but she never would. In the end I used to cry because I felt guilty. Then Nic would stick up for me when Lori was bullying me – no matter how horrid I had been to her. Nic and I could never be angry or upset with each other for long. That is our bond.

NATALIE NICOLE

When I was born in 1974, nineteen months after Nat, Dad already had three girls – he didn't want another child – certainly not another girl. He had nothing left to give. I was pushed aside. As a result I learned to keep to myself. I never made a fuss.

Lee, as the first born, was always special to Dad. Lori, born next, was very similar to Dad – that bonded them. And Nat was his favourite. Dad loved Natalie best and spoiled her. I accepted it as normal; that was the way it was. We called her Veruca Salt after the girl in *Willy Wonka and the Chocolate Factory* – the one who is always saying: 'I want this, I want that.' Demanding and powerful, what she wanted she got.

Nat was treated differently. When we fed the pigeons in Trafalgar Square, we both jumped in the fountain and got soaking wet. Going home on the bus, it was uncomfortable and cold. Dad took us into C&A and bought Nat a set of dry clothes.

'What about me?' I asked him.

'Yours will dry in the sun.'

I refused to cry. There was nothing I could do about it. Except pull deeper into myself. It made me self-reliant.

I was Nat's playmate; she couldn't see how much Dad's favouritism hurt me. I never said anything. When Mum was in Canada with Nat, Lori was like a mother to me; she protected me whenever she could.

NATALIE NICOLE

Things were not good between Mum and Dad – he did not make her feel loved. But I never thought they would split up again. When, after a few months, Mum went back to Canada I was horrified. She left us four girls with Dad. For the first time in my life, I was separated from my mum.

Nic was always sunnier than I was, lighter – she took whatever came along and made the best of it. She was happy inside herself and anything else was a bonus. For me, being separated from Mum was an agony. I felt a limb had been cut off. A part of me was with her all the time. I was cast adrift, bereft.

Dad, too, was lost without Mum; aimless and bruising. He wanted us to hate her as much as he did. Then he could get some power back, then he could feel vindicated and in control. The others went along with Dad's wishes. They rarely mentioned Mum, but I could not, I would not. I loved her so much, life without her was empty. I cried for her, longed for her.

One day Lori and Dad ganged up on me; Nic went along with them.

'Do you hate Mum?' they asked me.

I would not answer them.

'Do you hate her? Do you, do you?'

I would not betray her, but she was not around. They were – and I needed them to love me.

'Do you want to see her?'

I could not say anything.

'Natalie, do you want to see Mum?'

I was scared of my feelings, scared of their reaction. I took a piece of paper out of the drawer and, in tiny writing, I wrote my truth: yes.

Dad screamed at me. I was terrified. He was the only parent I had, my only security. He was red in the face, furious. I felt my world collapsing.

'I was just pretending,' I said. 'I don't really want to see her.'

With that Dad's face, his whole being, softened. I had said the right thing; I was accepted again. Dad put me up on his shoulders and we all went down the road together to get sweets.

Dad cut Mum's face out of all the photographs. When she rang, he would not let her speak to us.

'Your mother doesn't love you,' he told us. 'If she cared about you, she wouldn't have left you.'

Dad took good care of us. If we were sick, he would set the alarm so he could get up and give us our medicine at the right time. But he had a negative mind, he was always moaning and nagging. And he had a temper.

He was living alone and bringing up four girls, missing his wife but refusing to acknowledge it. Sometimes the pressure was immense. Nic and I clung to each other, in a casual sisterly I-can-take-you-or-leave-you way. We never told each other we loved each other – something that we find difficult even today – but we looked to each other for everything.

After a few months, Mum decided to move back in with Dad to bring us up. She arrived at the airport with bags of clothes. Fashionable, funky clothes she had selected for each of us with love. I remember the belt buckle she gave me. And the new satchels Nic and I got – mine had Donald Duck on the front, Nic's had Mickey Mouse. I treasured my gifts.

Back in my bedroom, I laid out my presents and loved them. They were perfect. They lived on top of the dressing table, joining the bag with the picture of the Golden Gate Bridge – the bag Mum bought me when she and Stanley had their first holiday in San Francisco. My favourite things.

Mum was home again. I treasured everything about her. I wanted to be with her all the time. I followed her from room to room, talking to her, claiming her attention. She was the closest person in my world – still is – the connection I felt with her then was absolute.

And I knew she loved me – not more than the others, we are all the same to her, her brood, her loves. But I loved her more than any of the others did, felt the biggest, strongest connection. I was utterly devoted to her. I put her on a pedestal. She was beautiful, a princess.

NATALIE NICOLE

Looking back, I see that being separated from Mum so early, I learned to distance myself. I was a quiet child, an observer. But whenever we had visitors I wanted to dance for them. While everyone sat around watching *Top of the Pops*, I danced the whole way through it, imagining I had an audience and a troupe of dancers following me. My imaginary audience gave me all the attention and validation I craved. I did intricate steps and rhythmic gymnastic moves. When I danced, I came alive.

I was an avid fan of the TV programme *Fame* and I loved the movie *Flashdance*. When I was given an audition at the Sylvia Young Stage School, I prepared a routine to my *Flashdance* record. I was move-perfect. But when I turned up for the audition, I discovered there was no record player.

'We have a tape recorder here,' Sylvia Young said. She turned it on and out came a piece of music I had never heard before. 'Can you improvise to this?'

Improvise? I danced with my whole heart – I even managed to incorporate a cartwheel into my routine. I desperately wanted to be given a place. I needed something to make me feel special. There was nothing I wanted more.

After days of waiting, the letter finally arrived.

'It's good news, Nic,' Mum said.

I could hardly believe it. My dream was coming true. The night before I started I got out all my new dance clothes and tried them on. My first pair of ballet shoes – housed in an orange bag with a ballerina on it – jazz shoes, tap shoes, a black leotard and pink tights. Nat, Mum and Lori watched me put my bag together as I told them over and over how excited I was.

The Sylvia Young Stage School had just opened and it was very small when I joined – just sixty pupils, only three of whom were in my class. It was the best school I'd ever been to. After my first day, Mum came to pick me up in our tan-coloured Toyota Tercell.

'I'm so happy,' I told her. 'I can't wait to go back.'

In the kitchen, we emptied my dance bag on to the floor. Like Cinderella I had come home with only one of each shoe, I had left the others behind at school.

Emma Bunton, now known as Baby Spice, was in the class below me. She was always a sweetheart – she looked exactly as she does now: sweet and fresh-faced. Denise Van Outen, who went on to become a TV presenter, was in the class above. Denise was prim and proper; she used to sleep with her hair in rollers and always came to school looking perfect. She was vain and full of herself, a typical stage-school child.

Letitia Dean, who plays Sharon in *EastEnders*, was one of the older girls at the school. She hung around with a girl who was identical to her; they looked like twins and could both sing really well. Letitia's mum was our school matron; she was strict but kind. If you were wearing eye make-up or chewing gum, she stopped you in the corridor. But if you were ill, Letitia's mum let you sleep in a bed in her office. When there was a particularly horrible lesson to be endured, the bed in Letitia's mum's office was a haven. Feigning a headache or stomach-ache, I knew I would be sent there.

I hated the public-speaking classes and tried to get out of them whenever I could. Although I loved to be watched when I danced, I felt self-conscious and inadequate giving a speech. Dancing was a release, an escape – I could get lost in my own world – and I was good at it. Public speaking was a torment.

Our teacher, Jackie Stoker, was strict and mean. We had to have a speech prepared and each week, randomly, she would select one of us to speak in front of the class. It was hell. If you did not have your speech prepared, she went ballistic. Her voice was so clear, every vowel pronounced. Being shouted at by her was vicious.

NATALIE NICOLE

I saw Nic having a good time at Sylvia Young's, so I begged Mum to let me go too. While most of the girls at Sylvia Young's were well-off, we were living in a flat in Kilburn. One day my class was taking part in a commercial for Nikon cameras and we had to be at the school extra early at 7 a.m. One of the girls lived two hours away from school and asked if she could stay the night. I was very excited.

We didn't have a spare room so Mum made her up a bed in the lounge, and the next morning Dad got up especially early to cook her scrambled eggs. We did everything we could to make her stay at our house as lovely as possible. But the following day at school she told everyone how small our flat was. I felt deeply ashamed. I tried so hard, but I ended up feeling worthless. It is a trap I can still fall into – hating everything about myself.

Mum worked hard to send us to private schools and

the children we mixed with were the children of doctors and lawyers. Our father was a car salesman. At stage school Nic developed a taste for a crowd. But I never felt good enough or pretty enough. The competitive atmosphere gnawed away at my confidence.

NATALIE NICOLE

Advertising directors would regularly come to the school looking for children to star on TV or at the theatre. Nat always tried her hardest – she was a grafter even as a child, she put her heart and soul into everything she did – but although she had a lovely singing voice, she never got the parts.

Nat's feeling of being let down by the school was highlighted by the fact that, initially, I was the youngest child at Sylvia Young's and this guaranteed me work. My first commercial was for a toy called Lights Alive. It was filmed in Covent Garden. I had just had my ears pierced – with gold studs – and I felt so cool. I loved the whole experience.

In the end, the company making the commercial went bankrupt and I was paid with one of the toys. It had revolving lights and Nat and I used it to create our Barbie discos. Nat and I spent hours dressing and undressing our Barbies in preparation for our disco.

More commercials followed and this helped pay the school fees at Sylvia Young's. I was cast as an extra in the films *Brazil* and *Santa Claus, The Movie* and sang in the West End musical *Joseph and the Amazing Technicolor Dreamcoat*.

Stage school was the start of finding a light inside myself. I was not good at school work; I was street-smart but in the classroom my attention span was minimal, I was always thinking about other things, looking but not listening, miles away. But when I danced I was in my element. At Sylvia Young's I began to feel I had something inside me – something worthwhile.

Nat and I danced at Sylvia Young's two days a week. Then, two evenings a week, we went to the London Studios, a dance studio in King's Cross. We were the youngest there. I loved dancing. Loved it more than anything. It came very naturally to me and I had such a drive to do it.

But the discipline side of being a dancer escaped me. When I did my bronze tap exam, I couldn't find matching shoes so one of my tap shoes had a really high heel and the other was flat. I tried to cover them up with woollen leg warmers, but when Mum saw that I was wearing odd shoes, she freaked. Without her saying a word, I knew how furious she was. The look on her face terrified me.

All the other girls had their hair in tidy buns and their tutus were pristine – even with matching shoes I could never have managed to look that neat. Appearance was part of the exam and Mum was convinced they would fail me because of my shoes. I was so scared but, in the end, I was awarded a Distinction – the youngest to get a bronze and, later, silver medals in ballet, tap and modern dance. It was a fantastic feeling – a mixture of pride in my dancing and relief that I had not let Mum down.

Often, I stood out in class at the London Studios because of the scruffy way I looked. Almost all the girls wore the standard black leotards and pink tights, but my favourite costume was Lee's leopard-skin bathing suit over ballet tights. I never looked neat, but I danced better than anyone else.

My dance teacher at the London Studios, Sandra Dorling, was caring – she never made me feel bad, but even she pulled me aside one day to say she felt my costume was too loud for ballet. Ballet is a very strict discipline – and I didn't want to offend my teacher by getting it wrong. I wanted to please her. I used to come home with my toes bleeding from where I had been dancing on them hour after hour. Sandra Dorling said bleeding toes were the sign of a good dancer – a dancer who does not quit. I stuffed the toes of my shoes with cotton wool and, the next day, I did it all over again.

NATALIE NICOLE

The person I looked up to – as well as Mum – was my older sister Lee. Nearly a whole decade older, she was cool, fashionable and exciting to be around. She had her own bedroom. It seemed huge. She loved the band Kiss and had painted their name in spiky black letters across one wall of her room.

Lee was a hairdresser and each week she would come home with her hair a different punky shade: blue, red, yellow, pink. She was always out – either partying or working in a nightclub. As she got ready each evening, Nic and I would sit watching her in the big mirror as she put on her make-up. She used to run around the house in her lingerie. She was so sexy.

I learned a lot from watching Lee. As if through osmosis, her sexiness and lust for life seeped into me. I loved Lee's things: all the glass and plastic pots and bottles. Liquids, creams and colours she put on her hair, face and body. The colours and textures of the clothes in her wardrobe, her jewellery, belts, scarves and bags. It was a world I could not wait to enter. Glamorous, exotic, grown-up.

Once I sneaked into Lee's room and tried on her favourite ankle boots: electric blue with tassles. I looked at myself in the mirror – I felt I was going to explode. I looked fantastic. Down the stairs and out into the garden. I felt huge and mysterious. I walked on to the lawn and felt the pointy heels pierce the grass. I looked down. Lee's precious boots were covered with mud.

I didn't know how to get dirt off boots. All I knew was that I had to get them back upstairs as quickly as possible. I hid the muddied boots under Lee's bed.

My fascination with Lee's clothing stemmed partly from the fact that I sometimes wore hand-me-downs. Lori got the new clothes, they were handed to me second and, when I outgrew them, they went to Nic.

One time Mum bought Lori a really lovely pair of beige corduroy trousers. I loved them and didn't want to wait until they were passed down to me, so I took a pair of scissors and shortened them to fit. Unfortunately, I cut them too short and ruined them for everybody. No one got to wear those corduroy trousers.

NATALIE NICOLE

I had been at Sylvia Young's for three years when Melanie Blatt arrived. On her first day, we both laughed at the same joke. We clicked straight away. Melanie and I found each other's eleven-year-old humour funny. We shared an extraordinary amount of likes and dislikes – including certain girls at the school.

Mel and I both had straggly brown ponytails and we slept in our school uniforms so we could spend an extra hour in bed. We were like two peas in a pod: inseparable best friends. The most precious thing I got out of Sylvia Young's was meeting Mel.

Once I got suspended for nicking someone's Wotsits – I got caught because my fingers were orange. Being a true friend, Mel took the week off to hang out with me. We perfected tap dancing on top of Mel's family's houseboat in King's Cross and composed a song with a tambourine and a guitar with only three strings.

For our end of term show, Mel and I performed a play based on the movie *The Revenge of the Nerds*. It was the story of two American nerds who were not accepted by the cool crowd. We dressed up in brown cords and thick tweed ties. We slicked our hair back and wore horn-rimmed glasses. The play was so good that, for years afterwards, girls called us the Nerds.

NATALIE NICOLE

The thing I loved to do most was sing. That was when something opened up inside me. I felt I could express myself – I could really let rip and there was a sense of freedom, as if I was soaring. Singing gave me a way to rise above what I saw as my inadequacies. It was a way to connect up to all the parts of myself – to feel rich instead of impoverished and wanting.

The only other thing I was good at was reading books. I was a boffin – into studying hard. I used to dream of becoming an orthodontist. I tore the tooth page out of the encyclopedia and spent hours drawing pictures of mouths and teeth. I wanted to get good grades and be a dentist.

In Canada I had been good at maths and they put me in a class with children a year older. But at Sylvia Young's nobody cared if you were academically bright or not. They all wanted to be actors and pop stars. If you weren't good at performing and dancing you were nothing. We did school work three days a week and the other two days were vocational. I stopped using my brain. What was the point? It only made me unpopular.

Worse, I was still not attractive – the cardinal sin. Most of the girls were blonde-haired, blue-eyed god-desses (Baby Spice Emma Bunton and TV presenter Dani Behr, for example). Being a gangly mousy geek with big ears set me apart. It was a miserable time for me.

I got some work – I appeared in *Grange Hill* and commercials, but somehow I didn't make the popularity grade. If you weren't blonde with lipstick, you weren't going anywhere. I was gawky. The school didn't give me the time of day.

Most of the students were girls and those who looked less than perfect lived with a lot of teasing. Weight was an issue – there was an emphasis on dancing and, therefore, a lot of time spent wearing lycra ballet tights. If you were even slightly heavy, you were considered overweight, and along with that went all the assumptions that you ate too much and were generally undisciplined and out of control. Fat was the very worst label a girl could have.

One girl joined the school overweight. She had a fantastic singing voice and a pretty face – but she was the biggest in our class. Everyone teased her and called her names. I laughed with them. But I agonized over it.

At home with Mum, I would go over what had

happened and how bad it made me feel. I felt for the new girl. I could understand her pain and so I felt guilty because I didn't stick up for her. I allowed her to be teased because I wanted to be a part of it. I hated being the one left out; to be included, even for a moment, was a sort of bliss.

It is frightening the way we criticized each other – we felt we had to be perfect and, oppressed, we took it out on each other. To any girl now I would say: do not get sucked into a destructive mentality. Girls need to support each other to feel good about themselves. The most important thing is how you feel inside.

When I was thirteen, a new girl, Samantha Janus, arrived in the class. I instantly thought she was cool. She was wearing grey ribbed tights with grey ankle boots. She read from her public speaking book with attitude, balancing on one leg. At the break I took my chance.

'Come and sit with me,' I said.

I told her about everyone in the class. She was as insecure as I was – she was just pretending to be hard. By the end of the break we were firm friends. Sam came from a tough school and I was intrigued by her attitude. She took no shit. She was ready for action.

Sam was my saviour. My first best friend. We did everything together. We have stayed close ever since – falling out spectacularly from time to time – but it is a friendship we always come back to.

NATALIE NICOLE

As Nat's best friend, Sam took the same liberties with me that Nat did. One day she asked me to go to Oxford Street with her after school so she could buy a birthday present for her stepdad. It was a vocational day at school and Sam decided to wear her tap shoes; I was wearing leather jazz shoes. After making me wait for hours in changing rooms while she tried on everything she vaguely liked the look of, Sam came up with a plan.

'Let's swap shoes,' she said.

'Yours will be too big for me,' I protested.

She would not listen.

'You have to wear them,' she said.

She forced her size 5 feet into my size 1 jazz shoes (stretching them out of shape for ever) and made me teeter the whole way home in her huge and noisy tap shoes. I accepted the treatment meted out to me. I felt powerless.

NATALIE NICOLE

Mum and Dad were still not getting on. Mum craved life, excitement, experience. Dad seemed shut down to life; frightened, he thought small, always saw the negative. I watched Mum shrivel again. The warm bright woman who had returned to us became shadowy and withdrawn.

Mum would lie on the couch and sleep; it was an effort for her to get up. Seeing her lying there like that one day, Dad went off to get his camera. He took a photograph of her – and afterwards he would show it to me.

'That's your mother,' he would say.

3 - CHEERLEADER

NATALIE NICOLE

When Mum asked me what I thought about moving to New York, I was horrified. I cried.

'You're young, you don't understand,' Lee said, but I did understand. It meant I had to leave school. I was twelve years old – I had been at Sylvia Young's for four years. I didn't want to leave. I had been to so many new schools; I knew what it was like to be the new kid and it frightened me.

'What about Mel?'

My best friend at school – Melanie Blatt. I didn't want to leave her behind. This was my life.

'Darling, I'm sorry. I can't stay with your father any more,' Mum said.

She tried to make it easier for me by giving me the option.

'You can stay here – with Dad and Lori.'

What was Nat doing? I needed to know.

'I'm going with Mum,' Nat said.

If I stayed in London I lost them both. It was a difficult decision. Going to America I would be losing so much, but I didn't want to live without my mum. Not again.

Mel and I promised to write to each other, but I don't think either of us could absorb what was happening. It was too much to take in. We didn't know when we would see each other again. The emotions were too big.

29

My most vivid memory is of our big blue suitcases on the platform at Victoria Station. Nat, Mum and I – all our belongings crammed inside cases – being shipped away. When we landed at Newark Airport, our suitcases were searched. In the customs hall, our lives were laid out on trestle tables in front of everyone.

Our stuff was squashed in. As one of the officers wrestled with the strap wrapped around Nat's case, she threw a hissing fit.

'If you take my stuff out, you put it back!' she yelled at the customs' officer. (They never forgot her. Years later, when we went back as All Saints, they said: 'Hello, Nat.' It isn't every day a fourteen-year-old girl lets rip in customs.)

I sat silently on the edge of the conveyor belt, embarrassed and sad.

In New York we stayed with Norman, a friend Mum had known and written to for years. He had a large nine-bedroom house which he had not decorated since his first marriage. It was very seventies. Orange and brown with a red velvet couch and shag-pile carpet everywhere. Norman had three sons, the youngest of which, Dean, lived in a room at the bottom of the house.

Dean was eighteen and worked in the games room in one of the hotels. He always had loads of quarters and Nat and I used to grab handfuls and spend them playing Pacman at the hotel where Mum worked. We rarely saw Dean – if he was not at the hotel, he was fixing his car in the garage. Occasionally he came upstairs to have dinner with us. I am sure he felt Nat and I were in the way.

There was a big white, skinny cat called Misty. That

was one good thing. A cat to stroke and play with. I always adored animals – felt happy, peaceful and 'right' with them somehow. Misty was a consolation for me when so much else was unknown.

NATALIE NICOLE

It was the summer of 1987. We had been in America for two weeks, when Mum took us to enrol at the local high school. Elenville High was cavernous. On that first day it had the size and ambiance of a prison. At Sylvia Young's there had been a hundred pupils – here there were thousands. Nic started to cry.

While we were sitting in the head teacher's office, a student walked in – a huge guy with a mohican gelled on his head in shades of brown and blond. He was scary.

'Oh my God,' I whispered to Nic. 'We're going to school with people like that – with men.'

NATALIE NICOLE

I started high school a day ahead of Nat. My first appointment was with my guidance counsellor, Ken Beck. Every child in the American school system has a counsellor; they are a good form of support – someone to talk to about classes and any problems you may be having. Ken Beck had a daughter, Melissa.

'You might get on with my daughter,' he said at the end of our first meeting.

He handed me my timetable – an indecipherable schedule of subjects, buildings and room numbers.

When I got to my home room the register was being called. I heard my name:

'Appleton.'

'Yes.'

'Beck.'

'Yes.'

I turned and saw a blonde girl with big blue eyes beaming at me. Melissa Beck. We clicked straight away.

NATALIE NICOLE

American schools are very divided. There are distinct gangs and each person fits into one and stays within it – dating within that group and hanging out with their own kind. Arriving at Elenville High was like landing on the set of the movie *Grease*.

First there were the prep or posh boys; they all wore football shirts and played football. The prep girls wore jeans that were tight at the bottom, with white pumps like the ones Jennifer Grey wore in *Dirty Dancing* – and big socks to match their sweaters. This was the uniform. You had to wear it to be accepted.

I turned up in boot-cut Levi 501s and Doc Marten boots and was quizzed.

'Why are you wearing flares – and what the hell is wrong with your feet?'

Then there were the 'greasers' – geeky boys who drove cars they made (and spent all day fixing). They wore acid-washed jeans and Metallica T-shirts – so did the girls. The rednecks or hicks wore flannel shirts, big boots and baseball caps with petrol signs. They drove pick-up trucks, chewed tobacco and hunted deer.

Then there were the black kids and the Puerto Ricans. The groups united only at football games. Then people from each gang would be on the same team united against a different school.

I found the segregation shocking. In England no one took any notice of the colour of your skin; but here being in a mixed race relationship was a bad thing. The atmosphere was frightening. I didn't feel safe. I made a point of speaking to everyone; I was determined not to be part of the divisions and rifts.

The school was deeply sexist too. Sage Rudman wanted to play American football. She was stronger than many of the boys on the team and the coach gave her a place, but she was bullied unmercifully. On the pitch, the boys teamed up against her and pushed her around. They used their combined physical strength to wear her down.

Sage used to come off the pitch covered in bruises. Eventually she quit. Any boy would have caved in under that amount of pressure. Football was a boy's game – not a girl's – and she was made to know it. At home, it was cool for a girl to be tough – I wore tracksuit bottoms, baseball jackets and chunky boots. Here there was an enormous pressure on girls to conform.

Attending a new school meant it was hard to know who to hang out with. When I had been there six months, I met Nicole Bagatta. We were both relegated to the bleachers – watching our classmates play because we had forgotten our sports kits. We got talking. At the end of the game she asked me if I wanted to go to lunch with her.

Nicole Bagatta had thin hair which she hairsprayed so it stood three inches from her head. You could see right through Nicole's hair. She was skinny with big boobs. She reminded me of Jennifer Love Hewitt in the movie *I Know What You Did Last Summer.*

Nicole taught me to volumize my hair. The cheapest hairspray you could get, Aquanet, cost a dollar and came in huge pinky-silver cans. I used to hold the can up and spray at my head for twenty minutes. Everyone did.

Eventually I got to know people in the cool crowd and I was accepted, but I didn't fit neatly into any one gang and ended up having friends in each group. I took turns with different gangs, but I was selective about who I really showed myself to, who was my mate. Everyone was shagging everyone else's partner.

Nicole Bagatta, too, was a loner; she did her own thing and she became my best friend at the school. Nicole was someone I confided in. I trusted her.

I always know instinctively who to trust. The few mistakes I have made are when I have not trusted my instinctive judgement. I can sense people's genuine motives. It is instant – immediate. It means I have few friends, but each is significant and lasting. I make deep connections. But they are rare.

NATALIE NICOLE

Nat and I wanted to fit in. We dyed our hair – I went blonde and Nat went red. The hangout at the time was the Burger King parking lot. I worked at my American accent. I remember practising and practising in front of the mirror, drawing out my vowel sounds, rehearsing as if for a play until the enunciation was just right. I knew it was the route to acceptance. I didn't want to feel like an outcast.

The first summer we were in America, Melanie Blatt

came for a visit. Seeing her at the airport, I realized how much I had changed – how very American I had become. I had lowlights in my shaggy permed hair. Mel was not into hairstyles at all and her long hair was parted in the middle. I wore American college sweatshirts and jeans. Mel was a hippy in a big floral Hawaiian shirt. I looked tanned and healthy. By comparison, very English Mel resembled a ghost.

The first thing I did was take her to a hairdresser to have her hair cut American-style – the look at the time was curly hair with a fringe.

Just before I left England, Mel had found out she had scoliosis. At the time, all we knew was that her spine was curved. Now I discovered it meant she had to wear a big plastic brace at night. It looked like a cross between a corset and a bullet-proof vest.

But nothing could crush our excitement at being together again. We had a great summer. I introduced Mel to my high-school friends – all of whom were a year or more older than we were. There was Melissa, my boyfriend, German (pronounced Herman) Flores, and his friend Keith Williams.

One night, out in German's car, Keith passed round a pipe. It had an unfamiliar sweet smell.

'What's that?' I asked.

'Weed,' he said.

I was scared to try it so I just pretended to inhale. But I got very stoned anyway – sitting in that car on the cliff with the windows closed. I remember laughing and laughing with Mel. We could not stop.

Later I told Nat – this was a huge mistake. Whenever we had an argument she would hold the information over my head.

'I'll tell Mum you smoked weed.'

Nat threatened me so many times that eventually I rebelled.

'Right,' I said. 'Right, I'm going to tell Mum, then you won't be able to threaten me any more.'

Mum was downstairs in the utility room, loading the tumble dryer.

'Mum,' I blurted it out as quickly as I could, 'I tried weed.'

I was impatient and scared, but the words came out smug and defiant. Mum did not respond straight away. She closed the lid on the laundry basket, and then said:

'Just because you told me, don't think that means you're going to get away with it. This is very serious, Nicole.'

I had expected a chat with Mum – I thought she would side with me, say Nat was wrong for blackmailing me, her little one. Instead she was more perturbed than I had seen her.

'You don't understand,' I tried to explain, 'I'm not telling you lightly. I'm telling you because Nat keeps threatening to and it's not fair.'

I left Mum at her laundry and went back upstairs. At least Nat could not use it against me now.

Later Mum came into my room.

'It's not cool,' she said. 'Weed is not clever. Are you sure you want to be smoking it?'

Mum has a marvellously respectful way of giving advice – a way of putting things so that you never feel lectured or belittled. She never condemned me or made me feel worthless; she never disciplined or punished me, instead she explained things to me. She always helped me to think for myself – to think before acting and anticipate the consequences of everything.

'Use your best judgement,' she said.

A lot of my friends were very rebellious and had strict parents that they were always complaining about. My mum was also strict – she did not agree with a lot of the things we did – but she knew she could not stop us experimenting and trying things out. Her empathy and reasoning meant I did not want to let her – or myself – down.

No matter what I had done, I always walked away from a talk with Mum feeling more valued. It was the way she spoke to me. I could not rebel against her. I had too much respect for her. She loved me. Whatever she said, it was for my own good.

Mum taught me to back off, to think ahead rather than go into things blindly. I have made a lot of mistakes in my life, but Mum's wisdom has stopped me from making many more. She is a force for good. In so many situations, I feel her sitting on my shoulder, giving advice the way she did when I was growing up. Think before you act.

It was hard living in Norman's house. He never looked Nat and me in the eye. I was open to him at first, I gave him a chance. But he really did not like the fact that we were there and he had to share Mum with us.

Nat fought with Norman right from the start. She said Norman was needy with Mum, greedy over her time and company. I began to see his jealousy for myself and it upset me. I rang Dad in London.

'Dad, I can't stand Norman. He's not there for me and Nat and he won't let Mum be there for us.'

'The door is always open if you want to come home,' Dad said. 'Come home.'

The more I needed Mum, the more I fell out with Norman. It was a vicious cycle. I grew to hate him. He was the grown-up, but he was behaving like a baby.

A year after we arrived in America, I went back to Dad in London and enrolled at Camden School for Girls. Nat came with me. Once again, we were inseparable. We stuck to each other like glue. Our closeness blotted out the pain of leaving Mum again.

But three months later we went back to America. We couldn't cope with the change. By then Mum and Norman were having a relationship, but things with Norman never got any easier for Nat and me – in fact, they got worse. As we grew into teenagehood, Nat and I needed Mum more than ever. Things were changing in our lives; we were having all sorts of new experiences and we needed Mum's advice. But Norman would not share her.

We had been in New York for two years when I got my first period. I was fourteen. I freaked out. It felt like a crisis. I asked Mum if she would sleep next to me. But Norman wouldn't let her. He had a fit. He had never had daughters so he didn't understand. He made it so hard for us to be with Mum.

Melissa Beck was my consolation – my best friend through high-school years. She helped make up for losing Melanie and was a haven from Norman's jealous tantrums. Melissa had one of those sponge brains that soak up information, but she had no street sense at all. She was totally gullible and didn't understand when guys treated her badly.

A great feature of the American high-school system is note passing. During class (especially Spanish at which I was very weak having only studied French in England) or hall study time (when we were meant to be doing homework or revising) I used to read and write countless notes. Then, when the bell went for the next class, there would be a scramble of note passing as replies went back and forth.

We used to sneak off to drink wine coolers or beers called 40 oz which came in huge bottles. We were too young to buy them legally so we used to get people to buy them for us or we used fake identity cards.

During the holidays and weekends we spent our time swimming and sunbathing. My friend Kim's parents owned the Nevele Hotel and Country Club and everyone, including Mum, had a job there. I used to babysit there at weekends. I earned twenty dollars a night – that was good money for five hours' work.

Teenagers came from all over America to work at the hotel. They stayed in the staff complex, Winter Lodge. It was like the lodge in the movie *Dirty Dancing* – a big college dorm. Everyone used to meet in the hotel in the Cousin Brucey Room. It had a jukebox and a games room.

We played George Michael over and over. There were mirrors all around the walls and we used to dance and go crazy, miming along to the album *Faith*. I started smoking menthol cigarettes – Newports. I never used to buy them; instead I would steal one from a friend's packet and puff on it slowly.

My best friend Nicole Bagatta and I had very different taste in men. She went for heavy-metal types, but I was into preps. And, unlike the girls, they loved my English accent. My first boyfriend was the boy Nic and I saw on our first visit to the school – the scary guy with the mohican – Tony Gina. He was half Italian. He was gorgeous.

Tony took me to the movies and we kissed. It was almost prom time. Prom was the talk of the school. When a mutual friend told me Tony wanted to take me to the prom, I was elated. I could hardly believe it: Tony and me at the prom!

I was visualizing what I would wear – I had it all worked out – a black strapless dress with a puffball skirt and cycling shorts because it was too short.

'There's just one thing,' my friend said.

'What?'

I was nonchalant, distracted, catapulted into the future.

'Tony won't take you to the prom unless you sleep with him.'

I was fifteen years old. I panicked. I was not ready to sleep with Tony. I was a virgin. That night, Tony invited me to the movies again. He had a new Toyota MRZ and he drove us to the top of Mount Cathalia – where all the couples went to make out. High on a cliff top overlooking the town, Tony started kissing me. Then he put his hand down my top. I had never gone that far. It freaked me out. I felt embarrassed and shy.

Tony drove me home. This was serious. I could not get it out of my head: Tony had touched my breast. I felt too embarrassed to tell anybody so it became a secret. Tony and I went on many dates but the threat of having to have sex with him to go to the prom stayed with me, I could not relax. Maybe that is why I developed a big crush on his best friend. Adam had green eyes, olive skin and the most perfect body. After Tony and I finished, Adam cornered me at the Nevele Hotel.

Adam was the brother of one of my friends, Kim. All the girls fancied him and I was no exception. Now he was talking to me, interested in me. When Adam kissed me, there was an electrical charge I had never experienced before. It was intense; even my fingers were shaking.

From then on, I was hooked. I wanted Adam to be my boyfriend, but Adam was no one's property. He liked to play around. I knew he could not give me what I wanted, but it didn't stop my body responding to his. When Adam was near me, the hairs would stand up on the back of my neck.

NATALIE NICOLE

Just before my fourteenth birthday, I auditioned to become a cheerleader. I knew I had a good chance because I could dance. My best friend Melissa was assured of a place as she was cute with blonde hair.

So we both joined the school elite. At Elenville High the cheerleaders were known for their looks and we made sure we lived up to that reputation. Our athleticism was displayed in short blue, white and yellow skirts as we danced, cartwheeled and juggled batons at the side of the game. We became a gang – me, Melissa, Elana and Chantelle. We used to compete against cheerleaders from other schools and we always won. They didn't stand a chance.

Once a week, I had a gym class at 8 a.m. In winter it was awful and I used to cut class and roll into the school at 9 a.m. As a result, the gym teacher failed me. Big deal. I didn't care. Not until I found out that it meant I was kicked out of the cheerleading team for a year.

'For a year?'

'When you fail your gym class that's what happens.' The coach was unrepentant.

So, for my sixteenth year, I spent the entire season sitting under the bleachers with my friend Chantelle, smoking and watching the other girls dance and kick for the school. Chantelle was the most beautiful girl, but tough, hard. She was always having fights. She used to flirt with the boys on the visiting teams. Outrageously. This would provoke jealous hysteria in the other cheerleading team, and then Chantelle would be up for a fight.

'Come on then' – standing up and shaking out her black hair – 'I'm not scared of you.'

And there I was beside her, just as brave, just as bolshie. I was fearless at that age. As long as Chantelle was there, I knew I was protected.

I was still dating German. When the students had to vote who was the most popular and good-looking boy in the school, German won – he was the Homecoming King. Everyone wanted him. A football player and a cheerleader – it was perfect. When he walked on to the field, he used to come over and kiss me before the game started.

It was a week before my fifteenth birthday. Mum was away for the day. German came over to my house with two friends. MTV was blasting out 'Sowing the Seeds of Love' by Tears for Fears. We danced around the house. German whirled me from room to room. We started kissing. I took him into Nat's bedroom because she had a double bed and mine was only a single. I had been seeing German for nine months. I thought: it is going to happen.

But I was not ready. As a result it was horrible, painful. I started to cry. I had ignored my body and now I was distressed and panicked. There was a heavy pressure to perform, there was an expectation that we knew what to do. Neither of us anticipated that sex could be like this.

There was no way for German and I to communicate with each other about what had happened. We had no language. People made jokes about sex and it was used as an insult, but it was never spoken about in a clear and direct way. He went home.

'I'm sorry,' German said.

The next day I woke feeling so different – something had changed; I was no longer a virgin. I imagined everyone knew. Becky Kinney had had sex, but she was the only one. I wanted my best friends Melissa and Kim to do it because they were the only people I wanted to talk to about it.

'Did it hurt?' Melissa asked me.

'It was horrible, but I've done it,' I said.

We had been brought up to believe that having sex was the most amazing thing in the world. We saw it on TV and at the movies, we read about it in books and magazines. No one ever told us it might be unpleasant or scary. That we might not be able to relax. That it might not be enjoyable at all.

Mum picked Nat and me up from school the next day. We were driving home when, suddenly, she switched the radio off and turned to me.

'I need to ask you something.'

'Yeah.'

'Have you . . .' She hesitated. 'Have you had sex?'

I felt I was on fire. Burning alive.

'No,' I said quickly. 'Of course not.'

I had that eerie sensation you sometimes get with parents when you think they can read your mind – that they know the very moment you do something you should not.

'Well, there was a condom on the floor of my room,' Nat said, 'and I haven't been in there so it was either you or one of your friends.'

I hunched down into the seat and looked out of the window miserably. I could not say anything. If Nat knew I had been in her bed she would go berserk and I could not risk Mum's disapproval. There was silence in the car after that. I felt sick.

Later, Mum spoke to me. She did not want to tell me off or give me a lecture. She wanted to make sure I was all right.

'You're not angry with me?'

'No. I'm just concerned,' she said. 'Are you sure about what you're doing? Are you ready?'

Here she was, again, giving me responsibility for my life and decisions. Providing me with pointers, suggestions. I felt ashamed of myself. I had let her down, put her in a position where she needed to speak to me like this.

'I'm pleased you used protection,' she said.

I did not have sex with German again for six months.

44

But Melissa and Kim soon caught up – then we discussed everything. It was such a girly time. We grew together.

Life was about football and cheerleading and partying on Mount Cathalia. As soon as you had passed your driving test, it was important to have a four-wheel drive truck. We could not afford one but Mum had a Nissan Centra – that was Nat's and my first car. There would be a line of fabulous trucks and jeeps and then Nat and I in our little car, straining to get to the top of the mountain. When we drove down, there was always the smell of burning brakes.

The highest point was the kissing point. Up at the top you could see out over the whole town. We would make a huge bonfire. Couples would cuddle around it, drinking beer, talking, hanging out, their faces flickering in the firelight.

There were lots of parties. And then there was Halloween. Halloween is a big deal in America. Two nights before Halloween is Devil's Night. Then everyone would get into gangs and stock up on eggs, toilet paper and shaving cream. We would wear dark clothes and go out on the streets to pelt other gangs – as well as the houses of teachers and people we did not like. It was a licence to be deviant, dodging other gangs and the police.

One night, covered in toilet paper and eggs, my gang and I were relaxing on the porch when the police pulled up outside my friend's house.

'What are you doing?' they asked.

My hair was so full of egg it looked plastic. I stank of shaving cream.

'We're doing nothing,' I said. 'Why don't you just go away and leave us alone?'

'If you don't hush up,' the policeman said, 'you'll

be in the back of this police car explaining this to your mom.'

I shut up. Instantly. I was being mouthy in front of my friends, but I was never more than a show-off. I liked to be around people who were prepared to get into trouble, but deep down I was too sensible for it. Mum had taught me well. I always knew when to back off.

NATALIE NICOLE

Nic and I had different friends and lived more separate lives at this time, but it didn't stop me feeling protective towards her. The school put on plays and, one Christmas, Nic had a part as a sailor in *Anything Goes*. She had a few lines and I rehearsed and rehearsed them with her.

On the night of the show, I sat in the auditorium waiting for her to come on. I knew she was really nervous and I shared that feeling with her. Next thing I knew, another girl was on stage doing Nic's lines. Furious, I stormed backstage to look for my sister.

I found Nic in tears. A boy had asked her out and she had mocked him, so he had punched her in the face. I was shocked – disgusted. Nic was not hurt, but she was shaken. I went after him. I made sure that boy never forgot the way he treated my sister.

I left school shortly after that. I was fifteen. Norman found me my first job – it was ironic that he enabled me to do what I loved most. I started work as a cabaret singer at the Nevele Hotel where Norman was Entertainments Director.

I bought tiered prom dresses and chopped them down to minis and used the excess fabric for hairpieces. Anything to look older. Every half an hour, I would alternate with other acts – comedians or singers. I sang songs by Gloria Estefan, Madonna and Paula Abdul. Also oldies like 'Tie A Yellow Ribbon'. I loved singing. When I found out they were going to pay me $120 a week, I was ecstatic.

I entered talent competitions and took advantage of every opportunity to sing. One day, a gang of us went to a huge adventure park and I saw a sign saying: Make Your Own Record. I chose a backing track – 'Out Here On My Own' from the movie *Fame* – and recorded my voice for the first time. It was a scratchy record, but I knew instinctively that this was one of the key events of my life.

NATALIE **NICOLE**

Nat and I spent the summer living in one of the hotel staff apartments. I worked for the Activities Staff, showing guests how to play basketball, baseball and shuttle ball. We worked really hard all day and then had parties – or went to discos and danced all night. It was the best summer of my life. I didn't know it was all about to come to an end. Once again, all I had built up was going to be pulled from under my feet.

Norman got another job – this time in Florida. Again I was leaving my school, my home and – most importantly – my friends. As in England, I had made genuine friends – friends I grew with and shared experiences with. We were doing the same things at the same time, learning together. Leaving them really broke my heart.

The night before we left, my friends had a leaving party for me. Too young to drink legally, we had a secret stash of alcohol. We were doing funnels – pouring cans of beer down a plastic funnel into our mouths so we swallowed the whole lot in seconds. I was also drinking tequila. I threw up and passed out. So did Melissa.

I had never been that drunk before. I managed to get home, but I woke in my own vomit. It was dangerous. I could have choked, but for once I didn't care about my bad behaviour. Mum was devastated, but I felt she deserved my anger.

'You're making me leave,' I screamed at her. 'I don't want to go and you're making me leave.'

All my friends came over that morning to see me off. I was nauseous and hung over. Norman had already left. Mum, Nat, me and our dog, Muffin, climbed into a car piled with stuff. The drive to Florida took twenty-four hours – the longest drive of my life.

4 - LOST AND FOUND

NATALIE NICOLE

When I was seventeen, everything changed again. Mum and Norman split up and Mum bought a house in Monticello, near Ellenville. The three of us moved back and spent the rest of the summer working at the Concord Hotel. It was lovely to have Mum back and Monticello is a holiday town so we partied hard. But, at the end of the summer, the town died. All our friends went back to college.

It was time for a change. Nic and I spoke about it as we said goodbye to our friends and thought of the autumn ahead. London. Back to Dad and Lori and a different life. We flew backwards and forwards between the two countries – between our two parents – so much we were equally at home in England and America. There was almost a feeling of choosing our lives.

The good thing about the move was that it gave me the opportunity to look around for a college where I could train to be in a band. Singing in the hotel in New York and experiencing warm audiences had given me confidence. I knew people liked to hear me sing. Now I wanted professional training. It was important for me to get a qualification.

A few weeks after returning to England, I enrolled at the Performing Arts College in North London. My days were spent learning dance routines and improvising scenes. The college taught me the mechanics of being in a band. And, best of all, long hours were dedicated to singing, to getting the most out of my voice. When I sang I felt my whole body was in sync – I was using the whole of me.

I was reunited with Samantha Janus and she introduced me to a whole new world: the Thursday Club – Jackys – on Wardour Street. It was Ladies Night, so ladies got in free. The Dream Boys were performing – male strippers; ten of them, in a troupe. Sam had started dating one of them, Mauro. Each week I went along with her to watch the show.

That was where I saw Carl. He was wearing white cycling shorts and boxing boots. He was beautiful. His muscles, his physique. He was hard to look away from – Carl's skin was dark and his body looked chiselled, perfect. He reminded me of my first love, Adam. At seventeen, Carl looked like everything I desired.

But he had a girlfriend. A brunette who would lock her body around his after the show. I watched them on the dance floor and envied her. I wanted to be her.

It was 21 February 1991. Sam was sitting on the bed in my room.

'Come out tonight, Nat,' she coaxed.

The relationship I had been in had just fizzled out and I felt like staying home. Home, with tea and sympathy from Mum. Going out involved effort. I was not in the mood.

'Carl and his girlfriend have stopped seeing each other,' Sam said.

A huge grin spread across my face as I started selecting and discarding items from my wardrobe. Cut-off black denim shorts, black thigh boots, Philadelphia hockey shirt – I loved that hockey shirt. I wore it all the time when I wanted to impress. It was lucky for me. I was feeling good that night, confident.

After the show, Sam brought Carl over to our table.

'It's Carl's birthday tonight,' she said.

It seemed especially significant to me that I was meeting him on his birthday.

I was giddy, but I managed to act cool. He sat down beside me. I wanted to lean towards him and run away at the same time.

'Happy Birthday,' I said.

We chatted around the usual stuff, but all the time something else was going on. There was an electrical charge between us.

At the end of the evening, Sam and I were climbing into a black cab when Carl said: 'Can I call you?'

He kissed me. As the door closed behind me and the cab sped off, I started screaming. Finally able to let out all the excitement and joy I had been containing. He was like Adam – but an Adam who liked me.

Carl and I met in Covent Garden after his show. I waited for him outside a bar. He arrived wearing a leather jacket with studs and metal badges, cowboy boots and jeans. Six foot, broad, body built to perfection. He took me to the Monkey Bar. Everyone was looking at him, looking at me, as he held my hand and walked me to the front of the club.

'Last song,' the DJ said into his microphone.

I recognized the first few bars, Oleta Adams' 'Get Here If You Can'. I held on to Carl's jacket and we danced. It felt good to be so close to him. We moved together easily. I didn't want the song to end. We left the club and walked towards the tube station to get a cab.

Carl said: 'I've got a present for you.'

He reached into his pocket and pulled out an Easter egg. He had come out from doing a show and been thoughtful enough to stop and buy me one. Back home, that evening, I kicked my Easter egg around the lounge, giggling with anticipation.

Carl rented a room in a house in Tooting Bec. He and three flatmates, sharing a kitchen and a cold bathroom. Carl's room was very small, his bed was tiny, like a cot, but we didn't mind. Each night, we clung together in his single bed.

Falling in love. Those first heady months when nothing exists for you outside of your lover's presence. We laughed a lot. At least one good belly laugh every day. That is precious. It felt magical to be so connected. It had been two years since Adam. Carl was the first love that loved me back.

There seemed to be something pure between Carl and I and yet, at the same time, it screwed up other parts of my life. My college work began to suffer. A morning off at first, then two mornings a week. It was hard to go back. I no longer had any interest in studying. All I wanted was to be with Carl.

I practically moved into Carl's bedroom and either sat around with him, or was waiting for him. I stopped seeing my friends – even Nic and my family. My life narrowed down to my existence with Carl. And life with Carl revolved around his shows.

Four months after we met, the Dream Boys went on tour around the country and I went with them. What had been fun when we first met was now doing my head in. The audience's reactions to his – my lover's body – tied *my* body in knots. As yet another woman reached forward to touch him, I felt sick. How dare they?

A certain type of woman goes to watch men strip – and when she does, an animal quality emerges. The man on stage becomes a piece of meat, up for grabs. Their lust has a possessive quality.

Carl would walk off stage with scratches on his body. But what could I say? I knew from the beginning that Carl was a stripper. This was his job.

Worse still were the Polaroid sessions after each performance. This was where the Dream Boys really made their money; charging each woman five pounds to pose with them and return home with a photo to prove it. The queues for Polaroids were long every night, and raucous. As each woman got nearer, her hysteria rose. The photo was an excuse for a mauling session. Everybody seemed to love it except me.

Carl used to talk to me about the other members of the Dream Boys. He told me about the women who waited for them after the shows. Quick and easy sex. It was hard for me to hear – I was friends with their girlfriends, and now I had information I would find hard to hide from them.

'What about you, Carl?'

'Me? I do nothing, babe, you know me.' Carl was always reassuring. 'Would I tell you what the others were up to if I was doing the same?'

'I hate watching what the girls do to you.'

'It's just my job. They can't have what you have, Natalie.'

There were times I was glad so many women wanted

him – they were after him and he chose me, night after night. It was such a hook.

'I want us to have a child,' Carl said.

Some time in the future, yes, I wanted to be a mother. But I was still a teenager and at college, training to be in a band.

'One day, Carl,' I said.

'No,' he said, 'not one day, now. I want us to have a child now. What are we waiting for, Natalie? We know we want to be together.'

Carl said it would make our relationship real. He said it would prove I loved him. He said a lot of things and I was young and thought he was the answer. Sometimes Carl talked about his upbringing – his mother never cared for him, she palmed him off on to his grandmother for months at a time. Carl had never had a proper family; he wanted to make one with me. And I wanted to make up for his broken family. I loved him. Loved him so much.

I drifted into it, without making a proper decision, by not using contraception. Each month when my period started, Carl was devastated. His emotions were so strong they took over mine. Soon I wanted a baby because Carl wanted a baby.

I moved in with Carl and, when one of his flatmates left, we moved into a bigger room in the house. I went back to Dad's house only when Carl was at work. Time away from Carl felt wasted.

We were struggling financially. Dad said Carl and I could stay with him and he would pay the mortgage. He turned a blind eye to the truth about Carl's job. As long as I was doing what I wanted, Dad was happy.

★

My period was a week late. I didn't say anything to Carl, but confided in a girl I had met at the club.

'I've got a home pregnancy test in my bag, shall I do it?'

'Go on,' she said.

I went into the bathroom. Carl was in Spain with the Dream Boys. My strongest feeling was of curiosity. I have the clearest recollection of sitting on the edge of the bath in the flat in Camden; I was wearing baggy dungarees with a T-shirt.

'Oh my God,' I said. 'It's turned blue. I'm pregnant.'

I was on the telephone to Carl straight away. My voice was so breathy it didn't take him a moment to guess.

'You're pregnant.'

I could hear his happiness. We both believed this was the best thing that could happen to us.

'I can't wait to get back to you,' he said.

When I told Nic I was pregnant, she was delighted, but I could see in her eyes she felt worried.

'Congratulations, Nat, I hope it's what you want,' she said.

'It is.'

'I want you to be happy.'

'I know you do,' I said. 'And I am.'

NATALIE NICOLE

It was around this time Nat and I really drifted apart. I felt I had lost her. When I found out she was pregnant I was excited, but Nat was so busy with Carl she didn't have time to be my friend. With Carl in her life she had no place for me. I felt left out.

I went back to New York. My other sisters, Lee and Lori, were living there with Mum now. It was lovely to be with them all again. I missed Nat and felt sad when I thought of her. She had gone from being a strong personality to a shell with no personality at all. She was totally different. Carl had her now.

Mum got me a job in the hotel where she worked. The four of us were now all employed at the Concord. Mum was the owner's secretary, Lori managed the health club, Lee worked in the golf shop and I had a succession of jobs – starting out as a waitress in the coffee shop.

Waitressing is the hardest job, ever. The customers are never satisfied and you work for your tips. When I worked as a cocktail waitress at the hotel pool, I always seemed to get the miseries. I would spend the whole day walking around with trays of drinks and, occasionally, a man would want to tip me. Then I would hear the complaining voice of his wife:

'You don't want to tip her. What do you want to tip her for?'

That summer I also sold ice creams by the side of the pool. I had a white cart with a big slot-in umbrella sunshade. I used to wheel the cart around or sit on a wall and wait for customers. One windy afternoon, I was sitting on the wall picking chewing gum off the sole of my shoe with a stick, when the umbrella lifted in the wind. Its thick metal pole knocked me on my forehead. I passed out.

When I came to, someone had stolen all my ice creams. I was called to the manager's office, but when I tried to explain what had happened, he didn't believe me. He was convinced the ice creams were stolen because I was sunbathing. I was fired. I had been an ice-cream girl for two weeks.

NATALIE NICOLE

With Mum and all my sisters in America, life narrowed down to Carl. While he did his shows, I sat at home and read pregnancy books, noting the changes in the size of my baby.

But Carl was becoming increasingly moody. He was unpredictable. In the flat everything had to be tidied away and he got very worked up if things were slightly out of place. One night, I didn't shut a drawer and he threw a fit. A few days later it was because there were crumbs on the table.

'Don't wear shoes in the house,' he would order.

There were rules for everything.

Nothing I did was good enough. I never got it right. I grew afraid. I learned to keep my mouth shut. Anything could set him off. Carl was taking steroids for his work. I blamed the steroids for his rages.

I made excuses for him. I was eighteen and having his baby. The baby would make everything all right. My mind went round in circles. I didn't know how my life had come to this. I didn't know who I was any more. I wanted to be a singer. There were still so many things I wanted to do.

I was two months pregnant when I went back to New York for my sister Lee's wedding. No one but Nic knew I was pregnant. I was scared to tell them, scared of what they would say.

I told Mum first. We were having tea in the kitchen.

She held my hand and stroked my face. She was sad. She knew what it was like to be a mum and she thought I was too young.

'You're throwing away your childhood, Nat,' she said.

I was afraid to tell Dad; I thought he might try to talk me out of it. One night we were having dinner at a wine bar in the hotel and Nic said:

'Tell Dad. Go on, Natalie. Now's as good a time as you're going to get.'

Dad was gentler than usual, buoyed on wine.

'Guess what, Dad?'

Nic cut in: 'Nat's pregnant.'

He was shocked. His baby Nat – the first of his daughters to fall pregnant. But Dad was happy for me, I could see that too.

Lee's wedding was at a hotel in upstate New York. I was one of ten bridesmaids. I was terrified of the camera, but I had promised to sing. When Lee and her new husband Micah took to the floor for their first dance together as a married couple, I went up on to the stage.

'For my sister Lee and for Micah,' I said. 'I'm going to sing "The Wind Beneath My Wings".'

Then I sang with my whole heart.

> It must have been cold there in my shadow
> To never have sunlight on your face
> You were content to let me shine
> You always walked a step behind.

As I sang I felt it again – sharply, keenly. All I wanted to do was sing. I felt complete. I was at one with myself. Carl disappeared. There was only the music and my voice. When I finished the song and looked at my mum and sisters, they were in tears.

I had missed them. I was desperate for someone to talk to me. I wanted one of them to pull me aside and give me time and attention, to help me get my life back on track. But it was Lee's wedding and there was so much going on. I got lost in the crowd and the busyness. I felt so alone.

Only Carl cares about me, that was the thought I carried close to me that night. I did not drink – fearful I might harm my baby I wouldn't even allow myself a glass of wine. Everyone seemed so far away, they were not connected to me. I left my sister's wedding party early, rang Carl and went to sleep.

A month later, Carl and I went on holiday to Cornwall. Our first holiday together. I thought being away from everything would bring out the real Carl. I was always trying to make everything smooth around Carl so that he could be happy and at ease. I knew there was a good person underneath all the rage and frustration. A good person who would make a wonderful father.

The first two days we went for long walks on the cliffs and had dinner in little pubs along the seafront. The sun was shining and we talked more than we had in ages. Carl was about to have the family he said he longed for. It made us feel very close.

I missed Nic a lot. I thought about how different our lives had become. While I was with Carl at the seaside, she was in America working as a waitress and living in the centre of our family. I wondered if we would ever regain our closeness. When I thought we might not, it pierced my heart.

Walking along the seafront, Carl started to pick on something I had done. He grabbed me by the arm, his nails biting into my skin through the thin fabric of my shirt.

'Stop it,' I said, 'you're hurting me.'

Carl started pushing me. He was screaming. People were looking. I felt embarrassed and ashamed. Carl had a magazine rolled up in his hand and suddenly he pushed it hard into my stomach. It felt like a metal rod. I buckled over.

A man ran up behind Carl and got him in an arm lock.

'Are you okay, love?' the man asked me. 'I've been watching you from the top of the road,' he explained. 'I'm an undercover policeman.'

The fear at what Carl might do to me switched now to fear of what might happen to Carl. I could feel my heart thumping.

'Tell him it's okay,' Carl said.

'It's okay,' I said. 'We're fine. I'm sorry.' I heard myself apologizing. 'It was my fault. He wasn't doing anything wrong. We were just having a disagreement.'

'That's right,' Carl said. He was red in the face.

'Please let him go.'

The man was looking at me. I felt desperate. The only thing that mattered was that Carl did not hate me.

'If you're sure,' the man said.

'Yes.'

The man let go of him and Carl walked towards me. He put his arm around me. I couldn't tell from his eyes what he was thinking or feeling.

'We're fine now thanks, aren't we?' Carl said.

'Absolutely,' I said.

The man walked slowly away and Carl and I kept holding on to each other. What if they had taken Carl to prison? How would I manage on my own? What would happen to our baby? The feeling we shared now was real – how close we had come to blowing the whole thing.

'I'm sorry, Nat. I don't know what happened there. I lost it.'

Carl rumpled my hair with tenderness.

'It won't happen again. I promise. I don't know what I was doing.'

Carl was charming and attentive, but I was devastated, totally bewildered that the man I loved and trusted could lash out at me. It was the first time Carl hit me – afterwards it seemed easier for him to do it again. He used to grab me by the arm. Friends would notice my arms were black and blue. Afterwards he was contrite – but he always blamed me, he said it was my fault.

'If you didn't wind me up so much, Nat,' he said. 'You know the things that drive me nuts. You do it on purpose, you know you do.'

There was always tenderness between us after the violence. As I lay in his arms, I made excuses for him, I blamed myself. I pushed Carl to the edge, made him get angry with me. It was not his fault. He had difficulties in life. I would do my best to be easier to be around. I would make a big effort.

But nothing I did made any difference. Carl used to come up behind me and I would stiffen, waiting for the punch, tensing all around my back. I screamed: 'Dad, help me, he's hurting me,' hoping Dad would hear, but Carl would put his hand over my mouth so I couldn't breathe.

Carl used to walk down the street with a cricket bat up his sleeve. I would walk along with my eyes down, not daring to look at anyone, paralysed by fear. I pined for my family in America. Most of all I pined for Nic.

One night she rang from New York, on her way out. Her voice. Her beautiful familiar voice as if she was there in the room.

'What are you up to?' she asked.

'Nothing much.'

I could hear in her voice she had plans for the evening.

'Lori and I are going to a party. How's it going with you and Carl?'

'Good – great.'

I was too ashamed to tell Nic – or anyone else. I could barely admit to myself that my wonderful dream of being with Carl had turned into this nightmare – that Carl had been hitting me and I had been putting up with it.

'Are you excited about the baby?' Nic asked.

'Very.'

I could hear Lori in the background.

'You and Lori hanging out now?'

'Yeah, we've got closer,' Nic said. 'I feel like we're only just getting to know each other.'

I felt a pang. I felt replaced.

'Have a tequila slammer for me,' I said.

She was gone and I was left alone again with Carl. Carl and I were having a baby, that meant we were together for ever. I felt completely trapped.

Rachel weighed 5lb 9oz when she was born. She had a mop of dark hair and green, green eyes. When I held Rachel for the first time I was in shock. This tiny, perfect thing in my arms was a person. A miracle. I was totally smitten with her – I thought she was the most amazing thing on the planet. Instantly Rachel was familiar to me. It was love.

When I left the hospital, I remember wondering whether I was allowed to take Rachel with me. I couldn't believe she was mine. Bringing a new baby home is the most frightening thing. I had Rachel's cot next to me the whole time. And I stared at her. This new being in my life.

I was fiercely protective. I used to lie next to Rachel, lick my finger and leave it by her face to check she was breathing. I was terrified of cot death. Frightened of anything that might harm Rachel or take her away from me.

I made so much work for myself. I didn't want any chemicals near my child so, rather than buy baby wipes, I boiled cloths in water to clean her. Rachel was so good and I enjoyed looking after her, but I couldn't help thinking that having a child was taking a big part of my youth away. I was nineteen and kept having the feeling this was not the life I was meant to have.

I love food, but I seemed to have lost my taste buds. Everything tasted like cardboard and it swelled in my mouth. Food was no longer appealing to me. I didn't want to eat. Looking back I realize I had post-natal depression, but at the time all I knew was that I was miserable and very, very tired.

When Rachel was two weeks old, Mum came to stay with us. Seeing her was the most fantastic thing. I would have fallen apart without her. She took care of me so that I could take care of Rachel. She made me feel better about myself and my life and that had a knock-on effect on my child.

When Rachel was seven weeks old, I took her out for the first time – to Brent Cross shopping centre. Mum was still living with us and she took Rachel from me and said:

'Go and have a walk with Carl. We'll meet you in Fenwick's in an hour for lunch.'

I arrived early at Fenwick's. I could not wait to see Rachel. There were lots of mothers and babies in the restaurant. Suddenly I heard a cry above all the rest – it was like a cat's mew. I could tell Rachel's cry over all the noise.

'Rachel must be near,' I told Carl. 'And she is crying.'

When Mum left, I missed her terribly. Having her around had made such a difference to my life. I wanted to move to America to be near her. I really needed her. But my life was here – in Dad's house with Carl and my new baby.

Carl was obsessed with his body; he trained all the time. I used to go to the gym with him most days and I worked really hard. I wanted to gain muscle. The house was filled with muscle magazines and trophies; I knew the names of all the famous body builders. I respected the effort and hard work they put in.

Lying in bed with Carl one night, I longed for reassurance.

'I still feel fat,' I said.

I wanted him to say I looked great.

Instead he said: 'You've just got to get rid of that,' and he pulled at the scant flesh on my hips.

'My hips?'

I looked at them with disgust. I had a flaw and focussed all my energy on it. It triggered old feelings of self-hatred. I felt ugly.

★

When Rachel was eight months old, Carl agreed to go to America with me. He was no longer working and we both hoped America would improve our finances. A few days after we got our tickets, we discovered that, if we wanted him to work in America I would have to marry him – to make him an American citizen.

'Don't do it, Natalie,' my father said.

'I don't want to,' I admitted. 'But we need money so he needs work papers. It's the only way.'

When we landed in America my first thought was of Nic. I was so excited to see her. Mum picked us up from the airport and drove us to her house in Monticello, near New York. I could not wait for Nic to come over. I hadn't seen her in six months.

She arrived late, with Lori. She had a huge bag of laundry which she dumped on Mum. She held Rachel.

'Oh my God,' she said.

But Nic and Lori couldn't stay long. They had plans with their friends. After about an hour, they got up to go.

'Bye, Nat,' they chorused at the door, 'see you later.'

They didn't want to spend time with me and my baby. That hurt so much. I felt deeply how much my life had changed, how far away from Nic and her life I was. Throughout our childhoods, neither Nic nor I had been close to Lori, but now everything was different. I had lost Nic to Lori. She had taken my place.

'How could she do it?' I cried to Mum. 'How could she just replace me?'

Mum was tactful, but honest. She could see what was happening between her youngest daughters.

'Nicole would argue that you let Carl take her place,' she said.

Carl and I married in a registry office in America. It

was a small affair, just Mum and my sisters. We went out for dinner afterwards. But, despite all our best efforts, Carl could not get working papers. He went for jobs as a male model, but he was unemployable.

'We need cash,' I told Mum. 'What are we going to do?'

Mum felt sorry for Carl – like me, she felt for his pain. But she had a bad feeling when she met him.

'You can leave him, Nat,' she said. 'You don't have to do this to yourself.'

NATALIE NICOLE

I never liked Carl – I hated his job and I never trusted him. But I didn't tell Natalie because I didn't want to cause her any more problems. I felt sorry for Nat. To me, she was like a prisoner. She should have been out enjoying herself with me.

I will never forget the afternoon I walked in on Nat and Carl when they were having an argument. The bedroom looked as if it had been hit by a tornado. Carl had torn the room to pieces; the cabinet was down and Nat was crying on the floor. I was shocked, horrified. I wanted to take her away, far away.

'What the fuck are you doing to my sister?' I demanded.

With that, Carl grabbed me and threw me across the room. He was huge – a body builder on steroids – and he was doing to me what he would have done to Nat.

Later Carl apologized, but nothing could wipe out the horror, the devastation I had seen.

'Oh my God,' I said to Nat.

'Don't tell anyone,' Nat begged me. 'For Rachel's sake, please.'

I wanted to tell Mum and Dad, but I also wanted to protect Nat so I did what she wanted. For her sake, I became part of the lie.

NATALIE NICOLE

I was so embarrassed that my little sister saw the way Carl treated me. I felt corrupted and dirty, so ugly. I would have given anything for Nic not to have seen me like that. As with all the other times, I tried to put it behind me.

By then I was working at the health club Lori managed at the Concord Hotel. I didn't want to leave Rachel, so I had her behind the desk with me, in her push chair. The hotel's rich American clients were intrigued.

'Is that your sister?' they would drawl at me.

'No, it's my baby.'

'Your baby?' Their tones were edged with disapproval. They clearly thought I was too young.

'You're not in college?'

'No.'

'You should be in college.'

I knew it, and their judgements only made it worse. My life was over. At least in London there were other young mums. Here, in a posh hotel in New York, the pressure was on to conform and all I could feel was that I had thrown my life away.

Carl too was buckling under the pressure.

'I have to go back to England,' he said. 'I've got work and make money.'

★

67

Carl moved back into Dad's house and Dad came over to stay with us for a few months. Dad had never stopped loving Mum. Never. Not for a moment. And she was fond of him. And of course they had us, their love for us. The friendship between them developed. Rachel had given them a mutual concern.

I spent the summer in America, then went back to join Carl. I wanted us to be a family, to make a life together. I still wanted to give it a shot, for Rachel's sake. I was no longer besotted with Carl, but I was determined to put all my energy into making our relationship work.

The first time Carl stayed out all night I thought he was having an affair. I confronted him about it, yelled at him, insisted that he tell me what was going on. It was not long before I realized it was not another woman that was keeping Carl out all night, it was drugs. Ecstasy, speed, cocaine. He was hanging out now with a bunch of E-heads at the Ministry of Sound.

I wanted to meet his new friends, but Carl wouldn't invite me because he knew I was against drug taking. So one evening Dad took care of Rachel and I went round to Carl's friend's house and took a quarter of an ecstasy tablet. I felt weird, frightened. People kept leaving the room and then coming back. They were doing cocaine. I flipped. I told them how dangerous it was, how they were messing up their lives.

Carl told me I brought everyone down. They did not like having me around.

'But I'm your wife, the mother of your daughter,' I said.

Carl did not care. He stayed out for nights on end. Sitting at home with our baby, I would telephone his friends.

'Is Carl there? Do you know where he is?'

On my twenty-first birthday, Samantha Janus wanted to take me to the Atlantic Bar. I asked Carl if he would look after Rachel so that I could go out and celebrate.

'No,' he said, 'I have plans.'

'One night,' I said. 'Please take care of Rachel.'

'No.'

So Dad took her, but I was unable to stay long with my friends as I had to get back. Dad was more of a father to Rachel than Carl. He did for her all the things that Carl refused to.

Almost at breaking point, I finally decided the time had come to leave. For years Carl had put down every one of my achievements and mocked my beliefs, so I squashed myself into nothing to please him. At the end I did not know who I was. I had to leave or Carl would destroy me. Whatever I did would never be enough. The problem, the demon, was his – not mine.

In England, I was too confused to be capable of totally breaking away from Carl so I went to America to be with my family. I had been with Carl for three years – three lost years. A blur of sadness and pain. Looking back, I see I was craving love and attention. I wanted to be special to someone so I switched off a part of myself – the part that was discerning and had my best interests at heart.

Now I was lost, diminished. I was twenty-one years old and felt like a shell. It hurt Mum to see me that way, she wanted to help me – to get me back to the way I used to be. All she wanted was my happiness, my peace of mind.

'You need to be a child yourself,' Mum said. 'You've

still got a lot of living to do. Go out and let your hair down, I'll look after Rachel.'

It was the most generous offer any parent can make. With her encouragement – and knowing I was leaving Rachel in the most safe, loving hands – I began tentatively to explore life again. Nic and Lori took me out to bars and helped me to meet people. I had missed Nic like mad – my bookend. It was hard to see her so close to Lori. I felt jealous and replaced, but also so grateful to be back in the world again.

In America, mixing with different people, I got some distance from Carl and slowly came back to being Nat. I no longer saw myself through Carl's eyes. I learned to trust my own instincts again. It was like coming back to life.

As I became emotionally stronger, I also became health conscious. I took up weights again and started cardiovascular training; I trained all the time – that became my hobby. It gave me clarity and took away stress.

Nic and I, too, got closer and I decided to go to London with her for a month. Leaving Rachel with Mum for the first time was hard. I remember getting into the car to go to the airport and Rachel was banging on the screen door of the house. She was three years old. The sight and sound of her pulled at my insides. As the car left the driveway, I could still hear her.

I felt sick, totally twisted up inside my own body. But what could I do? I needed to make a life for her – for us both. I needed a qualification. At that point, I felt I had nothing else to offer her.

In London, I saw a flyer for aerobics instructor training. It sounded exactly what I needed – a job where I could use my twin loves of movement and music. I trained for four intensive weeks at the YMCA and learned about nutrition and how the body works. I loved it.

I passed the course. This was the first thing in my whole life that I had seen through, that I had achieved. My first qualification.

I telephoned Mum in America. I was in tears.

'I did it. I passed.'

'Well done, Nat,' she said. 'How good do you feel right now?'

'It's one of the best moments of my life.'

That summer, I went back to America and started teaching aerobics classes – at fifty dollars an hour. One in the morning and one in the afternoon. A hundred dollars a day. I rediscovered my zest for life. I started to eat again.

Rebuilding myself was a slow process. My relationship with Carl was abusive. I put up with things that no one should put up with. To any woman or girl in this kind of relationship I would say: get help. Do not hide what is happening and do not hang about. Believe you are worthy of proper loving – being loved for who you are and treated with respect.

At eighteen I thought it was cool to have someone who was jealous and protective – at the time it seemed flattering. But I became a shell of a person because I was in a dominating relationship. I look back at who I was then and I feel so embarrassed and ashamed. I think we all have one destructive relationship in our life, and then we don't allow it to happen again.

5 - LET'S GET STARTED

NATALIE NICOLE

I was twenty years old and back in London, living alone and working as a waitress at the Sports Cafe restaurant near Piccadilly Circus. When my old schoolfriend Mel's father came in for a big football convention, I recognized him straight away. David Blatt. We hugged instinctively. When I had been studying at Sylvia Young's, he had been a second father to me, kind and present in a way my own father sometimes was not.

'You have to call Melanie, she'll be so happy to hear from you. Melanie's in a band,' David told me excitedly. 'Promise me you'll call her.'

'I promise,' I said.

I thought about Melanie all that shift. When I left for America, Mel and I had drifted apart. We had not seen each other in years, but bumping into her dad brought her vividly back to me. The more I remembered her, the more I wanted to talk to her. During my lunch break that day I called her.

'Melanie,' I said when I heard her voice. 'It's Nicole Appleton.'

'Oh my God!' she screamed.

Then I screamed too. We instantly fell into chatting, catching up. Neither of us wanted to get off the telephone.

'Let's meet really soon,' Melanie said.

'When?'

'Tomorrow.'

I put the phone down feeling very excited. Melanie was quick and funny and had an unusual view of life. I had few friends in London – on the move too much, never really settling – it would be lovely to be around someone who felt familiar.

And she was. When we met at Camden Town tube station, it was as if we had never been apart. I watched her come blinking into the sunlight in her big puffa coat and baseball cap.

'Melanie Blatt.'

'Nicole Appleton.'

Like names being called out of a school register.

We went for lunch at Caffe Uno on Tottenham Court Road.

'Do you remember we used to call each other –'

'Nerds,' I filled in the blank for her.

'That play we did.'

'Dressed in those baggy brown trousers.'

'And ugly tweed ties.'

We brought each other up to date in a jumble of words. Then Melanie said:

'I have to tell you about the band I'm in.'

I remembered how Melanie used to enjoy listening to Aretha Franklin, Stevie Wonder and Prince. I wondered what sound she would create.

'You have to hear our songs,' she said. 'I want to know what you think.'

The next day I went to Melanie's basement flat in Notting Hill, in the house she shared with her family. It was good to see her mum Helen and her sister Jasmine again.

Melanie's flat was cosy; there were two comfortable sofas and goldfish in a tank. She made tea and we sat on the bed. She put a video tape in the machine.

'I'm nervous,' she said.

'I don't know what to expect,' I told her. 'I'm excited.'

On the screen, I saw Mel and another girl dancing and splashing in puddles. That in itself was amazing. Seeing my old schoolfriend on TV. The song was cool. I liked it.

'It's called "Let's Get Started",' Mel told me.

'It's brilliant,' I said.

'We have one more song – "I Know Where It's At". I'll play you that another day,' she said. 'We were three voices,' she said. 'But the third singer, Simone Rainsford, has dropped out.'

I held my breath.

'What do you think?' she asked.

'Think?'

'Do you want to be the third voice? Do you want to be a part of this band?'

'Yes,' I said. 'I do.'

We hugged and then we danced around the room.

'Who'd have thought all those years ago when we played at school that one day we'd be in a band together?' Melanie said. 'It's wonderful – perfect.'

Mel filled me in on the band's history. The remaining member of the band was Shaznay Lewis. She was the songwriter. They had met two years earlier at ZTT Recording Studios, where they were both session singers. Mel told me they had called their band All Saints because the studio was in All Saints Road. She also said that they had been signed to ZTT Records.

'We released "Let's Get Started" as a single, but it fell out of the charts. Then a month ago they dropped us. You have to meet Shaznay,' Mel said.

I remember my first sighting of Shaznay. She was dressed entirely in black – black leggings and a black PVC coat. She had an amazing big, long ponytail that snaked down her back. We met at TGIs in Leicester Square.

Shaznay smiled at me.

'It's good to meet you,' she said.

We drank tequila slammers. By the end of the evening, we were all feeling excited and wild. Shaznay had a shyness about her. But also an openness and candour.

'I've asked Nicole to be in the band,' Melanie told her drunkenly.

'That's a great idea,' Shaznay slurred back.

The next thing we all knew, I was singing a Mary J. Blige song and Shaznay was saying: 'Yeah, let's do it.'

I needed to learn the band's songs and routines, so I spent all my free time at Mel's flat. It was delicious to be hanging out with Mel again. She was the way she had always been: fiercely intelligent with a wicked sense of humour – the thing I always loved most about her. And she was generous – like me, whatever she had she wanted to share and give away. We were always buying each other presents. We liked the feeling of making each other happy.

Mel was not as pure as the girl I hung out with at school – she smoked now and swore – but she was still Mel to me. Still familiar – even her smell was so known to me.

Mel was very close to her family, so I spent a lot of time around her mother and sister. With my family living in the States, it was nourishing to be included in a family – one that I already knew and loved.

Mel and I would sit at the dining-room table singing our hearts out. It reminded me of being on her family's canal boat when we were younger, pretending we were glamorous and famous. Her parents had been hippies then, choosing an alternative lifestyle. They were as special and interesting to be around as ever.

One night, we were lying on the bed in Mel's room, singing the words to a song into a tape recorder when Mel said:

'I'm so glad you're in the band. It's been hard working with just Shaznay.'

'Has it?' I was amazed. Shaznay seemed sweet to me.

'She thinks she's the best,' Mel said. 'She's always showing off and talking down to me.'

I was shocked – amazed that Mel would speak that way about someone we were working with – let alone a friend.

'You'll see,' Mel said. 'Shaznay is a control freak.'

I felt uncomfortable. I didn't know what to say, how to react. I had been working and paying bills for years – I had no space in my head for slating the people around me. It seemed petty, childish.

I liked Shaznay and I wanted to get to know her in my own way. Mel was trading on the fact that we had been friends at school. She was not giving Shaznay and I a chance.

'Shaznay's not like us,' Mel said.

'Like us?'

'She's too serious.' Mel wrinkled up her nose. 'She doesn't find everything funny the way we do.'

Later that evening, while we were having dinner with Mel's mum, Mel repeated her accusations about Shaznay. Helen – always fiercely protective of Mel – agreed.

'Don't trust Shaznay, Nic. Mel is always being pushed aside,' Helen said. 'Hopefully things will be better now you're around.'

I was new to the band, excited, impressionable, keener than I had ever been about anything in my life. I wanted the band to work, I needed it to. I told myself it was an honour Mel and her mum were being so honest with me.

'I hope I can make a difference,' I said.

Working at the cafe and counting on my tips to get me through, I ate meals at Mel's house and, gradually, at Shaznay's too. Shaznay's Mum, Del, is the best cook in the world. It was in her kitchen I learned to love Jamaican food: jerk chicken, plantain and spicy macaroni cheese. From my first mouthful, I was hooked. Everything Del cooked was so tasty. It was cosy at Shaznay's house too. The heating was always on full blast.

One night Shaznay invited me to stay. We sat up late in her bedroom, talking.

'Be careful of Mel,' Shaznay warned me.

'Mel?'

'Don't trust . . .' Shaznay hesitated. 'Don't trust what she tells you about me. When Mel and I were at ZTT, she got everyone to turn against me,' Shaznay said. 'I've got a feeling she might try to do the same with you.'

I felt sorry for Shaznay, for her predicament. What she most feared was already in motion. Mel was telling me stories about Shaznay and trying to get me on her side. And – as Mel and I were long-time friends – Shaznay knew Mel had the edge over her.

'Don't worry,' I said, 'I make up my own mind about people.'

'Mel is going to be jealous you stayed over at my place,' Shaznay said.

'That's ridiculous,' I said.

But the next day when I went round to see Mel, she was distant. I had the feeling I had done something wrong, but knew I hadn't. I felt like a prize shoved between them, both of them wrestling over me. I liked them both. I wanted us all to get on.

The more time I spent around Shaznay, the more I liked her. She was less humorous than Mel, less upfront and quirky, but we had a really good girly time together. We used to listen to music and gossip. When we got bored, we would call boys and giggle down the telephone. Other times, we listened to All Saints' music so I could become familiar with it, and Shaznay taught me the dance routines.

Mel was competitive with Shaznay but, to me, Shaznay was fascinating – she was unlike anyone I had met. My enthusiasm for Shaznay encouraged her to open up. Shaznay was fascinated by me too. She found me mad and funny. I had had wild times she could not imagine. I brought something out in Shaznay. She opened up when she met me.

'Come on,' one night I coaxed Shaznay and Mel, 'let's go to the Atlantic Bar.'

They had never heard of it.

'It's a bar and restaurant,' I told them.

I wanted them to get drunk with me and let their hair down. They both looked unsure. They were accustomed to dark, underground hip-hop clubs, and the thought of a fancy nightclub was alien to them.

'Come on,' I said. 'You only live once.'

Shaznay was wearing her black leggings and black PVC coat – I rarely saw her in anything else. There was a glamorous woman inside Shaznay waiting to come out. I knew it, but she wouldn't admit it.

Mel had a brand-new pair of trousers.

'Sod it,' she said as she zipped them up. 'They're much too long. Do you have any pins?'

'No.'

'Sellotape?'

Mel taped her trousers to fit.

'No one will know.'

I borrowed Mel's skintight silver trousers. We looked fabulous leaving Mel's flat that night. Dressed up together for the first time – the three of us looking our best. But when we walked into the long, smoky room filled with party people Mel and Shaznay froze. They were like rabbits in car headlights.

We had been there ten minutes when Shaznay grabbed my arm.

'This is not my scene,' she said. 'I don't like it here.'

'Me neither,' Mel said. 'We're leaving.'

I didn't take them back to the Atlantic Bar for several months and, when I did, it was with a big gang of people. They liked it better that time. By then they had begun to develop a taste for it. For glamour.

One night, sitting around Shaznay's house bored, we decided to go out – still in our pyjamas but with the

79

addition of baseball caps – to Browns nightclub in Holborn. It was a strange place – old men spending tons of money on pretty young girls. I loved the seedy late-night atmosphere and the feeling that, there, you could do whatever you liked. Shaznay liked it too.

A few days later, I went into a recording studio for the first time. Mel's mum – our perpetual chauffeur – drove Mel, Shaznay and myself to Professor Stretch's house in Slough. Prof was a friend of Mel's and he had built a recording studio in a garage at the back of his house. We were there to re-record 'I Know Where It's At'.

We arrived at three o'clock in the afternoon. Prof was in the studio. There was a mixing desk, a recording booth and keyboards everywhere. Ashtrays, Rizla papers, cups of tea and empty Pot Noodle cartons littered every surface. The air was thick with smoke.

Tall and skinny with a mop of thick blond hair, Prof had a spliff in his hand and smoked heavily the entire time we were there.

'Good to meet you, Nicole,' he said, shaking my hand.

He did not ask if I had been in a studio before.

'Into the booth then,' he said.

I felt shy and nervous; intimidated by the fact I was new and inexperienced. Everyone else in the room knew exactly what to do. I opened the sliding glass doors and went inside the booth. It was small in there; like being in a lift. There were two guitars on stands, a drum kit, a microphone and a big pair of headphones. It was very cramped.

Once the door was shut I felt utterly alone. Soundproofed, the booth was completely silent. I looked out of the window to where Prof sat at the mixing desk.

I put the headphones on.

'Levels all right?' he asked.

Levels?

'Are the levels all right in your cans?'

Cans? I didn't have a clue what he was talking about.

'Yes,' I said, 'fine.'

There is nothing worse than feeling like everybody but you knows the score – like being the new kid at school, the new girl who doesn't know what to do. Standing on my own in the booth with Mel, Shaznay and Prof all looking at me, I decided I would never ask what anything meant, I would learn it all as I went along.

I said a few words into the microphone and Prof and I made sure we could hear each other clearly.

Then he said: 'I need you to track the first line.'

Track the first line? In my headphones I could hear the music. Nothing else – Shaznay and Mel's voices had been hidden to make it easier for me to hear mine and not to sing flat. I was so nervous. I kept thinking to myself: please do it right, you can do this.

I sang the chorus a couple of times – it was just one line: 'I know where it's at.' It was strange, unnerving, just hearing my own voice in my ears. Then Prof was ready to start recording.

'Go,' said Prof.

'I know where it's at.'

'And again.'

'I know where it's at.'

'Oh my God.'

I stopped stunned, terrified.

'What?'

'You are a natural tracker,' Prof said. 'Listen.'

He played my voice back to me and I could hear it. 'Tracking' evidently meant singing a vocal and then singing the exact same vocal again so when they were played together the voice sounded thicker. I did it bang on. I had done it right.

We tracked the first verse. Prof got us to sing the same lines over and over. I was anxious about time. I was due at work. It was taking longer than I expected. At 5 p.m., an hour before I was meant to start my shift at the Sports Cafe, I rang my boss. She was a new woman, from South Africa; I barely knew her.

'I have to pick my mum up from the airport and her plane has been delayed,' I lied. 'I won't be able to make it in to work until later – or maybe not at all today.'

'If her plane has been delayed,' my boss said, 'why can't you come to work now?'

I looked at Shaznay and Mel.

'I'm at the airport,' I said. 'I have to wait to pick her up.'

'If you don't come in now,' my boss said, 'don't bother coming in at all.'

I held the receiver, my heart was pounding. I was in a borrowed studio in Slough with a band that had no recording deal – and my boss was giving me an ultimatum: my income or the band. She was making me choose. A decision had to be made.

'All right,' I said, with considerably more confidence in my voice than I was feeling. 'Whatever.'

I put the telephone down and turned to Mel and Shaznay.

'I can stay as long as you like now. I just quit,' I said, 'to concentrate on being in the band.'

'You've joined All Saints properly.' Mel was beaming.

'Now we're all working full time,' Shaznay said.

We hugged each other happily.

We stayed at the studio until late. We sang the song section by section, each of us putting our vocals down separately, in the same key. I learned that cans were headphones and levels related to the volume.

Then we 'stacked the harmonies', building them on top of each other like bricks for a house. Shaznay was good at low harmonies and Mel was good at high ones. I was a bridge between them. We laid down as many harmonies as we could.

Later, Prof played the naked track, just music, and I listened as Mel and Shaznay improvised in the booth, singing a whole bunch of adlibs – 'oohs' and 'aahs' – that Prof could intersperse throughout the song.

'Okay, Nicole,' Prof said when I went into the booth for the last time, 'now give me some adlibs.'

I put on the headphones but, at the last minute, my courage failed me. I felt stupid and shy. What if I sounded off-key?

'No,' I said, 'not yet.'

We had a long drive back. Improvising was something I would save for another day.

Over the next few days, Prof put all our individual tracks together and mixed the song, levelling and blending. He sent a copy of the demo to Mel. She rang when it arrived and I went straight over. A CD – a joy to hold in my hand.

'Listen,' said Mel.

I heard our three voices harmonizing. My body tingled.

'Mel,' I said, 'we're on our way.'

★

It was my earnings at the Sports Cafe that had ensured me, Mel and Shaznay could go out and have a good time. Now I could no longer afford to take us out. With my job gone, I was living hand to mouth. Mel was relying on her mum and Shaznay was on income support so I went to the dole office in Camden. I wanted to try to get some money to see me over this difficult patch. But clearly I gave the wrong answers to their questions. I came away empty handed.

Life hit a low point. I totally believed in the band and its potential, but I was broke. And I was miles away from my security – my family. When I lived in America I had been so well looked after. My hair was always done and there were good meals on the table. Now I was alone in London.

My hair had long dark roots. I lost loads of weight. I was living off coppers I had saved in an old spaghetti jar, tipping them out to buy Twixes and Pot Noodles because that was all I could afford.

I used to rummage around at the back of the kitchen cupboards looking for things that might have been left there. One day I found a bottle of green food colouring I had once bought to make a cake. I used it to dye a bowl of Ready Brek green. It was so successful, I later dyed a slice of toast. Anything for variety.

I could no longer go to the pub because there is nothing worse than standing at the bar expecting someone to buy you a drink. I used to ask people for cigarettes. Good days were ones where I put on a pair of jeans and found a pound in the pocket.

I hit rock bottom but I refused to give up – I really believed something good would happen. I had spent most of my life feeling unfulfilled. Now, with All Saints, for the first time, I was being creative in my own right. I loved being part of the band. I had found something that fitted me perfectly. There was no way I was going back to being a waitress.

But late one night, when I returned home from the studio in London and realized the only meal I could afford was a bowl of Ready Brek, I finally broke down. I called Mum in America. It was a point of honour with me to manage on my own, to make my life all right. I was resourceful, practical. Dad's uninterest in the early years – and being separated from Mum – had made me so. I was embarrassed at having to call Mum. I felt I was letting myself down, disappointing her, but I couldn't help it. When I heard her voice I wept.

'Here's something that might cheer you up,' Mum said. 'Your father and I just got married again.'

That made it worse. I was bawling my eyes out.

'What do you mean you got married again? All the family are there except me – I'm here on my own.'

Missing out on their wedding made me feel so alone, but then Mum told me they were planning on all moving back to London and I felt a huge sense of relief.

NATALIE NICOLE

It was the spring of 1995. I was twenty-two. Mum and Dad were looking after Rachel and I was newly arrived back in England. Nicole and I were sharing Dad's flat in Camden. We painted the living room dark turquoise.

Nic played me the songs she was working on. They were strong, melodic. I was so proud of her, so wanted her to be a success. It was a big sister thing.

I was happy to see Mel again. One night Nic took

me out to a bar to meet Shaznay. We got drunk on tequilas and I thought she was sweet. I praised the band.

'I love the songs,' I said.

I was a big fan of All Saints, but there was no way I could take the risk that Nic was taking – living on next to nothing, gambling for her dreams. Carl had promised to pay child support but the one cheque he sent me bounced. I had a little girl to feed and clothe. She was always my priority. Sometimes I sang – in the bath, listening to music on the radio. I still loved to sing but I thought the time for that was a long way off.

I needed a job. I had decided I wanted Rachel to go to private school. My parents scrimped so that my schooling was private. I wanted to give my child the best. Whatever job I had, I was only ever able to pay term by term, scrabbling together just enough money at the final moment, borrowing from my family, often doing without.

I had no qualifications, no experience of anything other than odd jobs. I wanted to work in an office – but an office where I would not get bored. I wanted to be challenged. Not for the first time, I wished I had graduated. We moved so much, I never got absorbed at school; it never seemed worth the effort. But I wanted to be using my brain. I wanted to remember that I had one.

Looking through the paper I saw an advertisement for a graphic designer, Sydney Austin. He was looking for someone to book models for him. I can do that, I thought. I telephoned the office and was given an interview the next day. Dad was back from the States so he drove me there. He parked outside and waited. It was

Mum and Dad on
their wedding day

Dad is very lucky to be married to our
beautiful mum

Where are we?

No cellulite!

With Lori and Lee

Bumping around in Brighton

Four sisters at Canada's Wonderland

Yummy!

Upstate New York

First school picture

My favourite picture of Nic and me on Hampstead Heath

The Fonz (Nic) and me 'trying' to be cool

Starting out in showbiz

Mum in her Sue Ellen days
with Lee

High school cheerleading days

Carl and my dog, Bugsy

I was just nineteen with beautiful Rachel

In the Catskills, NY

F*** off!

Living it up on holiday

First time in the recording studio

Recording 'Never Ever'
in Washington

The Olympic ice-skating team

In Boston freezing our asses off... Make mine a triple...

freezing cold, slush everywhere. I wore my pilot's leather jacket. I had a suntan.

'I won't be long,' I told Dad, 'I'll be in and out in a few minutes.'

I walked the two flights of stairs to Sydney Austin's office. There was a woman behind the desk. I looked around the room and saw that there were two girls in front of me. All I could think was my dad has turned the engine off to save petrol and he is cold out there.

'How long will this take?' I asked. 'My dad's waiting outside.'

Sydney Austin appeared at the door, he was showing someone out.

'Two seconds,' he said, 'why don't you come in?'

'I'm terribly sorry,' I told him, 'I didn't mean to be rude. I'm just worried about my dad.'

'It's fine,' he said, closing the door. 'Why do you want this job?'

I had no CV, no degree.

'I've got no qualifications,' I said, 'but I'm quick and I'm keen. I'm good with numbers. Test me.'

I did not hear anything for a week. I was convinced I had messed the interview up. And then Sydney Austin called me.

'Congratulations,' he said. 'You got the job.'

I was amazed. Sydney Austin was a successful and powerful man but he gave me a chance. He went purely, he said, on my personality – the enthusiasm I had shown at the interview.

I worked for Sydney for four months, but I was restless. I could not sit behind a desk. Sydney was like a father to me. He was tolerant, he looked away a lot, but the other staff resented me. We all knew it was unfair.

I took longer and longer lunch breaks, sunbathing in the park.

There was one aspect of the job I enjoyed – booking male models. I used to invite them to the office to see their portfolios. Occasionally, I would ask one out for a drink. Dating male models was fun. We would sit in a bar and I could feel the shift in power. Being in a position to employ them gave me energy. The tables were turned.

NATALIE NICOLE

Nat and I used to go out every weekend – mainly to the Pheasantry on the King's Road in Chelsea. We made friends with other people who went there regularly and our main reason for going was to dance all night.

Whenever we arrived at the club, Nat and I used to line up three shots of tequila and down them in one go. It got to the point where we would walk in and the waitress would come straight over to us carrying a round tray filled with tequila shots. Nat and I used to encourage everyone around us to join in.

'The first one goes down bad,' I would say. 'But the rest makes you feel great.'

Drugs were available, but they were of no interest to us. Instead, we would get through a whole bottle of tequila by doing shots. We drank guys under the table. We had a group of guys who were our friends and, for me, that filled 'the man spot' so I didn't need to date anyone. There were men I fancied, but I could never be bothered to do anything about it. Not being committed to anyone made it more fun. Nat and I used to go out and flirt.

We always dressed comfortably when we went out; my favourite outfit was dungarees, work boots and a tank top so that I didn't get too hot. Nat wore army trousers and her favourite best-buy-ever cropped brown top, which cost her £4.99. We were going out to play. Women in high heels used to say to us: 'I wish I'd worn shoes like you.'

My answer was always the same: 'I would rather have a hangover than blisters on my feet.'

The dance floor would be packed, but I wanted to use up my energy so I would jump up and down as high as I could, like a punk. Nat said I was like a pogo stick. At the end of the evening, I never felt drunk and I always knew what I was doing – which was just as well, as up to two hours could be spent waiting outside with the other revellers for a taxi to take us home. The next morning, Nat and I always went for a fry-up in a café. That was our weekend – and it was so much fun.

NATALIE NICOLE

Nic and I hung out a lot with Melanie and, occasionally, she came with us to the Pheasantry. Mel was excited, I could feel it, she was riding the crest of a wave. But she seemed to take every opportunity to say bad things about Shaznay. I listened to Mel telling me that Shaznay was a control freak and I tried to understand. Shaznay seemed kind to me. I knew they had a history of working together and I put it down to creative spats.

One night we all went out for dinner to the Arizona restaurant in Camden. Watching Shaznay it became clear that she was oblivious to what was going on – she had no idea how Mel felt about her. It was all going on behind her back.

I felt awkward. The whole thing was unnecessary. I felt additionally sorry for Shaznay because, when the four of us got together, she was in many ways the outsider. We had all known each other since school, we shared stories and similar cultures. If Mel was trying to unite us against Shaznay, then Shaznay would have very good reason to worry.

It seemed a good idea: to try to bring Mel and Shaznay back into harmony. They were the team on which my little sister's future depended. I did not feel I could just sit back and watch pettyness ruin Nic's chance of success. Mel's bad feelings had to be resolved. And the only way to do that was to talk – honestly.

'Mel,' I said, 'I think there are some things you need to say to Shaznay.'

Mel put down her fork and looked at me with malevolence.

'Things you need to get off your chest, Mel,' I said, 'to clear the air.'

Mel sat in silence for a long time.

'Well, Shaznay,' I said at last. 'Mel thinks you have a problem with her.'

Shaznay sat dumbstruck as, reluctantly, Mel itemized her catalogue of grievances.

'I didn't know you felt that way, Mel,' Shaznay said at last. 'I'm glad you're telling me.'

Shaznay reacted the way I anticipated she would: all Shaznay wanted was to work and do her music, whatever stood in the way of that she wanted cleared up and away. Mel and Shaznay spoke and, as they did, it became clearer that the issues were all inside Mel's head. Mel needed to speak about them and Shaznay needed to hear them. It was simple, obvious.

The atmosphere changed then, something lifted, Shaznay and Mel were coming through the other side. It was a relief for all of us. I could feel myself relaxing, unwinding, as the tension ebbed away. But then Mel turned to me and, instead of gratitude, what I saw in her eyes was fury.

'I can't believe you did that to me, Natalie,' she said.

'I'm sorry, Mel. I didn't mean any harm, I was just trying to help.'

Nic touched my hand, she understood, but Mel's eyes were blazing.

After that night, Shaznay was more sensitive to what Mel was feeling and they grew closer. But I had exposed Mel – I had put her in a situation where she had to talk directly about what she was feeling and she could not forgive me for that. Mel turned her anger on me. It was a side of her I had not seen before and it scared me. Mel had to have someone to feel negative towards and now that person was me.

NATALIE NICOLE

Mel and I went to see Chris O'Donald, who used to advise All Saints before I was in the band. We told him we wanted to do showcases, but we had no money and nothing to wear. He gave us a hundred pounds each as a favour and we bought three top of the range Adidas tracksuits.

We did a showcase for Sony. They thought we were great, but they wanted us to change our look, be more 'girlie'. The Spice Girls had just started and they wanted us to be part of the same bandwagon. When we said no to mini skirts, it seemed Sony lost interest. It was a huge blow.

Arguments flared. Shaznay decided to leave the band and do her own thing. Mel and I joined an acting agency, but they didn't find us any work. We even applied for jobs at the restaurant Planet Hollywood – we filled in our application forms and asked for three-hour shifts and weekends off – our applications went straight in the bin.

I went back to New York for the summer. I had been working with Mel and Shaznay for six months and I had All Saints' demo tape in my pocket. I played it at every opportunity.

'It's cool,' people said, when they heard it. 'But what's happening with it?'

'Right now,' I said sadly, 'nothing.'

I met up with my old schoolfriends – they were established in their lives, doing their thing.

'There's auditions for *Starlight Express* in Manhattan,' one of my friends informed me. 'Why don't you go up for it?'

'It's a great idea,' I said. 'I could get a steady job for a year, an apartment in New York, regular food, clothes, a life again.'

I came close to going for that audition – but my heart was still in All Saints. I knew it. I could not let the band go – we were too good.

'I'm going back to London,' I told Mum. 'I'm going to make All Saints happen.'

Even though Shaznay had given up on the band, I came back to London and started going out and taking the demo tape with me. I knew if I sent it to a record company they would just put it in the bin, so I carried it around with me, playing it to anyone who would listen. That whole summer, I took our tape out with me every night, playing it at clubs and parties, even when I was the only one in the room listening to it. The music I loved.

6 - COUNTDOWN

NATALIE NICOLE

I was jobless again. The afternoon Nic had her showcase for Sony, I took the time off work to support her. When I got back, Sydney told me:

'This is no place for you, pack your stuff.'

Sydney and I had had a special friendship. I had lasted as long as I could. It was right I was sacked. It was not fair I was getting away with so much. But now I was without work. It was at this point Nic and Melanie asked me to join the band.

'Shaznay is doing her own thing and we need three harmonies to carry on,' Mel said.

Singing – my great love. And I knew and vibed with All Saints' music. But I was torn.

'I need to provide for Rachel,' I said. 'I want all the best things for her.'

'Maybe you have more chance of securing her future by joining the band than by taking another crappy job,' Nic said.

Gambling my life with theirs, I felt scared but also strangely euphoric.

Our first attempt at writing a song together was one afternoon at Mel's flat. Nic, Mel and I lay on her bed with our heads together listening to the rap song 'I Need You' on Mel's portable stereo. We wanted to keep the original chorus, but change all the other lyrics to make them more in tune with us.

I came up with the first line: 'What's it going to take to get your attention?' Then we kept coming up with line after line. Mel came up with the bridges: 'Now it's time . . . you're flying high . . . don't deny.'

We wrote the whole song in an afternoon. Then we went into the studio to record 'I Need You' with Prof. Mel's mum, Helen, drove us to his place and hung around while we worked. We all loved her to bits and it was a bonus to have her there. Mel's mum is like family and gives the best hugs.

I went into the recording booth and put on the earphones. The first time I heard my voice through the microphone was strange. There was the music in one ear and my voice in the other. I knew how to sing live, I had been doing it all my life, but with recording the timing is different – I had to learn to follow the music closely, more carefully.

I sang the first verse:

> *Baby, now you're here with me*
> *I'll show you things you'll never see*
> *I'm gonna make you holler, make you scream*
> *Trust me baby, you're safe with me.*

I had to sing it again and, as I did, the words began to sound odd to me. The more I sang, the more my voice became contrived and orchestrated – too planned. Early on I discovered the first takes of a song are very often the best.

Nic, Mel and I took turns in the recording booth. It

took ages and we were starving. Helen had brought a tube of vitamin C tablets with her and we consumed them all. I am short-sighted and, at the time, I had a pair of big grey plastic snake-print glasses – I had had them since school. I left them behind at Prof's, but I never mentioned it. They were so ugly and cheap I felt embarrassed to ask for them back. (For the next few months, because I couldn't afford to buy another pair, I walked around virtually blind.)

NATALIE NICOLE

Four months after the disappointment with Sony, I gave our demo tape to John Benson. John was a regular in Browns nightclub and on the London party scene. He knew people. That was the reason I got him involved. He was doing me a favour, as a friend.

I met him at Miss Selfridge in London and handed the demo over.

'It's good, John,' I told him. 'Really good. You must be able to do something.'

He called later the same day, and said: '"Never Ever" is fantastic.'

John had connections everywhere. He pitched us to his friend, Tracey Bennett, Chairman-for-life at London Records. When Tracey Bennett said he wanted to meet us, it was time to tell Shaznay. I telephoned her and told her a record company was interested.

I had my work cut out, getting Shaznay back into a room with Melanie. They had fallen out badly. In addition, Shaznay had no idea that Nat was now in the band. She agreed to meet us to explore the situation.

'I'll come to the meeting, but I can't promise any-thing,' Shaznay said. 'I'm working on other things now.'

NATALIE NICOLE

A meeting was called at Melanie's house. Shaznay sat at the end of the beige velour couch, her body directed away from us, her eyes on the carpet. She listened to what we had to say but her body language and the few words she uttered let us know she was not really interested.

'It's London Records,' Nic said excitedly. 'It's what we have worked for and dreamed of. It's what you want, Shaznay, what you said you wanted.'

Shaznay looked at Nic for the first time.

'I'm not sure,' she said.

She was clearly angry we had gone for a deal behind her back.

'What were we meant to do?' Nic tried again: 'You walked out on us, you said you were through with All Saints.'

'So what makes you think I've changed my mind?'

'Because this is it, Shaznay. All the waiting is over. When I first met you, you said "let's do it".'

Shaznay looked up.

'Let's do it,' Nic said gently. 'We need your songs, Shaznay, we need you.'

In that moment, Shaznay held all the power. She sat so quiet and so still, I was convinced she was going to say no. The future for the four of us was riding on her answer. Without her, London Records would not want us. It was all or nothing. We were all holding our breath.

'Okay,' Shaznay said quietly.

No one reacted for a moment, all too stunned, too hopeful, too scared.

'You'll do it?' Nic's voice was trembling.

'Yes,' Shaznay said. 'Okay.'

'We've asked Nat to join the band,' Nic said then, gingerly.

'That's fine,' Shaznay said. 'I expected it. It's the most natural thing.'

The tension was still thick between us, but that afternoon we decided to make All Saints a four-piece band – and to put all our energy and enthusiasm together.

Three days later, we went for a meeting with Tracey Bennett. A wine bar in Chelsea. Eleven a.m. The place was empty. The four of us sat there in our big puffa coats, like caterpillars.

Tracey Bennett was a big man in a dark-grey suit that was too small for him. He looked like someone out of the group Madness. He had a big face, big eyes. When he moved he appeared to bounce.

When he spoke, Tracey Bennett commanded respect but, faced with us, he was patronizing. He treated us like little girls. I felt insulted – but knew even then I would have to get used to it. Welcome to the music business where men have all the top jobs.

'I think you're going to be big,' he said, shaking our hands in turn. 'I like what you do and you look good.'

Tracey Bennett stayed about twenty minutes. After he left John Benson could not contain his excitement.

'This is so excellent, girls,' he said. 'Isn't this great?'

He treated us to his grin – the one where his teeth did not separate. John Benson always spoke through a grin of nicotine-stained teeth. He was sweating now, as he always did, wiping his head while his eyes darted around.

'Excellent, excellent,' he said, and he rubbed his hands along his thighs like Vic Reeves.

First thing was a photo shoot to see what we looked like together – and then a showcase. Tracey Bennett offered us a Polygram contract and a million-pound promotion deal. We were ecstatic, but Tracey would not sign us unless John was our manager.

'But John is a playboy,' I moaned to Nic.

John sent us the contract he wanted us to sign. It was long and complicated. We decided to get a lawyer. Helen Searle was experienced and clear.

It took us three months to get the deal signed.

NATALIE NICOLE

It was Christmas 1996. I was ill with such a high fever I could not even celebrate. We were given £400 each. And Tracey gave us each a bunch of flowers with condoms inside. The message seemed to be, go out and pull. It felt insulting. We had a business relationship and I thought the gesture was totally inappropriate.

He had signed us up so we had thought he saw us as talented individuals but, at that most special moment, he made us feel the only thing that counted was our sexuality. This was to set the tone of our relationship with Tracey Bennett. We felt he always viewed us through the filter of his own prejudices about women and he only ever thought of us as good-time girls. He had no idea what we wanted, who All Saints really were.

John had a camera and he took photographs of us, of his lucky day. I felt such a mixture of emotions. Excited, of course, but nervous of what lay ahead.

That Christmas we bought each other baseball caps and Nike socks. Shaznay bought me a silver ring in a box shaped like an apple.

'I nicked it from Camden market,' she told me proudly.

The apple was red velvet with green leaves. I liked it more than the ring. It felt like a treasure. We were getting close again, putting the difficulties behind us.

That New Year's Eve, we went to the club L'Equipe Anglaise. It is a night that burns in my memory. The four of us dressed up and high on the prospect of the year to come. Nothing had happened yet, but we had a record deal – *a record deal* – and excitement rippled through us. The Spice Girls had made it big: it was the time for girl bands and we were something different – something unique – we knew it.

I can still see us on the dance floor. Shaznay with her big ponytail. Mel in her silver trousers. And Nic, there beside me, beaming.

'Your lives are about to change,' John Benson said.

And then the countdown to the new year began: *ten, nine, eight* . . . The four of us huddled together like rugby players . . . we did it . . . *seven, six, five* . . . we got a deal . . . *four, three, two, one* . . . 1997 – this is our year.

We were an island in a room full of excited people – people who did not know we were on the brink of a brand-new life. It made us closer, huddled around our secret. We were a team. And this was our celebration.

'This is it,' I said. 'Everything is going to change. From this day forward.'

'All Saints,' said Nic.

'All Saints.'

And four glasses chimed.

7 - THE FASTEST TRAIN IN THE WORLD

NATALIE NICOLE

Never ever have I ever felt so low
When you gonna take me out of this black hole?
Never ever have I ever felt so sad
The way I'm feeling, yeah, you got me feeling really bad

When I first heard 'Never Ever', I identified with it immediately. The melody evokes a poignant place of loss – a feeling of being deserted. 'When will you get me out of this black hole?' expresses the need we all feel, at times, for someone who can give us something to make us feel better. The words are about the desire to be rescued, but the melody is not desperate, it is gritty, feisty.

'Never Ever' is the best song Shaznay has ever written. She wrote it when she was at the end of a relationship and in pain. It was real. She felt exactly that way. It is a beautiful song. It is raw and honest; a mixture of vulnerability and the ability to cope, a grounded capableness. I think that mix represented All Saints – it is what made us attractive.

'Never Ever' was special right from the start. It was our favourite song and, as soon as the record company heard it, they said they wanted it to be the first song we recorded. London Records tracked down the guys who wrote the music and, as they were based in

Washington, the record company flew us out there to work with them.

Four days in a recording studio in America. We were all tremendously excited. Unable to sleep the night before, we telephoned each other constantly.

As we boarded the plane, excited and nervous, we videoed ourselves.

'I can't believe this is happening,' I told Nic. 'It doesn't feel real.'

Seated on the plane we ordered champagne cocktails. The combination of fizz and excitement was heady. Nic, Mel and I giggled and schemed all the way to Washington. Shaznay was quiet. She sat with her coat on, listening to her Walkman.

NATALIE NICOLE

Washington was bitterly cold. Two jeeps picked us up from the airport and drove us to our hotel. En route, we drove past the bar where they film the TV series *Cheers* and we all bundled out of the car and photographed ourselves by the Cheers sign.

The next day at breakfast everything was exciting and new. The four of us pigged our way through the hotel's menu: scrambled eggs, American cheese, pancakes, hash browns. It was very cold – too cold to go anywhere but the studio and back to the hotel. We all wore Adidas tracksuits and huge caterpillar coats the entire time.

Shaznay and Mel sang the lead on 'Never Ever' and Nicole and I sang the harmonies and choruses. At the end of our first day in the studio, the musicians Robert 'Esmail' and Sean the Maestro wanted adlibs for the end of the song. It was two o'clock in the morning – a full day of recording had taken its toll – we were all creatively depleted.

'I know you girls are tired, but it's the last thing,' Robert said.

Shaznay and Mel were slumped in chairs. Nic too had clearly reached her limit.

'I can't think of anything,' Shaznay said. 'I'm shot.'

Mel nodded. 'Me too.'

I was exhausted, but something was needed and I wanted to give it. I racked my brain.

'I've got an idea,' I said at last.

'Great,' Robert said, relieved. 'Go into the booth and see what you can do.'

Inside the booth, I put the headphones on and sang. The adlibs sounded good. Surprisingly good. I came out of the booth feeling proud. At the final hour I had managed to do what was required.

'Sound okay?'

'Brilliant, Nat,' Sean said. 'Well done.'

Nic looked at me gratefully. 'You did it.'

That night, Robert and Sean took us to a games room. We changed up money and played for hours on snow-boarding and skiing simulators. The beer came in frozen glasses and we drank and drank. It was so much fun. The four of us excited and on a high.

The next day, in the studio, Shaznay said: 'I've had

an idea.' Then, inspired by what she had heard me do the night before, she went into the booth and sang a bunch of adlibs.

Later that day, we piled into the studio to hear the finished recording of 'Never Ever'. It was a fantastic moment, the song sounded wonderful. Sharper, cleaner than any of us could have imagined. I sat there, looking forward to the end of the song. It was my first opportunity to show what I could do. I was very excited to hear how I sounded.

The song came to an end, the adlibs began – I heard Shaznay's voice – only Shaznay's voice. Her vocals had been put over mine. The ball of excitement and expectation in my belly burst.

At the end of the song, we all sat in silence. All Saints was about equality – about women being equal. I expected to live out that equality in my working relationship. I was shocked – this was the first sign of a hierarchy within All Saints.

NATALIE **NICOLE**

I thought: oh no, what now? Just editing Nat out of the song like that without any warning. Why didn't they let her know in advance? When Nat's upset she speaks her mind. I knew it was going to cause problems.

NATALIE **NICOLE**

Back at the hotel, our manager, John Benson, came to see me in my room. I needed to let him know why I felt let down. It was not that I resented Shaznay's talent or expected to take over the song or be the lead, but I had a valuable contribution to make and it needed to be recognized.

'Why did you make me rack my brain for an idea?' I asked John. 'Why didn't you tell me: "This is just to give Shaznay a guide, to put ideas in her head"?'

NATALIE NICOLE

This was a professional situation, one which needed diplomacy and openness. In Shaznay's room I looked at Mel for support. She was staring down at the carpet. Shaznay too would not meet my eyes. I was on my own. My allies, my pals, were ignoring me. We were working on our first song and, already, there were two gangs. It was the beginning of a destructive pattern.

I felt bad for Nat. Sick in the pit of my stomach, I walked across the hotel hall to her room. She was lying on the bed. I could see she had been crying.

'I have to tell you, Nat,' I said, 'they're threatening to kick you out of the band.'

Nat stared at me, her eyes confused.

'They wouldn't do that.'

'They would, Nat. They feel you should just do what you're told because you were the last to join the band.'

NATALIE NICOLE

I was shocked; I found it hard to believe what Nic was telling me. I had been devalued as an artist, I had reacted and now I was going to be thrown out of the band. I was being treated like a child. A child who had to keep her mouth shut. They were telling me I had no rights.

'Nic, do you think I was wrong?'

Nic's opinion of me was the one that mattered. I needed her answer. I needed to know what she thought. If Nic thought I had been out of order then I would listen to that. If she thought I had misread the situation, she would tell me. I could trust her.

Nic looked troubled and turned away from me.

'Your feelings are right, but this isn't the place to express them,' Nic told me. 'You can't behave like this, Nat. You've got to keep quiet. Keep your mouth shut. Cool it.'

NATALIE NICOLE

I felt terrible telling Nat she had to shut up. It hurt me. Nat always speaks her mind. It is part of her essence. She needs to be vocal, that is why she is such a great singer. She is honest, real. Crushing my sister's spirit was like crushing my own. But I was panicking.

NATALIE NICOLE

Sitting in my hotel bedroom, I felt bad, worthless. I felt humiliated. It was the way Carl used to make me feel. Like I was nothing. The worst of it was I was taking it. That evening in the hotel room in Washington, I realized there was nothing I could do. I was powerless.

I wanted to be a good role model for my daughter Rachel, an independent secure woman. What sort of example was I setting, letting people treat me like this? In that moment, I chiselled away a part of myself. It was the beginning of me not being there.

I did not want to be sacked – the band knew that and that was their form of control. And, knowing Nic would not want to lose me, their way of controlling her too. These then were the bare facts and I accepted them. All Saints was my life now and I had to do everything I could to make it work.

NATALIE NICOLE

The next day, only Mel and I turned up for breakfast. Everyone was avoiding each other. Even Mel and I could not talk about what had happened the night before. On the way to the airport and on the plane, too, the subject was taboo.

Shaznay, glad to be going home, sat alone again throughout the journey. Nat also sat apart, listening to her Walkman, lost inside herself. Mel and I got very drunk – so drunk that Mel threw up in the toilet.

'When we arrive at the gate can we get one of those buggy things they use to take old people across the terminal?' Mel said.'I feel so drunk I don't think I can walk.'

I laughed. Mel had a wicked sense of humour. Even in the worst circumstances, she always managed to make me laugh.

NATALIE NICOLE

I listened to *Dirty Dancing* on my Walkman – it is silly and I found it comforting. I wanted to be at home with Rachel, giving her a huge hug. She was what mattered. All Saints was the culmination of a dream, but it was not turning out the way I'd thought it would. The bubble of being in a band had burst.

NATALIE **NICOLE**

We recorded the rest of the album at studios in London. The record company arranged for us to be produced by top producer Cameron McVey. Cameron had worked with Massive Attack and his wife, Neneh Cherry. Our other main producer was Karl Gordon. We all loved KG to bits and ended up calling him 'the fifth member' of All Saints.

NATALIE **NICOLE**

When it came to recording 'I Know Where It's At', Cameron said Nic and I could sing the bridges. I went into the booth excited and nervous – my first All Saints solo. The music boomed through the headphones and I put my mouth to the microphone. Alone in the soft-walled box, I sang with everything I had inside of me.

Can't you see that there's no one on the streets

I came out of the booth glowing. I felt I had given my all, but I could tell, straight away, there was an awkwardness in the room. Cameron was hunched over the mixing desk, smoking a cigarette.

'You've got to fit in with the other vocals – with Shaznay and Mel,' he said.

I thought the way I sang brought variety to the song. I had been singing for years and knew my worth. Now I was being told to copy Shaznay and Mel. They knew the type of singer I was. Why had they hired me?

'I'm taking you off the solo,' Cameron said.

Again no one stuck up for my sister. In private, later, I said:

'Don't let them get to you, Nat.'

'Being in the studio is intimidating,' Nat said. 'This is making me lose confidence in my ability. It is making me scared to sing.'

I could see the damage being done to Nat. She was being made a scapegoat, a focus for the band's imperfections. When we left the studio late and Nat asked to be dropped home first so she could catch Rachel before she went to bed, the others made out she was making a fuss. Her reasonable requests were always being seen as petty demands.

A few days later, the head of publicity at London Records, Juliette Sensicle, conducted a mock media interview with us. We were each given a questionnaire with questions from our future fans such as: what is your favourite colour and who are your idols? When it came to the music question, I wrote that my favourite music is rock. Mel and Shaznay wrote that theirs was R&B and rap.

Juliette came back into the room and we read out our answers. When it was my turn, Mel looked aghast.

'You can't mention rock,' she said.

'Why not?'

'Because it's not what we're about. None of our tracks is rocky,' Mel said. 'You can't like something that we're not doing.'

'What do you mean?' I said. 'Liking rock doesn't mean I don't like what All Saints do. Do we all suddenly have to hide who we are?'

'This is not about you any more,' Juliette said. 'It's about the best way to present the band. There needs to be some kind of homogeny here, some way that you girls can be known and identified. I think you should stick to saying that you all like R&B and rap.'

'It feels phoney,' I said.

That night at home, I opened a bottle of red wine and sat by the window. I was so angry inside. What was real and true did not count. My individuality, who I was, what I cared about, was being systematically robbed, but what could I do? I wanted All Saints to work.

NATALIE NICOLE

To let people know that All Saints were coming, we made a short film. We drove around Leicester Square in a white limousine, our name, All Saints, flashing on one of the tallest buildings. Lighting up the building was expensive, so we had to shoot the whole thing in ten minutes.

When we looked up and saw our name flashing, we started to scream. We were too excited to do anything else. We wound the windows down and called out at the top of our lungs: All Saints, All Saints, All Saints. It was a total thrill. We wanted everyone to look up and see it.

As the limousine circled the block, we called our families.

'Quick, quick, drive to Leicester Square now or you'll miss it.'

It was the most magical moment. Who knew what would happen next?

> *If you want to have a good time*
> *If you know you've got something on your mind*
> *If you know that you wanna get on down*
> *No need to worry 'cause All Saints will be around*

Shaznay's song 'I Know Where It's At', written four years earlier, was our first release. I had loved the song from the start. I knew we had a hit on our hands. Everywhere we went there was a buzz.

We made the video for the song at an underpass near an old brewery. We wore Top Shop vests and baggy trousers. It was our first experience of working with a make-up artist and she plastered our faces: eyes and lips, dark and heavy. We looked like punks.

At the end of the video shoot, we changed into our own clothes and had our picture taken for the *Face* magazine. The four of us sitting in the back of an old Bentley.

Driving home from making the video, we were recognized for the first time. As our mini van pulled up at a roundabout, the people in the car next to us pointed and stared. We stared right back at them, as indiscreet as they were. Then we were all waving, our faces pressed to the window. Somebody recognized us. Somebody knew who we were.

Waiting for our first magazine article to be published drove us crazy – we were so excited to see it and to read what was written about us. We couldn't wait to share it with our friends.

We kept thinking the magazine was out when it was not; going into newsagents and scouring the shelves. When we finally saw our double-page spread, we looked like an advertisement for Adidas – without realizing it we had all put on our tracksuits. Mel used to go into newsagents, open the magazine on our double-page spread and leave it on the shelf so everyone could see it.

The *Face* said that we were streetwise, tough – something all the magazines picked up on straight away. We were not manufactured pop – our strength was that we were authentic. That is why it bothered me to compromise. It was important to me that we were real.

The album was finished, mastered by Cameron and Nelly Hooper. It was a fantastic feeling, exciting and scary. We needed a photograph for the cover. Jamie Morgan, the photographer, was flamboyant and camp; we assumed he was gay and did not object when he kept coming into the room when we were changing and flicking fluff off our chests.

'Come on, baby, give it to me,' he said as we posed for him.

When we found out he was straight, we were amused and annoyed. It was a lesson in not making assumptions.

My first real taste of success came shortly after, when I bumped into an old school friend, Josh, on the street.

'I've heard talk that you're in a band,' he said. 'Is it true?'

'Yes,' I said. 'We've got our first single coming out soon.'

I looked up and there, right in front of us on the wall, was a huge black and white poster: Nicole, Shaznay, Mel and I dressed as punks and slashed with barbed wire.

'There we are, there it is, there's our poster.' I could not contain my excitement.

'Holy shit,' Josh said.

Amazed and awed, Josh and I stood there, looking up at the poster – the first poster I had ever seen of us. The moment was highlighted by the fact that this was a road I knew well – the road I used to queue in once a fortnight to collect the dole. And there was my face – up there. *My face.*

I wanted to stand and stare at that poster all day. I wanted to grab hold of people as they walked by and tell them: 'It's me everybody, that girl there, it's me.' I wanted to scream: All Saints are here.

But more than any of that, I wanted to share this moment, this brand-new thing, with my sister Nic. I got straight into my car and went to pick up Nic and Mum. Then the three of us drove around London looking for posters. They were everywhere, all over town.

'We're going to be something,' I confided to Nic that afternoon. 'We're finally going to get what we always wanted. A chance to be something.'

It was the Smash Hits Tour, an opportunity for up and coming bands to travel the country, do interviews and perform live. Shaznay and Mel had been on the tour three years earlier but, for Nat and me, it was our first time and we were high on the prospect.

The first time we heard 'I Know Where It's At' on the radio, we were driving around the country doing promotion as part of the tour. We were sitting in the back of a Land-Rover, when suddenly we heard the presenter say:

'And now here is a song by a new group I think we are going to be hearing a lot more of. All Saints.'

We heard the opening line – Melanie singing: 'If you want to have a good time' – and then the four of us were jumping up and down and screaming. We had played the demo at home, but this was something else – this was public radio. People all over the country would be listening to it – listening to us, right this minute, right now.

We were making such a racket, it was impossible to hear the song – but our excitement was uncontrollable.

'That's us, that's really us, don't we sound brilliant?'

The windows didn't open in the back of the car and it was unbearably hot, but we didn't care, banging against each other and hugging hard. Then, with the song still playing, we picked up our mobile phones and started to call our families. We didn't listen to ourselves singing, the joy was in sharing the moment with the people we loved.

Later that day, we sang in front of a crowd for the first time. It was a fantastic experience. 'I Know Where It's

At' rang into the arena and the audience cheered. It was a lovely response. It gave me confidence. Singing on stage thrilled me – it was what I had always wanted to do.

NSYNC were touring with us, and the Back Street Boys, Aqua and Ricki Martin. It was our first opportunity to mix with other bands and we were keen to swap stories and learn as much as we could. At our first gig, Mel and Shaznay talked to members of other bands they had met on the tour before. Nat and I stood around behind them, waiting to be introduced, but they did not include us.

It was clear Shaznay and Mel did not want to share their friends, so Nat and I made our own. One night we hung out with Aqua. The next day Shaznay and Mel were scornful.

'Aqua?' The word dripped with derision. 'They're so uncool.'

'They were fun,' I protested. 'We had a brilliant time.'

I wanted to tell Mel and Shaznay all about it, but they made it clear that, because they didn't like Aqua's music, they had no interest in them as people. A new division began to form between us.

Mel really fancied JK from Jamiroquai and, one evening early in the tour, we got invited to a party where, it was rumoured, JK might be. Mel was so excited. When we arrived, there was no sign of JK but another member of his band – Stuart Zender – was there. Shaznay and Mel love Jamiroquai's music, so they spent the entire evening flirting with Stuart. When we got invited on to another party, Stuart took Mel in his two-seater sports car.

'Michael will give you a ride,' Stuart said, pointing to INXS' lead singer, Michael Hutchence. Oh my God. I felt nervous and shy, but Michael Hutchence was really lovely.

'Don't worry,' he said. 'I'm going anyway – I'll give you a lift.'

He had a black Cherokee. Sitting in the passenger seat, I didn't know what to say. He said he liked our music and I thanked him.

'I've always been a fan of INXS,' I told him.

I thought of the little girl he had with Paula Yates.

'Tiger Lilly is a cool name,' I said.

And with that he talked and talked about her. It was abundantly clear that he loved being a parent and got a huge buzz from his daughter. She meant the world to him. It was beautiful to hear.

That party was the beginning of Mel's relationship with Stuart. They were so into each other that night that Shaznay and I felt like spare parts and we went home.

NATALIE NICOLE

During the Smash Hits Tour, we all got on really well with the boys from NSYNC. We began to hang out with them, going out and getting drunk after our gigs. Shaznay developed a crush on Justin Timberlake and I felt very drawn towards Chris Kirkpatrick. Now we had crushes on guys in the same band we could be girls together, just girls. It gave us something in common – something light and fun. My relationship with Shaznay needed that.

Every time we arrived in a new hotel, Shaznay and I used to scour the guest list to see if NSYNC were staying in the same hotel. It was fun to behave like schoolgirls with a crush. Mel was busy with Stuart, so

Shaznay was happy to hang out with me, she included me. It was one of the last times.

NATALIE NICOLE

I was so glad Shaznay and Natalie were getting along. When there were difficulties over who sang what on a song, I stepped aside, I didn't fight. But Nat stuck up for herself – and for me – and that had made Shaznay and Mel dislike her. It was a relief when that tension was not around.

NATALIE NICOLE

The Smash Hits Tour lasted two months and finished off in Amsterdam. 'I Know Where It's At' was beginning to be played on the radio, and *Live and Kicking* flew their presenter Jamie Theakston out to the last show to record a thirty-minute interview with us. I had seen Jamie on television but, in person, he seemed much taller. At well over six foot, he towered over me.

It was a lively interview. Jamie was intelligent, witty and sharp-minded. A man with a quick mind is something that always gets me interested. Jamie made me laugh. He had a quirky, off-beat sense of humour. We sparred, set each other off. I really liked him. There was a buzz between us throughout the interview.

At the after-show party, I spent most of the evening dancing with Chris and the rest of NSYNC. Around 11 p.m. I walked to the bar where Jamie was standing with the *Live and Kicking* camera crew. Jamie called me over. He lined up a tequila slammer for me and I gulped it back.

'Come to my hotel,' he said, 'and have another drink.'

'I can't just leave the band,' I said, 'I'm in a foreign city and I don't even know the name of the hotel I'm staying at. I'll get lost.'

'I'll take you back,' Jamie said. 'Just come with me now.'

Walking through the streets of Amsterdam, I looked down and suddenly noticed Jamie's feet lit up by car headlights. He was wearing the weirdest shoes I had ever seen. They were lime green. They made his feet look huge.

In Jamie's hotel room, two single beds were pushed together to make a double. We sat on one each, drinking whiskey from the mini bar. Jamie was really drunk. His speech was slurred and it was hard for him to link his thoughts consecutively. I kept thinking: no one knows where I am, this guy is a stranger to me.

We had been in the room about twenty minutes when Jamie went to the bathroom. He was in there for so long I wondered what he was doing. Although he went in there fully clothed, when he came out of the bathroom, Jamie was wearing just his boxer shorts. And the smell was awful – he had been vomiting. He sat on the bed for a few moments and then he leant over to kiss me – and, as he did, the two beds came apart and he fell between them on to the floor.

Time to leave.

'See you later,' I said, and bolted for the door.

I managed to find my way back to the club and arrived just as everybody was leaving. I immersed myself in the crowd as if I had never been away.

'Nat, where were you?' Chris asked when he saw me.

'In the bathroom,' I said.

We all went back to our hotel together and carried on partying in Chris's room. The next day, I told the girls about my dalliance with Jamie Theakston and we laughed until we cried.

'He's a dumb ass,' I said, 'but a cute one.'

Even in his absence he was making me laugh.

I thought maybe Jamie would try to reach me – to apologize perhaps – but I didn't hear from him. That was okay; I was busy working. A few weeks later, Smash Hits held a party at a club in Leicester Square to celebrate the end of the tour. All the people involved were invited.

It was here I saw Jamie again. I felt instantly embarrassed, for both of us. Shy. But I walked straight over to him.

'Hi.'

'Hi.'

'How are you?'

He burst into a laugh that carried me with it.

'I just want you to know I'm so embarrassed,' he said.

'I can imagine. Do you remember what happened?'

'No, not really.'

It was too fun an opportunity to miss. I itemized every one of his humiliations.

'Why did you take your clothes off?'

He looked uncomfortable.

'Do you remember when you fell on the floor between the beds?'

'No.'

'You left a very horrible smell in the bathroom.'

We laughed.

I told him about the tour.

'I tried to contact you, you know,' he said. 'I was so ashamed I wanted to apologize. I called London Records but no one would give me your number. Did you get my message?'

'What message?'

'I left a message with a woman, asking you to call me.'

As it dawned on me that the record company had kept Jamie's call secret from me, I was furious. They had decided they did not want Jamie and I to see each other – not good for the image of the band, I guessed – a children's TV presenter.

'I'll give you my number now,' I said.

For our first date, Jamie and I went to a restaurant in Ladbroke Grove – 192. It was small and busy, with mirrors and bench seats all around the walls. We talked non-stop. After dinner, we went to the VIP lounge at Browns, the Red Room. We were sitting at a table sipping gin and tonic when a girl in a short silver dress came over.

'Hi,' she said, putting her hand on Jamie's arm, flirting with him. 'I think you're really great. And very good looking. I watch your show all the time.'

Jamie looked at me. I was very uncomfortable. He jerked his arm away.

'I'm glad you enjoy the show,' he said, 'but I'm not public property.'

In that moment, I felt so much respect for Jamie, and liking. Most guys like the attention of being a celebrity, they revel in playing one female off against another. Jamie was different and that one small incident sealed our friendship. I knew then I could get to like him. He was decent, respectful. He knew how to treat a woman, how to behave.

NATALIE **NICOLE**

Shortly after the Smash Hits Tour, we were sent to Germany to meet the staff of the record company there. They wanted us to make a presentation video – something to show everyone who we were. I am not quite sure how it happened but, for that video, we ended up tying German businessmen to their chairs with their ties.

It was during filming for this video that we heard the news that was about to transform our lives.

'I just got the midweek sales figures,' our tour manager, Johnny Buckland, said, hurrying into the room. 'It's good girls, it's great. "I Know Where It's At" is number four in the charts.'

Number four. We tried to take that in. Number four. That meant people were buying it – they were liking it. It was hard to believe. Being away from home made the experience even more unreal.

The *Big Breakfast* flew Melanie Sykes out to Germany to interview us. She was fun, bubbly and very excited for us.

'You guys have gone in at number four – congratulations,' she said.

She made us feel appreciated and it was great to appear on the *Big Breakfast* – a show we all watched. Our friends and families would probably see us. For the first time, it began to feel real.

From Germany, we went through Scandinavia to France. Then to Japan, where we had interviews lined up to the minute: 8.03, 8.07, 8.11.

'You are being played on the radio such a lot,' Mum told me over the telephone. 'And there are posters of the band everywhere.'

It was hard to take in. We went on the bullet train. Now that was exciting – and tangible – knowing we were travelling on the fastest train in the world.

The first time we appeared on *Top of the Pops* was a major moment for me. I grew up with *Top of the Pops* – it was an exciting and regular feature in my life. I never missed it. Most children dream about it, imagining they are their favourite pop stars performing on *Top of the Pops*. I was fulfilling a childhood dream.

At Elstree Studios all the dressing rooms are on the same floor. We walked along, peering into rooms trying to catch glimpses of celebrities. Paul Weller was performing that night, and the Lightning Seeds and Ocean Colour Scene – one of whom threw up in the dressing room.

Top of the Pops shares its canteen with the casts of *East-Enders* and *Grange Hill* so we saw lots of familiar and famous faces as we ate our lunch. Backstage in the dressing room a stylist showed us racks of clothes. We all decided on black trousers made by Dexter Wong and vest or T-shirt tops.

I felt shy walking on to the stage – nervous. But also very alive. All my senses vibrating. On total red alert. It was a fantastic feeling, singing for a live audience on a TV show we would watch at home. It was hot under the lights. For a decade I had been part of the audience, now the roles were switched. It was incredible.

On stage, Nic and I shot each other a look – and that said it all – *Can you believe this?* To share that moment with my sister – my playmate – made it doubly special.

NATALIE NICOLE

Mum and Dad taped the show and, after our performance, Nat and I went straight round there – so excited all the way at the thought of seeing ourselves on the video. We could not wait. Mum and Dad were excited too. We put the tape in the machine and there we were, watching a show that we would always watch, seeing the band and the audience and the presenter and then, suddenly, us. Nat, me, Mel and Shaznay doing the routine we had rehearsed in our choreographer's office – the routine we had been practising right up until the moment we went on stage.

That is when it hit us. Being in the studio we could almost pretend that it was not happening, but seeing ourselves on the TV made it real. Then Nat and I were jumping up and down, screaming and freaking out.

'That's us, that's us.'

'How did we ever get on *Top of the Pops*?' I asked Nat. 'It's the most incredible show and we are on it.'

'I never expected to be on *Top of the Pops*,' she agreed. 'It's like a joke – like we are pretending.'

It was special. One of those moments in a lifetime that stand out – and always will. A feeling, I guess, of 'I have done it.' Disbelief, excitement and fear. That night I remembered my teenage years and all my teenage dreams. Mum instilled in us that anything is possible. Here it was then: possibility.

8 - NEVER EVER

NATALIE NICOLE

Two months after the release of 'I Know Where It's At', we released our second single, 'Never Ever'. The video was inspired by a Fat Boy Slim video in which a fridge explodes in slow motion.

The clothes chosen for us were fantastic, but too old. Rails of basques, furs and long gloves. They were not right for the song or our image but the director, Sean Ellis, had very strong ideas about the way he wanted the video to look.

At the end of the video, things start smashing and falling apart. It was an amazing vision: fruit, furniture, the whole set shattering in the air so slowly you could see it break apart.

'That wall will collapse around you as you walk across it,' Sean told me. 'You have one chance to do it, so walk and keep walking until you reach the end. You can't mess up.'

Sean called: 'Action' and I started walking across the crumbling set. A pellet hit my leg – hard, sharp. I wanted to cry out, but we only had one take so I kept going.

When I got to the other side I realized why I was in so much pain – the pellet had ripped my trousers and my leg was bleeding. There was a nurse on set. She took me aside and cleaned the wound.

'No one warned me that if the pellets hit you they hurt,' I said.

'And you were wearing just those flimsy designer trousers,' she said. 'When stuntmen work with those pellets, they wear protective garments underneath their clothes.'

I always tried to get home so that I could see Rachel before she went to sleep, but Shaznay resented it when I wanted to leave the studio early to see my daughter. She made me feel I had to choose between the band and my child. On late nights, I used to climb into bed beside Rachel and hold her in her sleep.

Leaving Rachel to promote the band and our new single all over Europe was hard. I kept reminding myself that I was doing this to give her a better life. Rachel didn't understand why I was away from her so much and that was painful – for both of us. When I was away, I called her every day.

'Mummy,' she would ask, 'when are you coming home?'

She was four years old, she did not know what a day meant, let alone a week.

'Three sleeps and Mummy will be home,' I used to tell her, striving for a language she might understand. 'Three more sleeps and then we will be together.'

Her father was gone and now I was too. I wanted to make up for her father's neglect but, so much of the time, I felt guilty. Rachel looked just like Carl and I felt a deep sadness for her that he had walked out on her. His absence meant there was a double pressure on me to be there for her, to get it right.

After Europe, we went to New York to meet people from the record company. We were only there for a couple of days, but I was in the mood for going out so our manager, John Benson, and I went partying. We had a great time, a really full on night, but as I slunk back to the apartment it was daylight and the birds were singing. Tired and hungover, I knew I would be in trouble with the rest of the band. We had loads of work to do.

'What can I tell them to make them forgive me?' I asked John.

We racked our brains.

'Why don't you tell them you met someone incredible?' John suggested.

'Like who?'

And then the idea came to me.

'I'll tell them I met Brad Pitt.'

I concocted a great story, I even half believed it myself.

'You'll never guess who I met,' I said, as soon as they surfaced.

John, my co-conspirator, chipped in with: 'Yeah, you guys left too early last night.'

The girls were ready to be angry, I could see it, so with as much conviction as I could muster, I told them: 'Last night I met Brad Pitt.'

I waited a moment for the full impact to hit them.

'He was wearing a black hood and a leather jacket,' I said, enjoying the details. 'He smoked Marlboro Reds and asked if I wanted one. I tried,' I said, 'but I couldn't leave – it was Brad Pitt.'

The girls understood, of course. What girl would

leave Brad Pitt early because she had work to do? The only problem was the press officer was there and, it was such a good story, she leaked it to the papers. The *New York Post* ran a big article – it was on their front cover. The story even hit the papers in England.

'Oh my God,' I said to John later. 'I've never met the guy in my life. Brad Pitt will think I'm such an idiot.'

Another story that made the papers was my meeting with Johnny Depp. He was in England with Tim Burton, looking for locations for the movie *Sleepy Hollow*. I said one sentence to him, but the press turned it into a relationship. It made me laugh to think of old friends reading the papers and believing I had had relationships with Brad Pitt and Johnny Depp. I could imagine them gossiping: *What is it about her?*

'Never Ever' was on the radio for a couple of months, then it went straight into the charts at number six. We were invited on to another TV show. It was there I met Robbie Williams for the first time.

He was wearing a skintight T-shirt and orange glasses. He looked wild, cute – famous. Very famous. I felt intimidated. His fame made me shy. I had heard about Take That in America. Since I had been back in England, I had seen them on TV, in the newspapers, in magazines. They were everywhere. Huge fame distances people. It makes them seem 'other' somehow. Now here was Robbie Williams standing in front of me.

We were both diffident, but working in the music industry we had a foundation, a common base.

Rob said: 'I like your music.'

'I like yours too.'

There was no time to talk, to go further. Soon

we were standing on the stage, rehearsing our song. It was going well, when suddenly the head producer had an idea.

'Drop your tops to show as much flesh as possible,' he told us.

There were screens behind us and, with our tops lowered, there would be the illusion, on the screens, that we were not wearing any clothes. We looked at each other. We were not comfortable with the idea. There was no one there we could turn to.

We didn't want to ruin our chances so, reluctantly, we pulled our tops down a little. Mel was positioned on a box to add inches to her height and make us all appear equal. She got angry and began to curse under her breath.

'Do it again,' the producer said. 'You need to take your tops a bit lower.'

It was at that point we got the giggles. Pretending to be naked felt so odd, so unnatural – and the more we giggled and knew we were not supposed to, the more irrepressible our laughter was. Laughter lightened the situation. We were angry and this was our way of being rebellious.

'Get off and come back when you have got yourselves together,' the floor manager said.

'Yes, we need to talk about this,' I managed to say at last.

'We're on a schedule,' the producer said. 'Make it quick.'

We discussed our options. We did not want to sully things with the TV show, but we did not want to look naked – it was not us. We were scared that, if we went back, we would burst out laughing again. We took so long debating, it was too late to reshoot the image.

When we went on stage that night, I had to start the song:

A few questions that I need to know, how you could ever hurt me so.

As I sang I looked at the monitor and saw, projected on four huge backing screens, the film they had taken of us with our tops lowered. We looked naked and miserable. This was not what All Saints was about.

I didn't see Rob again for several months. We were asked to perform at the Hope Concert for the Princess Diana Trust. It was all boy bands and us. We were the only girls performing and we felt quite uncomfortable walking into the rehearsal. It was a room full of boys all showing off and practising their scales. They were all dressed up too, while the four of us were dressed down and comfortable in our everyday clothes. It was cold and I was wearing a puffa jacket, baggy trousers and a woolly hat.

Boyzone, 911 and Peter Andre were there. Gary Barlow, Take That's lead singer and songwriter, was sitting at the piano and he announced:

'Everyone come round the piano and we'll have a sing-a-long.'

Then he looked at us.

'It's your chance to show what you can do.'

He was so patronizing, I cringed. All of a sudden, a big bright sunshine came through the door. It was Rob. It was the end of November and raining outside; he was wearing a big fluffy coat. He looked like a wet bear. I thought to myself: that is someone to be impressed by.

Just by walking into the room, Rob changed the energy, changed everything.

It was the first time Rob had been in a room with another member of Take That since he had left the band. He had not had major success yet. At that time, Gary Barlow was seen as the most talented and promising member of the band.

Rob came straight over to us and gave us each a kiss, then he went and said hello to the others. He was a really down-to-earth guy and it shone through. He was so much more real than anyone there. He seemed totally out of place – just as we were. We did not fit in with all that manufactured pop – even though we shared the same fans.

I was having my twenty-third birthday party soon afterwards, so I plucked up courage and invited Rob along. There was something about him I liked. He was definitely the sort of person I wanted at my party.

When I first walked into the bar it was so empty – just the other members of the band, my sister Lori and her friends. I sat with them at a table and ordered half a pint of lager. The first person to walk in was Rob. It was early – about 8 p.m. He came straight over and wished me a happy birthday. He was with his friend Charlie. He also got half a lager and we sat there, chatting, mainly about rehearsals. I kept thinking: I am really happy he has come to my birthday party. It really made it for me.

Rob and I chatted for about an hour. It was very sweet. We were both sober. It was innocent and refreshing. I really appreciated that he came early and we had time together before everyone else got there. I got to know him a bit in that time. I knew I liked him. I loved his eyes.

People started to arrive. Mel was dating Stuart Zender, the bass player with Jamiroquai and the whole of Jamiroquai was there.

After being with Rob I didn't want to talk to other people. I found it hard to walk away from him. That was when I knew I was attracted to him. I kept looking over at him. He was talking to lots of people. I wanted to be with him, but I stayed away. I really liked him. As soon as I fancy someone I avoid them. I am terrified my feelings might be read.

I worried I might make a fool of myself – I didn't know what to say. There were so many pretty girls there – blonde girls in short skirts. As at school, they made me feel unattractive. I had come straight from a photo shoot for 'Under The Bridge' and I was wearing just black leather trousers and a black T-shirt. I knew I didn't stand out in what I was wearing – I felt I looked like one of the waitresses.

After a couple of hours, Rob came over to me and said he was leaving. Stuart Zender's birthday gift to me was a Polaroid camera.

'Will you take a picture with me?' I asked Rob.

'Yes,' he said. 'Sure.'

Rob pulled me close and hugged me for the photograph. It was lovely, full on, it felt electric. It was then I thought that maybe he was attracted to me. This was not just a hug for my birthday.

The Princess Diana Trust Concert took place the following day at Battersea Power Station. It was a huge event – ten different bands and an audience of three thousand.

I didn't see Rob, but I knew he was there and that was exciting. I was carrying around hundreds of Polaroids showing people the highlights of my party. I wanted to show Rob the photo of us together. I kept it at the top of the box so I could locate it quickly if I saw him.

An hour before the show, we had a final rehearsal. I left the dressing room, wondering whether Rob was around and whether I would bump into him. We rehearsed 'Never Ever' and I was walking off stage when I heard a voice twenty feet behind me singing at the top of his lungs.

It was Rob. We all turned round and he came over and said hello.

'Oh my God,' I said, 'I haven't got my pictures on me.'

I was wearing my stage clothes – a long coat – it had no pockets.

At the end of the evening, everyone was leaving. I had the pictures in my pocket and, as we walked out of the main door, I heard Rob shout:

'See you later!'

I turned round.

'I have a picture to show you,' I said.

He walked over and I showed him the Polaroid.

'It's a great picture,' he said. 'I like it.'

I smiled.

'See you then,' Rob said.

'Yes – bye.'

Later he told me he was touched by the sweetness of me showing him the picture. I left feeling satisfied.

The next night, we gathered around the TV to watch the Princess Diana Trust Concert. It was presented by Denise Van Outen and we were amazed not to hear our names mentioned at the beginning on the list of performing artists. As we watched the programme, the horrible truth dawned on us.

All through the show Shaznay had been in a terrible state. She had lost her voice. Before we went on, we plied her with cups of hot honey and lemon and John called in a professional voice coach to try to get her through. But when we came out on to the stage via steep stairs, Shaznay was shaking so much she looked like she was going to fall. Her voice was awful that day and, as she was the main singer on the track, there was nothing we could do to cover up for her.

We had been axed from the show. I felt ashamed and deeply embarrassed.

NATALIE NICOLE

I could not stop thinking about Robbie Williams. I had a sense that he liked me and I wanted to see him again. I asked my manager, John Benson, to get Rob's phone number for me, but I lacked the courage to use it. What would I say? How would he react? I liked the fact that I had his number, that I could call him if I wanted to.

A week later, I opened the paper and saw that Rob had been on a date with Denise Van Outen, who was a class above me at the Sylvia Young Stage School. I knew that they had flirted together on the *Big Breakfast*. I told myself I was not upset or angry, I just wanted to be Rob's friend.

That night I went out to a party and got very drunk. I was coming home by myself in a black cab. Suddenly the moment seemed right – or at least, right enough. I dialled Rob's number. Quickly, almost without thinking – before I could change my mind. His roommate Charlie answered.

'Hello, is Rob there?'

'No,' Charlie said, 'he's just gone out to get some milk.'

'It's Nicole from All Saints,' I said. 'Can I leave my number?'

One second later Rob called me back. Not out at all, just screening his calls. We were both clearly happy to be speaking to each other.

'I'm going to a studio in the country to work on my album,' Rob said. 'Why don't you drive down tomorrow night and have dinner with me?'

It would be a crazy thing to do. I had only met him once. I hardly knew him.

'Okay,' I said.

The next day I could barely think about anything else.

Nat was concerned for me.

'You're crazy, don't go,' she said.

I booked a taxi and a beaten-up Nissan turned up, precarious on the icy roads. The taxi was noisy and smelt of damp. It was snowing. I was wearing a pair of white hipster trousers, a black top and a big green parka coat. I was freezing.

Rob said the journey would take forty-five minutes; it took an hour and a half. I kept thinking to myself: this is the middle of nowhere. You are nuts, Nicole, what are you doing?

When I finally arrived at the farmhouse, I paid the driver quickly. I did not want Rob to see the dilapidated car I had driven up in. Rob greeted me at the door.

'I've saved dinner,' he said, 'so we can eat together.'

Rob was wearing tight grey trousers that looked uncomfortable. All tight and tucked. I could see everything.

'Let's go and eat in the dining room,' he said.

I followed him. He was carrying two plates covered in cling-film. That night the cook had made a roast dinner: roast potatoes, gravy, Yorkshire pudding – all the trimmings. It was difficult to eat. I did not know how to act. I wanted to be myself and friendly but I was feeling very nervous. I was acting like girls I loathe: no personality, just agreeing with everything.

'What about Denise Van Outen, then?' I found myself asking.

'She sent me a bird with a card saying: "Can I be your bird?"' Rob told me. 'I gave the bird to my mum.'

After dinner we went into the studio where Rob was recording. I met the rest of the band: four older men, seasoned musicians Rob hooked up with after he left Take That. They were all really friendly and tried to make me feel comfortable. I was still so nervous.

Rob went into the recording booth and I sat on a sofa and tried to look busy. I did not want to just stare at him. I picked up a book, but quickly put it down. I felt like a spare part. In the recording booth, Rob did something wrong and said into the microphone:

'I'm being distracted by the beautiful person behind me.'

Suddenly included, I laughed and leaned back, banging my head loudly on the shelf behind my head. I went red with embarrassment. Instantly I hated myself.

I reached for another book and started reading. It was a book full of disjointed words – rhyming words to be used for writing song lyrics. I tried to be engrossed. After about an hour, Rob came out of the booth and we all walked down the road to the pub. I felt more relaxed then and less like an accessory.

We got very drunk, drinking pint after pint. Finally I felt like myself. Rob and I were much more relaxed and happy with each other now. 11 p.m. It was then I realized I must be staying the night – even though I had brought nothing with me and I had a video shoot for 'Under The Bridge' first thing in the morning.

We left the pub and stood outside. Rob had not held my hand or anything. It was cold, I put my parka hood up. It was snowing really hard. Rob took my hood down and kissed me.

Back at the farmhouse, Rob and I sat on a couch watching television. We were so wasted we passed out on the couch. All I kept thinking before I passed out was: I have a video to do tomorrow, I must wake up. The couch was narrow. Eventually we roused ourselves and went upstairs to Rob's room. I slept in a T-shirt and black belly-warmer knickers – I really had not thought beyond arriving at the farmhouse. I turned my back to him. He made the situation funny, we laughed.

I kept saying: 'Could you please make sure I get up in the morning?' over and over.

Someone woke us up at 7.30 a.m. There was thick snow outside the farmhouse and I had to get back to London. We drank strong black coffee out of big mugs.

Suddenly Rob stood up and, with a perfect imitation of Liam Gallagher's voice and walk, strode across the room with a cigarette hanging out of his mouth, saying:

'I'll check if the cab is here.'

I laughed.

The car arrived and Rob walked me to the door.

'I'll call you later,' he said.

It was a slow ride back to London in the snow. At the video shoot, I was regaling everyone with my night's adventures when one of the stylists arrived with the newspapers. And there, on the front page of the *Sun*, was a photograph of Rob with Denise Van Outen, under a headline proclaiming that they were now an item.

Rob had told me the truth about him and Denise, but I had a hard job convincing everyone, especially Natalie who was very protective.

'He's a celebrity pop star,' she said. 'Don't be naive. Please be careful, Nic.'

Rob called that afternoon.

'I had a really good night last night,' he said.

'Me too.' I felt triumphant.

I thought I would hear from Rob again in a day or two, but nothing. I was determined not to call him. I began to feel I should not have gone to the studio – not all that way, just because he asked me to. Part of me felt I should have played harder to get.

A week later, I was getting ready to go out for dinner with Mel, when the telephone rang. It was Rob and he sounded completely wired. He was off his head.

'Hello, Nic,' he said. 'Could you come and get me? I'm at a party.'

'Where?'

'In North London.'

'Are you all right?'

'Yes, I just want to get out of here. I want to leave. I've been up all night.'

I rang Mel and told her. She was annoyed that I was dropping everything for Rob, again.

'But he sounded really desperate,' I said.

I got into a taxi and went to the address Rob gave me. It was the house of one of the guys in his band. Rob was lying on the couch, he looked as if he had been to hell and back. No one else was there. Just a couple of people clearing up.

Rob needed a bit of care. He found it hard to reveal his vulnerability; being out of it was almost an excuse to show that side of himself. We left and went back to his place. It was two nights before New Year. I stayed over.

In some ways this is when Rob and I started seeing each other, but we were not ready yet for anyone to know, so we spent New Year's Eve apart. Rob did a private show at the Atlantic Bar. Zoe Ball is a sweetheart and she invited me to go with Nat, Jamie and Samantha Janus to her party.

When we arrived, it was very dark. There was a DJ and sixty people having drinks. At midnight we gathered round to do the countdown to the new year. Everyone gave each other hugs. In my heart, I wanted to be with Rob giving him a new year kiss, but I ended up giving it to Samantha Janus instead.

NATALIE NICOLE

Jamie and I embraced for the countdown, we hugged and kissed. It was very romantic. New Year's Eve 1997 – exactly a year since we were toasting the genesis of All

Saints. One year on, we were established in the public eye and our music was selling well. Professionally we had achieved so much.

And yet I was still concerned about the same things. I had come to a New Year's party with my best friend and my sister and I was the only one with a boyfriend. I worried how they felt.

NATALIE NICOLE

On the morning of 2 January, I was caught by press photographers leaving Rob's house. The next day it was in all the papers.

'What is Nicole Appleton doing leaving Robbie Williams's house first thing in the morning?'

It was the first picture they got of us together.

My first thought was: thank goodness I took a change of clothes with me. At least I didn't walk out wearing last night's clothes.

NATALIE NICOLE

All Saints were busy with magazine covers and telephone interviews. We were doing masses of promotion and were extremely busy every day. There was no time for anything else. We were up and on the ball every day. No partying because we had found we could not play and work as hard as we needed to.

'Never Ever' went into the charts at number six. I told myself I would be satisfied if it stayed at number six for a while – but I was gutted when it went down to number nine. That's it, all over, I told myself.

The next week, our manager told us that 'Never Ever'

was climbing again. Slowly over a period of nine weeks, it climbed and climbed. It was unbelievable at times; fervent hope battling self doubt.

NATALIE NICOLE

People like to be able to relate to songs, especially if they are actually in that situation. When you are going through a difficult time in a relationship and everything feels hopeless but you cannot stop longing for that person to call you so you can speak about it and sort it out – that is what 'Never Ever' is about.

Most days we were at Pineapple Studios in Covent Garden, perfecting the dance routine for 'Never Ever'. When it came to filming it for *Top of the Pops*, we decided to dress up in suits. We looked very formal.

We filmed the routine three times in one day – with three costume changes. Everyone had a feeling the song was going to be around for a while, so they wanted a choice of films to show.

The only thing that bothered us was that they put us on a tiny diamond-shaped stage. We were shoulder to shoulder. I was very nervous. The stage was so small we couldn't do our routine properly.

Rob and I had the same fans and, although we only wanted the best for each other, there were difficult moments. The song 'Angels' was Rob's baby; he released it at a point where he felt it was make or break for his career. I remember lying in his bed early the Sunday morning after its release. His manager called to tell him the chart positions. Rob sounded excited on the telephone. It sounded like good news.

'That was my manager,' he said, turning to me. ' "Never Ever" is number one.'

'Never Ever' had been in the charts for nine weeks. It had been steadily climbing – but number one – and in the week Rob released 'Angels'. I always thought 'Never Ever' was a number one track. I didn't think about it actually going to number one, I just thought it was a top, top song.

Rob was really pleased for me. I was too but I tried to contain myself. I did not whoop and jump up and down as I wanted to. Rob had had competitive feelings since he had left Take That, it was really important to him to prove himself. I did not want to rub in my success, to make him feel bad.

Rob rang his mum. 'Nic's number one.'

She was delighted. I spoke to her on the telephone and she was loving and very sweet. I didn't call anyone. I did not want to make it a bigger issue than it was.

NATALIE NICOLE

'Never Ever' sold 770,000 copies before reaching number one – more than any other single in chart history. It took so long, I began to feel doubtful. But obviously it grew and grew on people.

Going to number one was easily the best moment for me – performing on *Top of the Pops* at number one. The crowd were singing along with us. It was our moment, our time. Mel and Shaznay cried tears of joy. We were on top of the world.

I couldn't wipe the smile off of my face – I could not even do our routine properly. I just wanted to sing and look at everyone. It was a feeling of achievement, of success. It was over so quickly – three minutes of my life. I wanted the moment to last for ever.

I went straight from *Top of the Pops* to meet Jamie at a charity event. I am most comfortable in trainers and combats but, thinking I ought to dress up, I wore a mini skirt and high heels. Struggling to get to Jamie, I tripped over Chris Eubanks's crossed legs and landed on the floor. I was so embarrassed, but on such a high from All Saints' performance I sat there with a big grin on my face.

NATALIE NICOLE

So many times in my life, people dismissed and patronized me. Going to number one felt like a monumental 'fuck you' to them all. It was intensely satisfying. With our single at the top of the charts, all those disbelievers would know how well we were doing. Our song would be in their heads. They would have no choice but to think of me and eat their words.

NATALIE NICOLE

No drug, no drink, no sex can touch the feeling of having a number one single. I was laughing inside myself. Like Nic, I felt smug and self-satisfied. I was euphoric. To make 'Never Ever' number one, a lot of people had to buy it. I wondered how many people had the record – how many people knew about All Saints, knew about me.

People began to recognize me in the street – and they knew my name. I would hear them calling out: 'Natalie, Natalie.' Jamie and I were in Safeway's and the cashier said to me: 'All right, Nat?' It blew my mind. Complete strangers knew my name.

One time, Nic and I got slated in the press – the usual stuff, calling us vacuous party animals, saying we had no talent. That day we performed at Gay Pride and, when we were walking through the crowd to our car, two teenage girls ran up to us.

'Don't worry,' they said protectively. 'We're going to call the newspaper and complain.

'Fuck them,' they continued. 'You and your sister have done so much for us.'

Bad press always hurts – you imagine people, hundreds of people, believe it. These heartfelt words from complete strangers were something we needed to hear; they chased the demons away. Contact with fans is always like that. It reminds you why you do what you do – lets you know you are loved no matter what the press say.

'Can we give you a hug?' the girls asked.

'Of course you can.'

We wrapped our arms around each other.

We performed 'Never Ever' everywhere – all over the world. One of my friends went to a big dinner party with Rory Bremner. She told me they put our record on and they were all singing along, saying 'Never Ever' was their favourite song of all time.

Three months after 'Never Ever' reached the top of the charts, we were invited to perform at the Brits. I didn't sleep at all the night before. I was terrified. We had no idea whether we had won anything – just singing at the awards ceremony felt scary enough.

The Brits was our first performance in front of an audience of top stars, but the most scary person for me to sing in front of was my boyfriend, Jamie. Loved ones always make me nervous – you cannot pretend in front of the people who really know you, if you make a fool of yourself, they are the first to know.

Getting ready backstage, there was a lot of tension. I walked out of the dressing room and saw Spice Girl Emma Bunton in knee-length boots and a sparkly dress. She looked brilliant. The Brits was the Spice Girls' domain – they were the big girl band.

'Hi,' I said.

'All right, Natalie?'

Shaznay scowled at me. I went to school with Emma – she was the little kid who sat next to me in singing class – but Shaznay and Mel felt embarrassed by Nic's and my connection to the Spice Girls. Again, they didn't rate their music, so they looked down on the Spice Girls as people.

NATALIE NICOLE

It was the first time I saw all the Spice Girls together. I also saw Dave Stewart walking around; he was wearing big earphones with spikes on them. David Bowie walked past us too. I was surprised at how short he was. He was wearing heels.

NATALIE NICOLE

We had loads of clothes to choose from for the Brits – glamorous versions of the casual clothes we usually wore. As we got ready to go on stage I was so scared I thought I was going to pass out. I stood next to our tour manager, Johnny Buckland.

'It's only being broadcast live to six million people,' he said.

I started to shake. When I am nervous I get aggressive. Johnny knew that.

'Don't worry,' he said. 'Hit my arm.'

I drew my fist back and punched him in the arm. It helped to relieve my stress. Then Johnny massaged my shoulders. I walked on to the stage scowling and squinting my eyes so that I couldn't see the audience. I was terrified.

We sang 'Never Ever' and, for me, it was an emotional performance. Jamie was in the audience and my mum – sitting together at our table. Afterwards I went straight to Jamie and sat on his lap.

'Well done, Nat,' he said, kissing me. 'You were great.'

Shaznay whispered to one of the minders who then came over to me.

'It's not a good idea you sitting on Jamie's lap,' he said. 'Why don't you sit on KG's lap instead?'

This was not the first time I had been asked to hide my affection for Jamie. Weeks earlier, when the BBC sent Jamie to America with us to do an interview, the same thing happened in the airport. We were told to stop holding hands because it was upsetting Shaznay.

'You are drawing too much attention to your relationship,' the minder said. 'Attention that will be taken away from the band.'

Now I was being told it was cool for me to be seen on our producer's lap, but not on the lap of my boyfriend. It was not the image Shaznay wanted to present. Sadly, silently, I moved away from Jamie.

Then, on stage, I heard Alan Partridge say:

'The prize for the Best Video goes to the talented and not unattractive All Saints for "Never Ever".'

Oh my God. I leapt up. I was so surprised, elated. The others stopped to kiss and hug, but I went straight to the podium. I only arrived a few seconds before the others, but I could see by the looks on Shaznay's and Melanie's faces that they were angry with me.

'I would like to thank our record company for believing in us,' I said.

Then Shaznay pushed me to one side – as if she thought I was trying to steal the limelight.

When we got back to our table, the jokes came thick and fast.

'My God, Nat,' Mel said. 'You ran.'

'Did you go and get *your* award then, Natalie?' Shaznay said.

'I didn't realize there was a rule,' I replied, 'for how long you took to get to the podium.'

When 'Never Ever' won the Best Single category too, I let the others go up first. The only person I wanted to hug was Nic. But nothing they could say or do could spoil this – it was the most exciting moment. It felt like a reward for all the lows – for all the pain and the bitchiness Nic and I had had to endure.

NATALIE **NICOLE**

In the Best Single category, we had been up against the song Elton John wrote for Princess Diana, a version of 'Candle In The Wind'. We never expected to beat that. Shaznay made a speech and she started crying, then we all did. Our mascara-stained cheeks made the front page of virtually every newspaper in the country. We had achieved what the Spice Girls had achieved the year before. We had been on the music scene a little over twelve months.

Rob was up for four awards, but in the end he didn't win anything. We left together. I was on cloud nine – but so aware of Rob's pain. He didn't say anything. He is good at keeping things inside, but I knew he was hurting.

NATALIE NICOLE

The next day, Nic and I relived the Brits together. It was then, in each other's company, with no need for hiding and no need for pretence, that we could really feel our success – our incredible success. We were wild, ecstatic, exuberant.

'We did it,' Nic told me.

My sister and I.

NATALIE NICOLE

After the Brits we started getting invites to fashion shows and top designers sent us clothes. It was fantastic. Fans started waiting for us wherever we went – sometimes waiting hours to see us. It was hard to take in – that level of success. It was as if we were no longer ordinary people – to some we were seen as celebrities, as stars. No matter what we felt inside, it was an image we had to preserve. We owed it to our fans, to the people who bought our records.

We were invited to nightclubs and premieres. When we showed up at the door, the chain would be removed to let us in. I couldn't help thinking about all the times

I used to go out, worried that I would get turned away from places – nights pre-All Saints, when I always had a contingency plan – the pub or playing pool – just in case I didn't get in.

One of the places we were regularly invited to now was Browns – I had been there before, but never in the VIP area. Now I was in one of the most famous night spots in London where all the celebrities went. It felt so good to walk inside the door to the VIP area – a door I could only look at before. I enjoyed being recognized as I walked in and being treated as special, but I never felt as comfortable as I had in the days before we were famous.

In the VIP area – as in all the trendy places we now frequented – the people all wore expensive high-fashion designer labels. Their hair, nails and make-up were flawless. We didn't wear the clothes they were wearing, so I felt we didn't fit in – either with their look or their attitude. We always went out to have a good time but, for the people we were mixing with, the objective was to see and be seen. Sometimes I pined for the nights out Nat and I used to enjoy before we were famous. They really were a lot more fun.

NATALIE NICOLE

We made friends a lot easier now. People wanted to know us. It was great to get all that attention, but there was always a voice in my head saying: don't be fooled. I had a good time with the people we met, but I kept a firm hold of my old friends. As always in my life, I knew who to trust.

★

On the face of it we had it all. As we wrote our own songs, All Saints were seen as a feisty foursome, insisting on authenticity and doing it our own way. But behind the picture of the four of us as supportive equals, Nic and I were feeling increasingly as if we were the second-class members of the band.

In interviews and public appearances, we tried to hide the undercurrents: we were close friends crossing our friendship with a working relationship. But with such different personalities in the mix, the group equilibrium was always compromised.

Shaznay was the songwriter and people looked up to her. Mel was the main singer, she carried most of the solo lines. Nic and I felt we were treated like backing singers. It was hard, sometimes, not to feel bitter.

It was as if we were still schoolgirls vying for top dog position. The initial tensions between Mel and Shaznay shifted into a conflict against Nic and me. When Nic decided to wear a cowboy hat, Shaznay and Mel mocked her. But when Shaznay decided to wear a cowboy hat, suddenly it was cool – no one laughed at her.

It was as if Mel and Shaznay were the queens and the people in our entourage were courtiers. When Shaznay or Mel expressed an opinion, the courtiers agreed, but when Nic and I said something they would look at Mel and Shaznay to see how they were reacting and, from there, they took their cue. The power of the group.

It was an alienating experience. Nic and I felt we were not valued. We were made to feel our contribution was worthless. But, at the same time, we were mates. We absorbed the conflicts between us because we were a sort of family. And, as in a family, competition does not stop the love.

After the Brits promotion around the world started in earnest. We had punishing schedules working twelve to thirteen hours a day, and were often homesick. On a bad day, we ran up two-hundred pound phone bills talking to friends and relatives back home.

Through it all, Rob and I used to laugh all the time – that's why we lasted as long as we did. We both kept each other amused because we shared that hunger to entertain. If you can find a man who can make you laugh like your friends do, then you're sorted.

In the beginning, Rob and I were both really busy and, like Nat and Jamie, we didn't get much chance to see each other. We were both promoting our albums in Europe and it was wonderful when we could manage to be in the same city at the same time.

After doing the video for 'Booty Call' in Los Angeles, I landed in Paris. Rob and I were both doing a show there in a big stadium along with stars such as Rod Stewart and Lionel Richie. We hadn't seen each other for ten days. Arriving at the hotel and knowing he was in the same building was so exciting. I couldn't wait to see him. My heart was pounding. The hotel had a really long hallway and I remember I saw him at the end of it. We ran to each other and I jumped into his arms. We stayed in each other's hotel rooms the whole time.

What I loved most about Rob was his sense of humour. And his generosity. He went to Sri Lanka to do work for the charity UNICEF and ended up playing football with young people he met. He is a very kind person. He is not a mug – he is smart with his money – but everyone is always welcome at his house and he never takes what he has for granted, he is always helping people out. He is a genuine person.

Rob and I brought the best out in each other, but our relationship was under a lot of pressure. I was starting out in a band in turmoil and I would come home to Rob full of problems. It was embarrassing – the band was doing well, but we were not getting on and I was miserable. It is no fun to have someone around who is crying all the time.

Rob was kind and sympathetic – he had been there himself. But ironically that is what made it so difficult. I would start off talking about All Saints and end up helping Rob out with the horrors from his own past with Take That. My pain uncovered his. Rob was never accepted in Take That. He told me how he had been teased for being overweight, and all the rules and regulations he was expected to live by.

One night we sat on the roof terrace in his flat in Notting Hill and he burst into tears talking about Take That. Bad management, the power of band members – he had seen it all before. I knew Rob's problems went a lot deeper, but it was hard for him to go that deep. He didn't want to be with his pain.

In Japan, when I had a huge row with Shaznay, I rang Rob in tears. I knew I was pushing my luck, I knew it was hard for him to hear all this and that he had had enough, but he was my boyfriend, I wanted him to be there for me.

'This is doing my head in,' he said. 'Leave the band – I did.'

'I can't.'

'How much do you have to take?' He was angry now. 'How sad do you have to get?'

9 - BLUE

NATALIE NICOLE

Despite the sometimes abrasive atmosphere, I had been friends with Mel from school and we were close. We were both in steady relationships and would talk about what it might be like to have babies. We lived so much in each other's pockets that our periods were in sync.

We were promoting 'Never Ever' in Vancouver when Mel and I realized that our periods were a few days late. We decided, together, to take a pregnancy test. We took turns to pee on the paper strips and watched, in astonishment, as they both went blue. Quickly (as they always do when it is positive) mine was vibrant, bright, pregnancy blue, Mel's was a smudge.

'We're pregnant.'

It was the most extraordinary moment. It was late at night and moonlight made the snow outside look blue. We did not move. Just sat there grinning as if our faces would crack. All these years of friendship, then musical success together and now this – *this* – our friendship was such a totally splendid thing.

'By my calculations, it means I conceived on Valentine's Day,' I told Mel.

It felt such an amazing omen.

We hugged. Hugged and hugged.

'Let's not tell anyone for a while,' Mel said at last. 'Let's have it as our secret.'

It was like being kids again, sharing something that no one else knew.

'Except Nat,' I said. 'I have to tell Nat.'

'The others won't like it.'

'They'll freeze us out,' I said, 'big time.'

Thoughts of the inevitable hurricane to come sat there alongside our joy. Mere moments after our ecstatic discovery, the fear of displeasure, of being out of favour.

'They'll see it as a threat to the band,' Mel said. 'I know it. It will compromise our image.'

I agreed. It was a time before any of the Spice Girls had become pregnant. Pregnancy for pop stars was not yet cool.

I telephoned Rob. It was two in the morning. He was tired and sleepy, but it was lovely to make contact, as we did every day – to check in, to get our fix of each other. It was hard, always, being apart.

'How are you?'

'Good, tired, you?'

'Yes, the same – and excited,' I said.

'Excited?'

'I have some news, something to tell you.'

Rob was silent.

'Mel and I both did a pregnancy test a few hours ago and I'm pregnant.'

'That's great, babe.' His response was immediate – warm and enthusiastic. It was exactly what I wanted to hear. Even without voicing it – not allowing it – I knew then that I had been afraid of Rob's reaction. We had been together for three months. A part of me feared he would not be into this – and all it entailed.

'Is it okay with you?' I asked him.

'I'm really happy about it,' he said. 'It's what I want.'

That night, Mel slept in my room at the hotel and we stayed up half the night, giggling and planning. It was like a dream: having babies together – babies that would grow up together, as we did. We were so excited. It seemed possible, then, to have everything – career, man you loved, baby. Life could be that good. We were riding on all that potential and possibility.

We had cereal and glasses of milk for breakfast. It was a really happy morning for me. But I was scared to tell John that I was pregnant, scared of his reaction.

'I'm not frightened of him,' Mel said – which was partially true. 'I'll tell him first, if you like, then you can gauge his reaction.'

We left Vancouver, heading for Australia. Mel and I sat up at the back of the plane. The date was 25 March. It was Mel's twenty-third birthday. That just added to the intoxication – it felt momentous.

'If only they knew we were pregnant,' we would whisper and then laugh.

The plane landed for our stopover at Los Angeles airport and we made our way to the huge food hall to wait for our connecting flight. The food hall was crammed with restaurants and bars.

'I'm going to tell John,' Mel said.

'While you tell him, I'll tell Nat.'

We squeezed each other's hands.

'Good luck,' I said.

'It'll be fine,' Mel said. 'Don't worry, you'll see.'

'Come on,' I said to Nat. 'Let's have a look in the gift shop.'

It was one of our favourite airport pastimes, buying strange knick-knacks.

'Nat,' I said. 'I have something to tell you.'

'What?'

She looked panicked and excited, even before I spoke.

'I'm pregnant.'

Nat screamed and threw her arms around me.

'That's fantastic,' she said. 'Are you happy?'

'Yes, very.'

'And Rob?'

'He's happy too.'

We were beaming at each other.

'Does anyone else know?' Nat asked.

'No.'

'Oh God,' she said. 'What about John?'

'Nat, I have something else to tell you.'

I watched her expression change to accommodate another bombshell.

'Mel's pregnant too.'

NATALIE NICOLE

'Mel's pregnant – for fuck's sake, do you two have to do everything together?' I said. 'How did you plan it?'

'We didn't,' Nic said, 'it just happened.'

'I'm jealous,' I said instantly. 'Two best friends getting pregnant together.'

I was happy for my sister – a baby for our family. But I was also in shock. I was relieved Mel was pregnant too. I knew that would make it easier. I was excited. I could not stop staring at them. The Nerds were pregnant. It made me laugh.

Nat and I left the gift shop and started walking towards Mel and John. They were sitting at a table. Twenty metres away, John's voice reached us. He was shouting and wiping sweat from his forehead. Mel was in tears.

'Oh my God,' I said. 'Oh my God.'

I wanted to run – out of the food hall, out of the airport, away from John and Mel, but Mel needed me. I had to be there for her. I walked over to their table.

'You're a fool,' John carried on. 'How long have you known Stuart – nine months, ten? You're letting everything go.'

I put my arms around Mel.

The plane was boarding. We all started walking towards the departure area. John did not stop. A constant voice in Mel's ear.

'You haven't known Stuart long enough to have a child with him. You're so stupid, so naive.'

On the walkways, passengers were staring. I felt embarrassed, ashamed. I wished someone – anyone – would make him stop.

At one of the payphones along the corridor wall, Mel said:

'Go on without me, I'll catch you up.'

As we moved towards the plane, I could hear her.

'Stuart, Stuart, it's me, it's just terrible, it couldn't be worse.' She was crying into the phone.

Nat looked at John aghast.

'It's not about sentiment,' John said. 'It's about what is best for All Saints. Best for you. Shaznay's not going to like it.'

'Don't tell Shaznay, John,' Mel said.

'Why not?'

'I want to tell her myself.'

'When?'

'Soon.'

'It's not your place to tell Shaznay,' Nat said. 'You don't have the right, John.'

Nat looked at me wide-eyed. I knew what her expression meant: all this and he does not know about you yet.

Another payphone. Again, Mel hung back, this time to call her mum. She was crying and shaking all over. My heart hammered and hammered in my chest. Dry tears squeezed behind my eyes. Melanie was doing this for both of us, but I would receive the same, it was only a matter of time.

'What did Stuart say?' I asked her.

'He said: don't listen to the others, you're going to have this baby.'

'Mel, is there anything I can do?'

'No, just make sure he doesn't tell Shaznay.'

'How am I meant to do that?'

'I don't know,' she said. 'I don't know.'

Mel called Stuart again – right up until the last possible moment, making contact with the people who loved her and were happy for her. I knew the pain of leaving that behind. Some days were definitely worse than others. Some days you dragged your whole being on to the plane – every fibre of you longing for your own bed, a cup of tea made by your mum, a quiet night in.

Shiara Juthan, John's assistant, put her arms around Mel as we boarded the plane.

'Don't worry, honey,' she said, 'everything will be all right.'

We all loved Shiara. Warm, helpful, honest, she was a friend.

On the flight, Nat swung herself into the seat beside me and we whispered together.

'How are you?' she asked.

'Terrified,' I replied. 'I never imagined he would act like this.'

'Me neither. And he doesn't know about you yet.'

'I know,' I said, 'I can't bear it.'

'When are you going to tell him?'

'I don't know.'

'Today?'

'I don't know, Nat.'

Shaznay walked past us, she didn't stop to speak.

'She's pissed off,' I said.

'I know.'

'John's told her.'

It was obvious.

'How could he do that?' Nat said.

'It's going to be awful when we land.'

When we landed in Australia, Mel and I got off the plane like zombies. Sunglasses on, heads down, we could barely speak. The future looked bleak. Tracey Edenshaw, who worked in the London office of the record company, was there to meet us. One of the kindest people at London Records, she saw instantly that Mel was in crisis and wrapped her arms tight around her.

'What's this then?' she asked. 'Anything I can do?'

We told her about Mel's pregnancy.

'There's something else, Tracey' – suddenly I was blurting it out – 'I'm pregnant too.'

'Nicole, that's wonderful.'

Tracey Edenshaw's immediate response was so warm and positive I burst into tears.

'It's fine,' she said. 'Fine. As long as you do your work, it doesn't matter if you have children. Bands work it out. It's not always possible to pick and choose the right time to have a baby – things happen.'

Travelling from the airport in a mini van, talking to Tracey, I felt the first glimmer of hope since Mel's confession to John. Things might work out okay.

At the hotel, John called a band meeting in his room. Shaznay sat at the back not speaking, not engaging with anyone. Mel had not told her she was pregnant, but it was clear she knew what the meeting was about. Shaznay would not look at any of us.

'I've called this meeting because the band is in danger of collapsing,' John said. 'Today Mel told me something which can only harm the band. I need to make it public. Mel says she's pregnant.'

With that, Shaznay started screaming. Screaming and screaming.

'I can't believe you're pregnant.' She spat the words at Mel. 'We're going to look so stupid. Have you thought about the responsibility?'

I felt the blood thumping in my ears, my face was hot, red and hot. I wanted to stand up, but I could not. I had to speak. Mel needed me to speak. I was tearful, terrified.

'I'm pregnant too.'

The words were out. They could never be taken back. John started to laugh, then he turned on me.

'I don't believe you,' he said.

'It's true.' I tried to make my voice strong. 'I'm pregnant too. We both are.'

Shaznay started screaming again. It was frightening. I thought she was going to hit me.

'You idiot,' John said. 'Have you any idea what you've done?'

'Done?'

'Robbie Williams is a pop star,' he said. 'He's just using you. He'll be with someone else tomorrow and someone else the week after that.'

'That's rubbish.'

'Is it?'

Mel and I were both crying now, while Nat looked on, open mouthed.

'I would have expected this of Nicole,' Shaznay said, with all the contempt she could muster, 'but not of you, Melanie. I thought you had more sense. I expected more from you.'

It was Mel she was really furious with – her ally, Mel. Even at this point, when we were both guilty of the same sin, the same All Saints betrayal, there was a scale of hierarchy and I was at the bottom of it. All I wanted to do was go home.

John turned to Nat.

'You do realize your sister is making a big mistake, don't you? You won't escape from its impact.'

John called a meeting with Nat. I do not know what he said to her, but I know she went in there as my loyal friend and came out convinced our entire future depended on making me give up Rob's baby.

I laid on my bed. I was so full of emotion, so drained of everything else. Jet lag added to the concoction and I longed so much for home.

I telephoned Rob. He offered to arrange a flight home

for me, but I wanted to finish the promotional tour. We had three days left. I could last that long. I wanted to do it for our fans.

'We're having this child,' Rob said.

I loved the confidence in Rob's voice, the certainty.

'Nothing and no one can stop that.'

Mel and I clung to each other and to our certainty, when we were together, that we were doing nothing wrong. She called me into her room.

'Promise me,' she said, 'promise me, whatever they say, you will remember you want to have this baby. Don't let them bully you into giving it up.'

'No way.' I was clear. 'I want this baby.'

'Me too.'

That night, standing on Sydney harbour, I felt closer to Mel than I ever had.

'Fuck them.' We made a bargain. 'We're having our kids.'

The next day at the record company, the Australian staff were very supportive.

'You will make beautiful mothers,' they said.

It was fantastic to return home to Rob, to someone who wanted this baby every bit as much as I did. We were very close at that time, happy. We loved being around each other, planning ahead. Rob was buying a flat at the time. He took me to see it. Standing outside, we looked up and he pointed to one of the front windows.

'That will be our baby's room,' he said.

Rob took me to see his grandmother at her house in Stoke-on-Trent. She was very sweet, so happy for us.

Rob put his hands on my belly and said: 'This baby is saving my life.'

It was an answer for him, a reason for his life. If it was a girl, he said, we would call her Grace. He wrote a song about her – it's on his album.

Grace, I'm not yet born
Come embrace
A soul that's torn
I have so much to give you.

Mum was supportive of me, she wanted for me whatever I wanted. But one day I went to visit her and I could see she had been crying.

'The record company telephoned,' she said. 'They told me you are making a big mistake and that Rob is bad news.'

'They telephoned you?'

'Yes, they want me to help you change your mind, help you think about the repercussions on you and Nat.'

'I can't believe they involved my family,' I said.

'Are you sure, Nic, really sure you want to have this child?' Mum asked.

'What have they done to you?'

We were both crying.

I cried for hours on the couch that afternoon. Mum and Nat trying to reason with and soothe me. I wanted one person – just one person in my family to tell me to do what was right for me. I felt so frustrated. No one but Rob and Mel understood what this baby meant to me. Why did I have to keep proving myself, keep avowing my right to live my life the way I wanted to? Wasn't that the example we were trying to give with our music and our lives? Freedom to do as you please.

'Don't make me choose between my child and this band,' I begged them. 'Not you. Not my family.'

A month after our return from Australia, we went to New York for a week. We were still a band split in two halves, but this time it was another shifting alliance: Mel and I in one camp, Shaznay and Nat in the other.

NATALIE NICOLE

We had been sent a tape of songs by Burt Bacharach and asked if we wanted to take part in a tribute concert in New York City celebrating this incredible man's music. The list of artists taking part was formidable: Luther Vandross, Cheryl Crowe, Dionne Warwick, Chrissie Hynde. Shaznay and Mel said no because it was not their type of music, but I was keen to take part so, for once, I was singing the lead. Nic, Shaznay and Mel were singing backing vocals.

This was my chance. Most of the songs had already been allocated but there was one available that I knew and loved: 'Always Something There To Remind Me'. The show took place in front of an audience of famous people at the Radio City Music Hall. I was terrified. I wrote the words on my hand just in case panic made me forget them.

'Don't worry,' Elvis Costello said to me, just before I went on stage, 'when I did the Freddie Mercury tribute concert I also had the words written on my hand.'

My tactic for extreme fear is to be extra-confident – to be absolutely determined that the audience are not going to get to me. I looked out into the audience and saw top model Christie Brinkley in the front row. That scared me, but I knew it was good to make contact with people's faces, to sing to people and psyche them out rather than have them psyche me out.

I started to sing and I was in my element. This was what I was born to do. I sang the third verse wrongly, so I cut a bit and sang the second verse again. I came off stage filled with nerves about the way I had sounded.

'That was fantastic,' John Benson said.

Then he hugged me. I had pulled it off. I had been given a chance to shine. Maybe they would realize now that I had something to offer.

NATALIE NICOLE

It all came to a head the next day. There were so many different agendas and excuses being thrown at me. I really wanted to have Rob's baby. What was wrong with that? Everything it seemed. John had hit the roof; so had Shaznay. The band was split down the middle. The record company had even called my mum to talk about it.

I was called into a meeting in the record company offices on my own whilst the others were wandering around helping themselves to CDs and posters (one of the perks of the job). They wanted to talk to me about my pregnancy, and the meeting ended with the record company asking me – did I want them to organize an abortion for me? They said that, if so, they could organize it for the very next day, and that it would be quick and easy – I would be out of the clinic the same day.

I was left speechless. Even the record company had an interest in my private life. After the weeks of pressure

Has anyone seen our eyelids?

Benson with the beautiful Melanie Sykes

My first Polaroid taken with Rob at my birthday party

Rob after 'Let Me Entertain You' video at Jamie Theakston's house

Baywatch in Brighton

One of the last pictures
taken of us

With Jamie in Venice

Enjoying the
view

About to fly in a Very Small plane with Johnny Buckland, our tour manager

Happier times with Mel on Sydney Harbour. Just found out we were both pregnant.

'Cheese!' with Lionel Richie

My relationship with Travis was short but sweet

With Lee and Rachel at Disneyland

With Rachel on
sports day

I had been under, I was so battered. I felt weak. The fight went out of me and I just gave in. Like a robot I agreed to an appointment with the doctor. I was going through the motions. This was not what I wanted but I just had no fight left. A wave had been created and I felt I had no choice but to ride it – unconsciously, without choice or desire. Everyone else was bigger and more insistent than I was. I did not have the energy, the wherewithal, to fight them.

Shiara came into the room and sat down beside me. She put her arm around me. I knew she had been sent in because she was a woman. She was perfect.

As we left the building, I told Mel what had happened.

'You're not going through with it.' Her eyes were blazing. 'Tell me you're not going through with it, tell me, Nicole.'

'I don't know.'

'You don't know?'

'I'm confused,' I said. 'I don't know what's right any more. It's been made to seem really easy. We're a new band. It's a bad time.'

'I don't believe you.' Mel was disappointed in me, disappointed and disgusted too. 'You want this baby. You have a right to it. Have you no spine? How can you do this?'

'Don't hate me, Mel.'

Mel walked away, she would not talk to me.

When I told Nat about the abortion she shrugged her shoulders. She wanted to avoid the subject. She didn't want to talk about it.

Back at the apartment, I telephoned Rob and told him what had happened. He was silent for a long time.

'I'm going to do it,' I told him. 'I'm going to have the abortion.'

'Are you sure that's what you want?'

I could not answer him. I did not know.

'I'll support you whatever you decide,' he said. 'I'm coming out on Concord, I'll be with you tomorrow morning.'

When Rob arrived at the hotel, the record company took him to his room and presented him with an Issey Miyake coat.

We sat up all that night in my bedroom talking. Rob was hugely supportive. I had been trying to hide my feelings but, with Rob, I could be myself.

'I don't know what I'm doing,' I told him. 'I don't know whether I want to go through with it or not. Mel won't talk to me; she thinks I'm spineless. Nat's freaked out about Rachel. It's all such a mess.'

Rob held me as I cried. It was the one time I wished for media intervention – saw a benefit in being public property.

'I wish the press in England would find out I'm pregnant,' I said. 'Then no one could force me to do anything.'

The next day, while the others all packed to return to England, Rob and I met a doctor. He did not know the first thing about me. He did not even ask about my blood type, rhesus negative, which is rare. He was not interested. All he seemed concerned to do was to get me in and out of his private clinic as quickly and quietly as possible. He asked perfunctory questions about my choice. Then he examined me.

'You're carrying into four months,' he told me.

I tried not to picture a four-month-old foetus. This was not a baby yet, this was an okay thing to do. Rob held my hand. I knew this was hard for him too. He was putting his feelings on hold to support me, but he was not an automaton. It hurt him. It was crushing us both.

'This is at a late stage. If we don't do it now,' the doctor said, 'it will be too late.'

'All right,' I said. 'All right.'

It was not a proper decision. I was panicked. I no longer knew my own mind. I had lost confidence in my ability to stand up for myself and for my unborn child. At that point I felt it would have taken superhuman energy to say no.

'It's a painless operation,' the doctor said. 'We will keep you awake so you can return to work almost immediately.'

Rob went to sit in the waiting room. The doctor led me into a tiny little office and I sat in a chair like the ones at the dentist. There was a big scanning machine on my left.

'You will stay awake and sitting up throughout,' the doctor said.

I nodded.

'Let's just have a look and see if anything is there,' he said jovially.

I looked across to the scanning machine. I saw something that looked like a small kidney bean. I wanted to say no – *NO* – but it seemed impossible.

'There it is,' the doctor said.

He prodded the bean with a plastic flashlight. Then he gave me an injection inside my vagina.

'This is to numb the area,' he said.

Maybe the anaesthetic was too light or maybe my body was putting up its last fight for my baby. The pain was excruciating. I felt as if my body was going into labour.

'I can feel everything,' I gasped.

'Don't be ridiculous,' he said. 'You're just imagining it.'

It happened so quickly. I heard the vacuum-cleaner noise of the suction unit, saw its long plastic tube and I watched the bean move from one side of the screen to the other.

It was gone. So quick. I wanted him off me. I should have stopped him. It was done.

There was blood everywhere. My body felt raw and emptied. Rob. All I wanted was to see Rob. I wanted to weep and weep. I felt so sorry for myself, for the mess that was my life. Suddenly, horribly, I realized what had happened – with a clarity that rocked my entire body. My baby was gone.

I fainted on the table.

'It's very common to faint,' I heard the nurse telling Rob as I came round. Rob passed me a glass of water to sip from, and two painkillers.

'I want to go home,' I said.

'Okay, babe.'

'Now.'

Rob lifted me up. I was weak. In shock. I wanted to be as far from that place and that doctor as possible. Rob half-lifted, half-carried me outside to the record company limousine and we drove back to the apartment.

'I can't believe what I've done,' I said over and over. 'I want to kill myself. I want to die.'

'It's all right.' Rob didn't know what to say. 'It will pass, babe, you'll see.'

'We can't ever put the clock back.'

'No.'

'It's irreversible.'

My stomach was cramping and cramping with labour pains. I doubled over in the back of the car.

'Are you all right?' Rob asked.

'No. It hurts so much.'

'Not far now.'

Rob gave me another painkiller, another swig of water. He was an angel, but I barely noticed him, I was too focussed on my own pain, my own failure. I felt I had nothing, nothing that mattered.

The apartment in Trump Tower looked empty, vacant. The others had packed up all their stuff, ready to leave on that afternoon's flight. I was hoping someone would hug me, but they were running about, retrieving bottles of this and piles of that. I lay on the sofa. Rob put his arm around me. Nobody asked how I was.

I listened to Shaznay talking about all the fabulous things she had bought during her shopping trip. Mel avoided my eyes, avoided me altogether. I wanted her to hug me. I wanted her – her of all people – to understand. But she could not be near me. I understood that. Didn't she realize the person I had hurt most of all was myself?

Nat came into the room and gave me a hug. She was the only one who had the guts to come to me.

'Are you okay?' she asked.

'I feel terrible.'

Nat looked at my face.

'Does it hurt?'

'Yes – masses.'

'God, Nic. I'm so sorry.'

Suddenly Nat was crying.

'I didn't mean for this to happen to you,' she said. 'I didn't want to hurt you. I'm so sorry.'

'It's too late, Nat,' I told her. 'I love you, but I just want to be left alone.'

She got up off the couch.

'I'm in a lot of pain,' I said. 'I don't know what's been done to me. I don't blame you.'

NATALIE NICOLE

When I saw Nic lying there in a foetus position, on the couch, I realized fully what she had been through. I was instantly devastated – *devastated* – about what had happened to her. She was white, with huge dark shadows around her eyes. The guilt began then. I did not stick up for her enough. I had let her down. My little sister.

When I asked her how she was, Nic put her arms up and hugged me. My heart broke into a thousand pieces. My jaw was trembling. There were no words for how sorry, how wretched I felt. It is a guilt I still live with. Some things can never be undone.

NATALIE NICOLE

Within ten minutes, the place was bare. Nat, Mel, Shaznay, Shiara, John, the people from the record company – everyone had gone to catch the flight home to England. The apartment felt stark, lifeless. Just Rob and me and this huge great emptiness.

Then, only then, I found the strength in me that I

would have needed to say no, to fight for my rights. I could have stopped it, should have stopped it. This was the beginning of torturing myself. It was the worst day of my life.

'Shall we lie down?' Rob asked.

Rob and I lay on the bed and held each other gently. The pain was so sharp still, so acute. I could not forget what had happened even if I wanted to.

'At least I can eat all my favourite foods again.' I tried to make light of it.

'Yes,' Rob said. 'As soon as we get back I'll take you to Nobu.'

Nobu is my favourite Japanese restaurant.

'And you can have yellow tail jalapeno, lobster salad and chocolate box pudding.'

We lay there together, cracking jokes, trying to lighten the atmosphere. It was horrible, uncomfortable, wrong, so wrong. Before we had plans, a future to look forward to with a child we had created. Now we had nothing. Just a dead thing between us. We no longer knew how to be with each other, what to say, how to stop the pain.

Rob had wanted this baby. I replayed scenes of him touching my belly and saying: 'You are saving my life.' I did not know if he forgave me. To this day, I still do not know. The abortion must have symbolized everything he hated about how this business can control your life. It had so overwhelmed me that he had lost his child.

We stayed the night in the apartment. Restless, fitful, neither of us slept. The record company had booked us on to a flight. Seven hours to England. It felt impossible. What if I haemorrhaged? Rob made a phone call and got us on to Concorde.

'The flight will take three hours, Nic,' he said. 'Do you think you can make it?'

'I think so,' I said. 'I have to get back.'

The band were booked to do a gig the following week in front of the Sultan of Brunei. It was important that I be there. In the midst of it all, work was my saving, something to occupy my mind, a reason to put one foot in front of the other and walk out of the door. My career – the band – I had done this, all this, for All Saints. I would become a workhorse; work was all that mattered, being dedicated, a success.

When I got home, I went straight to see Mum and we cried together.

'Oh, Nicole,' she said. 'I'm so sorry, so sorry for you.'

She felt my pain as her own. I knew that. It was a sweet relief to be around her, to have her hold me and love me.

10 · PRINCESS

NATALIE NICOLE

I had the abortion for the band – the future of the band. I believed I had to do it to save All Saints. Back in London, in rehearsals, no one mentioned it. It was as if it had never happened – my pregnancy, my abortion, my constant and overwhelming pain.

I was thin and bleeding constantly. I looked in the mirror and I was grey. I had been told not to travel for two weeks but, one week after I got back from New York, we flew to Brunei where we had been booked to perform a private concert for Princess Hamida's twenty-first birthday.

The royal family had their own bowling alley, disco and amusement park – which the people of Brunei could use for free. It beat Disneyland. In the centre, there was a huge choreographed fountain that was beautifully lit. The palace was like an NCP car park full of Lamborghinis and Ferraris. The royal family even had jerseys from every football team – all of them signed.

We were each given our own mansion with servants and gold carts to drive around in with Capital Radio playing. The guest mansions were like something out of a fairytale. Marble everywhere – even on the roads. The rules were we were not allowed to show our arms or to point at anything.

The palace staff could not do enough for us. One day

Shiara and I fell asleep by the pool. When we woke, we were surrounded by trays of our favourite food: cocktails, crisps and M&Ms.

For her birthday, the princess was given a diamond the size of a bowl. One day she took me driving in her custom-made Ferrari. It was an automatic hatchback; once the company made it, the family paid for the mould to be broken.

I asked her: 'Princess, you have everything. What do you want?'

'I just want to laugh and be happy,' she told me.

We were performing alongside Janet Jackson and we did two shows – one for the public and one for the princess. There were wild monkeys everywhere. It was swelteringly hot, like a sauna. Nat could not breathe and had to be taken in an ambulance to the hospital. There was a team of top doctors there from all over the world – flown in and paid to be there just in case they might be needed.

We had to meet in Janet Jackson's mansion to get our gifts. We each received a jewel-encrusted watch. Mine was covered with emeralds and Nat's with rubies. I tried to enjoy myself and hung out, mainly, with Shiara. After a few days, Mel flew off to meet Stuart in Bali. We barely spoke.

When I got back from Brunei, I went for my after-care check-up with a doctor in London.

'Something is wrong,' I said. 'I'm still bleeding and the pain is acute.'

'It's nothing to worry about.'

'It feels serious,' I said. 'I don't feel right.'

'It will pass.'

'Am I dying?' I asked the doctor.

'Dying?' He was dismissive and cold. 'You're imagining it. You are fine.'

Looking back, I believe everyone's concern was that the doctor would confirm I was fit enough to perform with the band. What mattered was our success and money-making. I felt powerless.

I was seen out partying all the time and earned a glamorous reputation but, in reality, I was drowning sorrows I could not talk about. I would be out with people, wanting to tell them what had happened, but I could not. I was silenced by my fear of the record company.

No one wanted to talk about it. I felt I had let Rob down, so I could not talk to him either. I remembered how good I had felt when I was pregnant. He told me I was saving his life. I had betrayed his trust.

NATALIE NICOLE

KG gave us a backing track with the music for 'Under The Bridge'. It was a rock song and, as I love rock, the plan was for me to write the words to go with it. But we were so busy I never had the time – the space in my head – to write it. So we decided to record a cover version, just as the Red Hot Chilli Peppers had done originally. I really liked the finished version, and the video we made for it is my favourite. I love the special effects.

As Mel is part-French, she came up with the idea of us covering Patti Labelle's 'Lady Marmalade' as well. The record company decided to release our third single as a double A-side: 'Under The Bridge' and 'Lady Marmalade'.

We had to perform both sides of the single for *Top of the Pops* and we were exhausted. Our tour manager, Johnny Buckland, said he had some Pro-Plus, a caffeine stimulant, in the car and that that might help. I took one and it was great, but I came down from it as quickly as I had gone up, so I took a second pill. I got the shakes, badly. I thought I was going to faint on stage. I did not like feeling so out of control.

A week earlier, in America, when I expressed my exhaustion, a doctor had been brought in to give me a Vitamin B12 injection. It worked – within moments I was up and raring to work. But it was scary, artificial. When the body says it is tired it needs to be listened to, not drugged into action.

Jamie was the presenter of the show that night. It embarrassed me to perform in front of him, but I was getting used to it. At that time, Jamie seemed to be presenting everything we were on. It became the norm. I grew to like having him around; it was a comfort. It was a treat to be able to have a hug during work.

When I found out our third single had gone to number one, I was in Brighton staying with Jamie and his family. Jamie hugged me. He was very proud.

'Well done, darling,' he said.

The DJ, Foxy, telephoned me and I had to speak to him live on Capital Radio.

'How does it feel to be number one?' Foxy asked.

Again there was that feeling of unreality – that we had hit the jackpot. It felt so good I did not trust it. To Foxy, I made it all sound much simpler.

'It's great,' I said. 'We are all thrilled.'

And we were. Jamie and I went to a local pub and celebrated together – All Saints' second number one.

We were happy together. The secret of our relationship was that we did not see each other very much so the times we had together were always special.

With Jamie, the basis was friendship and respect and, at that time, I felt more comfortable and happy with that than with anything else. Jamie is the only boy in a family of girls, and that means he is very comfortable around women.

I liked the sweetness of Jamie's face and his lanky body – even though, as I was only five foot five, it meant I had to look up at him and spent the majority of our relationship with neck problems. I rarely mentioned it. At over six foot, Jamie felt he was too tall, and had a problem with his posture because he hunched so much.

We were cosy with each other, very, very normal. When the world went mad and suddenly All Saints were in every paper and on every TV programme, whizzing all over the world and behaving as the pop stars we were expected to be, Jamie was an oasis of normality. He knew me before I became famous, he knew who I was – good and bad – and he liked me for me. That was immensely valuable and reassuring.

Jamie lived in a small one-bedroom bachelor pad with a mountain bike hinged to the wall and funky designer chairs made of steel that looked like crowns. He had lampshades shaped like the everlasting gobstoppers in *Willy Wonka and the Chocolate Factory*. We are both pretty down-to-earth people. When we started going out, we knew we would have long periods apart – it upset us both but we tried to keep it in perspective. Jamie bought me a handmade leather-bound book of love poems with gold inlay.

When I came back from touring, he used to come to

the airport to surprise me. We had a fun relationship. Just to see each other was a rare joy – snatching a few days before I was off again. When we were together, we just stayed at home enjoying each other's company. He had flowers and a meal waiting for me when I came back. He cooked for me all the time. He was very giving.

Jamie's favourite menu was pasta with pesto sauce and grated parmesan – and a glass of wine. It amused me that Jamie always served small portions that left me peckish. I am used to large portions of food – my mum always heaps our plates – but Jamie never gave me enough food. It got to the stage where I used to contemplate eating before I went round to his place. Instead I used to try to fill myself up on wine.

Jamie and I developed a passion for Cheddary spread and we used to have it most mornings, piled on top of crumpets. He always brought me breakfast and coffee in bed. A sweet man gets under my skin.

Jamie is very intelligent and had opinions on everything. Sometimes I found him condescending, needing to be the smartest one. He was always keen to give me advice – it could have driven me nuts – but he did it in such a sweet way, I could not help but be drawn to him. We had a lot of respect for each other.

At times, Jamie was a bit competitive. All Saints were in every magazine on a weekly basis and Jamie felt the need to show me his press cuttings every time he was featured – as if he needed me to know he was in magazines too. It was silly. It didn't matter to me. I was very proud of his work and watched all his shows.

'You don't have to prove yourself to me,' I told him once. 'I think you're brilliant.'

But he never believed that, not totally. He got into

radio by doing the traffic on Greater London Radio to help out a friend in a crisis. It was not until he teamed up with Zoe Ball that his career really took off. On the Saturday morning show, *Live and Kicking*, Zoe taught him about live television and he rekindled her enthusiasm. When Zoe left *Live and Kicking*, Jamie felt he had to leave too.

I was thrilled for him when they teamed up again for *The Priory*. They have the same sense of humour. He is quite measured and she has a wonderful infectious ebullience. Together they work really well.

A month after our success with 'Under The Bridge' and 'Lady Marmalade', we performed at the G8 Conference. It was informal. We performed in T-shirts and trainers. We shrieked 'Hi, Tony!' from the stage. Later we met Bill Clinton. I said:

'We love you, Bill, don't ever leave.'

He was happy that we spoke to him and he said he liked our work and would like a copy. We gave him a signed CD single. We wanted to send him more music so Nic said:

'What's your address?'

He said: 'The White House.'

That made us laugh. He said he liked my Caterpillar boots. He is a big guy, quite sexy. He does have a charismatic male aura. At that point, his reputation was untainted by the scandal with Monica Lewinsky and meeting him was exciting. I was totally in awe. I had never been in awe of anyone before. In photos my eyes were wide open and my pupils were totally black.

We met Tony Blair too. He was very sweet. It was nice to meet him. But meeting Bill, the most powerful man in the world, was amazing. I never thought I would get close to Bill Clinton, shake hands with Bill Clinton – the American president.

NATALIE **NICOLE**

We were fantastically busy, but I was still bleeding. There was something very wrong with me. I lost two stone in weight. I went to see another doctor, and then another, to try to find out why I was so unwell. I had thyroid tests, an HIV test. Everything came back negative. I wanted to see another doctor, but I was scared they might go to the newspapers. This is the power the business has over you.

Months after the abortion, a large bloody clump fell out of my body. Horrified, I put it in a jar and took it to a doctor Mum found for me. When she looked at the contents of the jar and listened to my story, she was silent. Afterwards, I could see she was in shock.

'These are tissues that have been left behind,' she said. 'Your abortion was incomplete.'

'Incomplete?'

'What I don't understand,' the doctor said, 'is how come it took you so long to visit a doctor.'

'I have been visiting doctors,' I told her. 'They never checked anything. They just gave me blood tests and said I was fine.'

I thought of all the times Rob and I had sat in doctors' offices only to be told I was malingering. Fobbed off by doctors when, all the time, the abortion was incomplete.

'Worse,' I confided, relieved finally to have someone who believed me, who gave a damn, 'they made me feel I was making the whole thing up, a hypochondriac. I knew –' I started to cry now, a mixture of fury and relief and pain, blind pain. 'I knew something was badly wrong, but no one would listen to me, nobody cared.'

'This explains why you have been feeling so ill,' the doctor said; she was furious. 'This is why you are losing so much weight. Your body is having to flush itself out.'

Finally, someone was giving me answers. She did tests, asked questions about my blood type and symptoms.

'Before they did the operation did they give you a rhesus injection?' she asked.

'No. Why?'

'Because of your blood type.'

'They didn't even ask what my blood type was.'

The doctor was appalled.

'It is standard procedure,' she informed me. 'You have to have a blood test before an abortion to see if you need a rhesus shot. For your rare blood type, you needed the injection to protect any future foetus. It could have caused an infection in your womb.'

'What does that mean?'

'At worst,' she said, 'it could mean you might not be able to have a child.'

I was horrified, violated by what I felt was the power of an industry that leads a woman to sacrifice her child to keep a band together. My life had been in the hands of a doctor who had taken less care of it than he would a stray dog's.

In consultation with this doctor, I realized that at four months I was too far gone for the procedure the doctor had implemented. I required an altogether different operation – but it would have taken longer and I would have been more ill afterwards – there's no way I would have been able to return to work so soon.

'What about counselling?' the doctor asked me.

'Counselling?'

'Were you offered any counselling to help you cope with the emotional trauma of having the abortion?'

'No,' I said. 'All that was important was that it was hushed up.'

I needed answers. When I got home, I called the doctor in New York.

'I need to see my medical records,' I said.

'I'll see what I can do.'

He called me back several hours later.

'I'm sorry to inform you,' he said, 'but all your files were lost.'

Lost? Not lost, eradicated. They did not want me – or anyone else – to know the truth.

Shortly afterwards, the news broke that Scary Spice was pregnant and then Posh Spice. They were seen as 'girls' – carefree, single, and wild – yet the news was greeted with delight. Two of the Spice Girls were pregnant – congratulations – two pregnancies in the same band. For the first time, I wished I was in their band – that I was a Spice Girl. No one knew what I had sacrificed – and, as time went on, I realized nobody cared.

Mel said that if they pressurized her to abort her baby she would leave the band.

'I'm having this baby,' she said.

And, somehow, her defiance, her certainty, made it okay with everyone, even Shaznay. I watched Mel's stomach grow, heard her excitement, watched the support she received. I used to rub her tummy, feel her baby kick. Mel did not feel guilty. She stood by her word and she was proud of it.

'You're an idiot,' she said.

And she was right.

I would look at Mel and think: I would be that big. I tried not to torture myself, but it drove me crazy. I did my utmost to block it out of my head. I could not talk about it.

11 - LOVE IS WHERE I'M FROM

NATALIE NICOLE

Rob and I had shared a unique experience and I deeply valued his support. We grew closer. Trying to cheer each other up, we had lots of really good times together. We used to rent videos and go for picnics on Hampstead Heath. The top room of Rob's house is like a playground and we used to play music up there really loudly and pretend to be DJs. We also fooled around with his huge soccer bean bag and life-size stormtrooper from *Star Wars*. We were very much in love.

In the summer Rob proposed. It was early in the morning. I had just got back from Japan. Five a.m. I went to his house. He was in bed and I was tiptoeing around; the next thing, I felt him stirring and shifting.

He got out of bed and down on one knee.

He had a beautiful ring for me – antique with emerald-cut diamonds. It was too big, but I put it on anyway and then I did not want to take it off.

'Will you marry me?'

'Yes,' I said. 'Yes, I will.'

It was so early, I could not call anyone except Nat who had flown from Japan with me.

Rob took me on holiday to St Tropez to celebrate our engagement and to try to get over the abortion. On the plane coming back, he put a pen into my hand and said:

'Write your feelings down. Just do it. That's what

a song's about, that's what will get to people's hearts.'

I put words down on post-it notes. Loads of feelings. The title came quickly: 'Love Is Where I'm From'.

And the first verse:

> *How could I not see it*
> *Guess I was young*
> *My mike sounded nice*
> *So did every song.*
> *You had a certain power*
> *I felt alone*
> *Now the tables have turned*
> *I'm sure that I've grown.*

'You should record it, Nic,' Rob encouraged.

'The record company would never pay for me to have studio time,' I said. 'It's a wonderful idea but –'

'I'll book a studio for you.'

I sat in silence.

'And Guy Chambers,' Rob said excitedly. 'My musical director, we'll bring him in to work on the music. It will be great, Nicole. It's time you started to make your own music.'

In the studio, a few days later, Rob paced up and down, listening, occasionally throwing song lines and words at me.

> *I'm not fighting my own war*
> *No room for you inside my head*
> *Try to understand we live and learn*
> *Or crash and burn*
> *I cannot be wrong*
> *Love is where I'm from.*

As I sang, Rob felt inspired to join in and contribute to the lyrics. Guy did the music, so we decided to split the copyright three ways.

'Is that okay with you, Nic?' Rob asked. 'It started out as your song.'

'Of course it is,' I said happily. 'If not for you, I would never have had the chance to record it at all.'

I had an idea.

'Wouldn't it be great if the rest of the band came in and sang the harmonies,' I said.

'Yes,' Rob said. 'Why don't you call them?'

I rang Shaznay.

'The song sounds great,' I enthused down the telephone. 'It would be good if you could come and do the harmonies.'

'Yeah, all right,' Shaznay said. 'When?'

'Today or tomorrow.'

'I'll be there,' she said.

I waited for Shaznay to come. Two days passed. She did not call or try to make contact. I cried in the studio. I was embarrassed in front of Rob and Guy that my own band could treat me like this, be so uninterested and unsupportive. So disrespectful. *Band* – never had the word seemed more of a joke.

At the end of the second day, I rang Mel.

'Shaznay didn't show up,' I told her.

Mel came to the studio. She couldn't bring herself to say Shaznay had done wrong – that would have meant taking sides with me. But the fact that she came showed she felt for me. Nevertheless, Mel did not arrive as a professional. Her whole attitude was that of a friend doing a favour for a friend who was upset. She was humouring me.

I gave the finished tape to *London Records*. I didn't know what they would make of it – make of me. I only knew I liked the way the song sounded – and Rob did. We were excited and nervous. We thought we had created something special between us, but the record company's opinion was the one that counted. I needed them to take it further to realize this dream.

Three days later the DJ Pete Tong, our Artists' Representative, telephoned me.

'We think "Love Is Where I'm From" is fantastic,' he said. 'We are very excited about it. We think it could be a single.'

A single. I let the word sit in the air for a moment. I was thrilled and incredulous. I wanted to call Rob and tell Nat all at the same time. It was the first song I had ever written – and it was a success.

NATALIE NICOLE

When Nic asked me to go down to the studio and do harmonies on her song, I wanted to support her but I thought – what is the point? Unless Shaznay went to the studio, I knew it would be a waste of time. Without Shaznay's agreement, nothing could happen.

NATALIE NICOLE

Rob and I had been engaged for two months when things first started to go badly wrong between us. All Saints had been to Mexico and Argentina and were flying to Brazil, when I looked out of the window of the plane and there was a big thunderstorm. The sky was flashing with lightning. I had a horrible feeling inside me. I started to shake. Something bad was going to happen in Rio.

That day in the hotel room in Brazil, when Rob told me over the telephone that our relationship was over, I thought about the baby I had given up, Rob's child. Now I had lost Rob too. Angry, despairing, panicked, the pain was so acute because I had totally blurred the line between my personal life and the band. I was a puppet, never doing what I wanted. There was a grave-yard in my stomach. It was all my fault.

That day, I truly wanted to walk into the water and disappear, truly wanted to put all that pain behind me. The rest of the time in Brazil, I did not eat. Weight was falling off me, I looked awful. I did not like sleeping by myself so I was always in Nat's or Mel's room. I did not want to know whether or not Rob had called me – I could not face the disappointment. I wanted someone with me all the time. I did not want to be alone.

Flying home, Natalie comforted me as best she could.

'Don't take him back, Nic,' she advised sagely. 'There's no excuse for what Rob did to you.'

Two days later we were performing on the beach at Blackpool for Capital Radio. It was raining and there was a picture in the paper of Rob in the South of France – surrounded by girls and winking at the camera. We did loads of interviews that day for children's television and I hid the truth about me and Rob from them all.

When I got back, there was a message from Rob's roommate Charlie.

'I just want you to know that Rob loves you,' he said.

Fifteen minutes later, Rob called.

'It's true,' he said. 'I've told Charlie off for calling you – it's none of his business. But I do love you.'

I was quiet.

'Did you see the pictures in the papers?' he asked.

'Yes.'

'It's not true,' Rob said. 'None of it. I miss you.'

I missed him too.

'I want to see you,' Rob said.

I wanted to see him too.

'Okay,' I said.

We went to my favourite Japanese restaurant, Nobu, and ate loads of sushi and got drunk. Then we went on to another place and got even more drunk. The press caught us walking out with me on Rob's back. We were back together.

I never knew why Rob had broken up with me – that was why I took him back. It was such an unsatisfactory ending to a love that had felt so special – so huge. When he told me it was over, a part of me did not accept it. It did not make any sense to me.

It was August 1998 and we released our fourth single 'Booty Call'. We flew to Los Angeles to make the video. This was the most enjoyable video we ever made. We filmed on the old sets at Universal Studios. We lived in huge luxurious caravans, equipped with videos and couches. We felt like film stars – a feeling heightened by the fact that our caravans were parked by the clock tower from the film *Back to the Future*. We used to sunbathe in front of the clock; it was a marvellous feeling.

After our first day's filming, with my back a little sunburnt, Shiara and I went across the road to Tattoo

Mania, to get tattoos. I was born in the Chinese year of the tiger, so I wanted a Chinese tiger on my back.

The finished tattoo looked much bigger on my back than it had in the book. I was in so much pain and beetroot because of my sunburn. Everyone ended up getting tattoos there. Nat got a maple leaf on her hip.

Shortly after, Robbie proposed again, this time in the back of a car. We were on our way to a friend's party in the East End. I said yes.

NATALIE NICOLE

Before a live performance I always warm up vocally and stretch. I am a perfectionist. The moment just before a live performance is like diving into cold water. You hesitate and are filled with doubt and uncertainty, but once you dive in you are fine – there is no going back.

The fear before going on is the fear of rejection – what if the crowd hate me? At one gig, Mel C was on before us and I watched bottles being thrown at her. She was out there on her own and I felt terrified for her – terrified for me. Walking on to the stage I shake, always.

I never wear my glasses on stage – and that means I am virtually blind. But I always notice when someone puts one finger up and I sing to them directly, with anger. Once when we went on stage, there was a huge banner saying 'Pure Whores'. It made Shaznay and Mel feel uncomfortable, but I thought 'rock on'. I loved it.

Performing at Party in the Park to a crowd of eighty thousand people was a fantastic experience. There were so many people, I could not see to the back. Just a sea of faces. It reminded me of a packet of hundreds and thousands, only these were people. As we went on stage, a huge cheer erupted. The energy was amazing – it surged right through us, from them to us.

The crowd is like the key to your car; if they turn you on you can go and go. If they are there to have a good time it shows and it is infectious. This crowd's energy made me want to give them a show to remember. In that moment, all my fear disappeared. I put everything I had into that performance. I felt powerful, in control. There was just the audience and me.

The stage was huge, so we had to make bigger movements, take bigger steps. Nevertheless, it reminded me of being at home dancing in front of my bedroom mirror – that feeling of being free and in touch with myself, in my element. I sang with a smile – a huge great smile.

After the show, we were unwinding in our dressing room, when Johnny Buckland said: 'There are some people here who want to say hello.'

A pretty guy walked in and then another and then the actor Kevin Spacey – all of them dressed in black suits and white shirts, like penguins.

'Hi,' Kevin Spacey said.

I felt the way I did when I met Bill Clinton – overwhelmed and awestruck – except with Bill Clinton I was prepared to meet him and we were in a line-up; this was Kevin Spacey just walking into our dressing room.

In interviews, whenever I was asked who my favourite actor was, I always answered without hesitation: Kevin Spacey. I had seen him in *Usual Suspects* and *Seven* and I thought he was one of the greatest actors ever – subtle and unique. Now here he was. Oh my God. I wanted to say: I think you're great – I wanted him to like me – all that stuff a fan feels when they are confronted with their hero. Instead I stood there like an idiot as he said:

'I have been trying to get in here for ages. I saw Lionel Richie out there and wondered why he was allowed in and not me.'

The silence was uncomfortable. Kevin Spacey kept clapping his hands together.

'I just want you to know I think you're great,' he said, 'and I want to invite you all to come to a show I'm doing, *The Iceman Cometh* at the Old Vic.'

'Sure, yeah,' I said, finally finding my voice. 'Of course we'll come.'

When he left, I had the feeling that I had been in a dream. I never expected Kevin Spacey to be a fan. There were so many things I wanted to say to him. Why did I behave like such an idiot? I could not stop thinking about him, talking about him. That night, when I went to bed, still full of him, Jamie had had enough.

'Shut up already,' he said.

Two days later, I went to a bar and Kevin Spacey was there – sitting at a table with loads of people hanging around him.

'Nat!' he called out to me. 'Come here and sit down. Everybody move.'

I crawled under the table and sat next to him.

'Get her a drink – a tequila,' Kevin said, putting an arm around me.

We ended up drinking loads of tequila.

'One more shot,' Kevin kept saying, while I kept repeating: 'I just think you're really great.'

I began to feel ill – really ill.

'I'll be back in a minute,' I said, crawling under the table and making my way to the toilets. Once there, I slid down the wall outside and sat on the floor. The room was spinning. The next thing I saw was Kevin's shiny Prada shoes in front of me. He started swaying with me, saying: 'Just go with it, Nat.'

But I felt too ill. Somehow I managed to get to the cloakroom for my coat. Then, with tequila dripping out of my mouth, I got myself into a black cab. I was so drunk, I had to ring Jamie on my mobile so he could give the driver directions to my house. Then I lay on the floor of the cab, oblivious to the fact that Kevin had run all the way through the bar to stop me from leaving – and was kicking over dustbins because he didn't know where I had gone.

Over the next month, while he was in town, Kevin and I had dinner together many times. Usually with Shaznay – his other biggest fan – and Kevin's assistant. We were just friends, but Jamie felt threatened – he even wrote me a letter telling me he did not like me hanging out with Kevin. Kevin does a brilliant impression of the actor Christopher Walken and he left it as the message on my answer machine. When Jamie called he was not impressed, and threatened to end our relationship if I did not delete it.

After that, I kept my meetings with Kevin a secret from Jamie. One night after dinner Kevin was driving towards my house to drop me off, when we saw a figure standing in the middle of the road. We were several feet away but, at six foot three and with his hands on his hips, Jamie was unmistakable.

'Reverse,' I yelled.

Immediately, instinctively, Kevin put the car in reverse and screeched back along the street without even looking behind. It was like a scene from a film. Then I got out of the car and walked towards Jamie with fake tears in my eyes.

'I can't believe you don't trust me,' I said. 'I can't believe you're checking up on me.'

I felt bad about lying to Jamie, but nothing was happening between Kevin and me – and I desperately wanted to make the most of my opportunity to hang out with him – he was my idol.

Kevin went back to America and I did not hear from him until, months later, his assistant called me.

'Kevin would like you to go with him to the premiere of his new film, *The Negotiator*.'

'I'd love to,' I said, 'but I'm touring.'

'He will send a private plane for you,' his assistant said.

I called a meeting with the band to see if it could be arranged.

'No one has seen Kevin with a woman,' I said, 'so if I am seen with him, it could help the band in America, help get us noticed.'

But despite all my best efforts to sell it as a bonus for the band, Mel and Shaznay said no.

After that, Kevin kept calling.

'What are you?' he asked. 'Dead?'

NATALIE NICOLE

I was a big Jerry Springer fan and, when he came to London to do *An Audience with Jerry Springer*, the four of us jumped at the chance to go. We had a good table, pretty much at the front, and it was fascinating to hear Paula Yates interview him. At the end he was surrounded by paparazzi, but I really wanted his autograph so I stood in line waiting. Paper was scarce, so people were asking

Jerry to sign their sleeves and T-shirts. I was wearing jeans and asked him to sign the back pocket.

'Thank you,' I said.

Jerry took hold of my hand.

'Would you meet me at my hotel?' he asked, and whispered the name of the hotel and his room number.

I felt embarrassed, awkward. Don't do that, I wanted to say to him – you're old and I don't fancy you. I ran back to the others and was in the middle of regaling them with the story, when Jerry showed up next to me.

'You know I meant what I said,' he told me. 'It isn't a joke.'

A group of us went to Saint Bar in the West End and I was totally amazed when, a few moments later, Jerry Springer walked in. Apparently he had asked someone where we were going and followed me. Angry and embarrassed, I could not face another run-in with him and I went home.

NATALIE NICOLE

Jerry Springer came to sit with us at our table. He kept looking at me intently. It made me uncomfortable.

'How old are you?' he asked me.

'Twenty-six.'

'Twenty-six?' He sighed, and smiled at me. 'I've got socks older than you.'

It was at that point I decided to leave.

'I'm going now, to find Nic,' I assured him. 'We'll meet you at another bar. Stay here with Shaznay.'

When Shaznay rang me later she was furious.

'Natalie, where the hell are you?' she fumed. 'You are so dark, leaving me with him.'

As Shaznay told me how she ended up dragging Jerry Springer to two bars, I laughed and laughed.

'But you love Jerry Springer,' I reminded her. 'And you had him all to yourself.'

NATALIE NICOLE

A few months later, Jerry was back in England for an awards ceremony. When he walked into the bar I was at, I was convinced he wouldn't recognize me, but he came straight over to my table with his co-presenter, Dani Behr.

'Hi, Nicole,' he said.

The people at my table were chuffed to meet him and immediately made a space – right next to me.

'I remember you,' he said quietly. 'I should do a show about being dissed by an All Saint.'

NATALIE NICOLE

My relationship with Jamie came to a head when I heard, from a friend, that she had seen him kiss another girl at a party. I rang Jamie and told him to come over. He was devastated, saying it was absolute rubbish, but my friend was adamant that it had happened.

'I thought we trusted each other,' I told him. 'Fidelity is respect. You don't cheat on someone you love.'

Jamie started to cry. I started to cry.

'What did I do to deserve it?' I asked him. 'I'm a good person, I was good to you.'

Jamie denied the whole thing vehemently, but I trusted my gut feeling, my intuition. He had cheated on me – I knew it. I reached for a tub of moisturizer that was on the table beside me and threw it at Jamie. It opened in mid air and thick pink cream splodged his face and shirt. For days afterwards, the room smelt of strawberry.

Jamie and I had never really had a fight before. I was away and we were apart so much that, when we did see each other, we never rowed because it was always delicious. Being separated kept the relationship alive and fun, meant there was always something to talk about.

This, then, was our first big fight, but Jamie did not fight back. He let me rampage and he had tears in his eyes as he said over and over, 'It's not true.'

After about half an hour, I told Jamie to go.

'Get out and don't come back!' I yelled at him. 'I don't ever want to see you again.'

When Jamie had left, I cried. Tears I would not allow myself when he was there to see them. Rage gave way to pain. I was so hurt, so stunned by his betrayal. My relationship with Jamie was the first in my life that had not been stressful.

I drank myself to sleep. When I woke up for a few peaceful moments I thought that Jamie and I were still together, then I remembered. It was a horrible feeling. Jamie was no longer there to put his arms around me. It felt unbearable. Fortunately I had work – Nic and I had a photo shoot with David Bailey to do that day. I would throw myself into my work. That's how I would cope, that's how I would feel okay about myself and my life. I had work to do.

At David Bailey's studio in Camden the day's papers were strewn across a coffee table. Front-page headlines informed the nation that Jamie and I were no longer together. According to them, I had punched him in the face and knocked him out. An old friend was even quoted as saying I had a violent temper. Juxtaposed were the sweet cuddly children's TV presenter and the wild and crazy Appleton sister. I did not stand a chance.

'Jamie keeps his squeaky clean profile and I look bad,' I said, 'but it's totally untrue.'

'You didn't hit him?' Nic asked.

'No,' I said. 'We had an argument and I slapped him – trying to get him to tell me why. But I didn't hit him. I wish I knew who'd said it. It makes me look like a complete neurotic freak.'

When both partners are high profile, media attention can become a third party in the relationship.

'What will you do?'

'What can I do? The words have been written. If I go to the papers and give my side of the story they'll only bring it up all over again.'

'You have to let it go,' Nic agreed.

My eyes were swollen and, although I tried to keep it together, I continued to cry throughout the shoot.

'Broken up with your boyfriend then, have you?' David asked.

I knew I looked stupid, but there was nothing I could do about it.

'I'm sorry,' I said. 'I'm not feeling too great.'

'You'll meet someone else soon,' David said. 'Forget about him.'

He played love songs the entire afternoon and did his best to make me laugh. David is naughty, mischievous, like a schoolboy. At one point, when I had to run to the toilet to cry and came back with mascara leaking down my face, he remarked dryly:

'Pass Nat the razor blades.'

It sounds unkind, but it made me feel stupid. It was useful in a brutal, male kind of way.

That night Jamie went along to the TV Awards without me. Televised live, it was too painful for me to watch, knowing I should have been there with him. Friends had told me how sad Jamie seemed, how desperate, and I did not want to see his pain. Mum saw the programme and, as soon as it had finished, she telephoned me.

'I don't know quite how to tell you this,' she said, 'but when Jamie got up to give his award, he got a standing ovation.'

The papers had cast me in a jealous and aggressive light. Now a room full of people were applauding Jamie out of sympathy. I felt humiliated, betrayed all over again. I felt judged.

'They clapped him?' I could not believe what I was hearing.

'It's because of what the papers are doing,' Mum said. 'Fanning the fantasy that you beat him up.'

'It's disgusting,' I said, 'vile. I hate them all. I hate the world.'

I stayed at Nic's house for comfort. The next day, when I went back home to get some clothes, photographers were camped outside my house. As I struggled to find my key in my bag, they snapped and snapped at me.

'Please,' I begged them. 'Please. I just need a bit of peace.'

Two days later, the front page of the *Daily Mirror* asked: 'Was Jamie Careying On With Mariah?'

'Have I stumbled upon the real reason for All Saint

Natalie Appleton's sudden split from children's TV star Jamie Theakston?' Matthew Wright asked. He then went on to tell the nation – and to inform me for the first time – that a few days earlier when BBC's *O-Zone Special* sent Jamie to New York city to interview 'gorgeous pop diva Mariah', Jamie and Mariah shared an early-morning limousine ride.

'It's not the first time Jamie, 27, and Mariah have met. Jamie interviewed her earlier this year and, I hear, attended one of her parties in Los Angeles. After meeting on Tuesday the pair went their separate ways – or so they would have us believe . . . So imagine my spies' surprise when they spotted Jamie with Mariah, 28, inside her chauffeur-driven limo at 7.30 a.m. on Wednesday.

'Jamie was sitting next to her on the bat seat,' says my source. 'They both looked really smug. Who knows what they were getting up to during the night – but it was still strange to see Mariah and Jamie together so early in the morning. The car dropped Jamie at his hotel. He looked knackered – I guess it was the jet lag.'

The *Mirror* then set up a table:

Mariah vs. Natalie		
28	AGE	23
Divorced	STATUS	Divorced
£90m	SALES	£10m
£25m	WORTH	£2m
8/10	SEX APPEAL	9/10
5/10	CREDIBILITY	10/10

We were releasing our fifth and final single from our first album, 'War of Nerves'. It is my favourite song on the album – the emotions are powerful and it gives me chills. Filmed at the Met Bar, it is also my favourite video.

A month after we split up, All Saints were booked to appear on Jamie's Saturday morning show *Live and Kicking* to promote 'War of Nerves'. It was important that we appear. Jamie and I had had no contact since the night I threw him out of my house. Seeing him on the set of the Saturday morning TV programme was strange, uncomfortable.

Jamie looked shifty and embarrassed. We did not know what to say to each other. I kept thinking: it is good TV, the estranged couple together for the first time in front of the cameras. Did they want me to appear for the sake of good television? Television was also good for the band and our single – I knew it worked both ways.

I was sad, angry and deflated thinking how Jamie put his career before everything else. I wondered if that was all he cared about, or if he was feeling anything seeing me again.

12 - LOSS AND LIMOUSINES

NATALIE NICOLE

To have a hit single is amazing – but there is something very special about releasing your first album. An album is the test of a professional artist. It is judged by criteria that matter. It defines whether you are taken seriously as an artist or not.

Our debut album, *All Saints*, was finally ready – it was a tremendous feeling. When the album went to number two in the charts it was a validation of our music. I was in the band because I loved the music – so, apparently, did everyone else. We were on a high. We felt so good about what was happening that Nic and I resolved to put our difficulties with Shaznay and Mel behind us.

The record company threw us a party to celebrate the album's success. They hired a huge hall in London and men on stilts, jugglers, magicians and balloon makers. The hall was packed. Everyone was there; Donatella Versace even flew from Milan for it.

But the party was painful as well as fun. It was clear, as the party coincided with Shaznay's birthday, that the record company were making more of her birthday than the success of the rest of us. The record company loved Shaznay – who could blame them, she wrote 'Never Ever'. But the unequal treatment was unnecessary. It felt extreme – unkind. It was as if we were invisible, our skills totally unseen.

I thought, with a pang, of the album cover. Nic and I had been given an allotted space to say thank you but, when the album came out, we saw Shaznay had twice as much space. Even our manager John Benson had a list of thank-yous printed – as if it was his album.

The album sold more than five million copies and became one of the biggest-selling albums of the year. Success came quickly, but it did not go to our heads. We had a strong sense of what All Saints stood for. We turned down a multi-million-pound sponsorship deal from Pepsi (the Spice Girls' sponsors). When offers came from magazines to pose in skimpy clothes, we said no to those too.

We were independent women. We did not fall in with the programme that said pop stars belong to the highest bidder – and female pop stars show off as much flesh as they can. We stood for something different.

NATALIE NICOLE

People imagine pop stars in their prime are immune to life's pains. The idea is that we have everything and that protects us. It is not true. As the time approached for Mel to give birth, I began to feel very vulnerable. It was a reminder of the child I never had. I could not talk about it – I could barely own up to it myself.

I was really happy for Mel and could not wait to see the baby but, at the same time, I knew it would hurt. It was hard. Mel gave birth to a daughter, Lillyella. I held her and I wept.

Mel took six months out to be with her baby and the rest of us carried on promoting All Saints as best we could without her. But once the baby was born, for me everything came to a head.

A month after Lillyella's birth, we were invited on to Jools Holland's New Year's Eve show. During the sound check, Shaznay and I had an argument about the future of the band.

Once we started shouting at each other, there were so many other feelings waiting to be expressed. If Shaznay had been more of a friend, she would have defied the management and supported my desire to have my baby. But she did the opposite. She was anti motherhood and All Saints mixing and that played a major part in how things got played out. I hated her. Hated her and her complacency. It takes a lot for me to lose my temper, especially in public, but I had been sitting on so much for so long.

The microphones were still on. There were lots of bands there: the Corrs, Texas, Catatonia. They were all looking at us. Shaznay and I were wearing baseball caps and arguing so closely the brims were banging against each other. Other bands argue behind closed doors, but, as usual, we were fighting in public. We could be so stubborn with each other.

We went down to our dressing room and the fight escalated.

'I've had enough,' I told Shaznay. 'Everything is your way or no way at all.'

Shaznay started putting me down, trying to make me feel small and insignificant as always.

'If you don't like it,' Shaznay said, 'you know where to go.'

It was the final straw. I had given up my baby for this band, but the sacrifice went totally unnoticed.

'I've made up my mind,' I said. 'I'm going to finish this. Shaznay, I'm leaving the band and that's the end of it.'

'What are you going to do?' Shaznay taunted. 'Go off to Robbie?'

'He cares about me a lot more than you do,' I said.

Rob was in Amsterdam; in that moment I decided to get a ticket and fly to him.

'Yes,' I said. 'I'm going to see Rob.'

I looked at Nat.

'The band is over for me,' I said.

John Benson came running towards me, sweating. We were a week away from our American tour.

'Please,' he said. 'Please just do America.'

'Absolutely not,' I said.

I turned to look at our staff and crew, all the dancers, musicians, make-up artists and hairdressers. I wanted everyone to know what I had decided, I wanted to make it final, unshakeable.

'Goodbye,' I said. 'It has been nice knowing you all.'

Then I went back upstairs to do the show – and I enjoyed it. I sang and danced with a new freedom, a fresh verve. Tom Jones asked us to sing a song with him at the end of the show. Shaznay said no because she was not into his music, but Nat and I agreed. We thought it would be fun. Besides, our dad really likes Tom Jones and we knew he would get a buzz out of seeing us singing with him.

With an hour of the show still to go, Shaznay's performance was over; she got her coat ready to leave.

'Where is she going?' I asked John.

'She's going to see her boyfriend.'

'Before we finish?' I was outraged. 'This is the

problem,' I told him. 'Double standards. Whenever we wanted to leave early and see our boyfriends we weren't allowed to, but now she has a man in her life, all that has changed.'

I turned to Shaznay.

'You're so unfair,' I told her.

I was giddy with power, heady with the freedom that I could walk away from all this, that, for once, they needed me. Singing with Tom Jones, I had the time of my life. I was free.

When Rob greeted me in Amsterdam, I told him: 'I've left the band.'

All the times I had had to fight Nat's battles for her, running between her and the other members of the band, trying to keep things smooth. It was over, all over.

'They have turned me from someone secure and happy into someone insecure and unconfident,' I said.

'Leaving my band was the best thing I ever did,' Rob enthused. 'Look at me,' he said. 'I'm here and I'm stress-free. Use me as an example. It is worth it. It really is.'

NATALIE NICOLE

I begged Nic not to leave. Mel had taken time out and we were a week away from our American tour. America was important for us. It was bad enough when it was going to be just the three of us, but with only two of us now, was there any point in going at all? Nic was ruining it for all of us. I tried to get her to stay, but she was adamant. She had had enough.

The next day, Shaznay and I discussed the best way of honouring our commitments. The two most ambitious members of the band, neither of us wanted to let the tour go. It was our dream. We decided that we would hire two backing singers.

'We need outrageous women,' I said.

Shaznay agreed and we were delighted when we managed to hire two of Chaka Khan's backing singers. Shaznay said she was happy for me to sing lead with her. At last, I was getting a chance to sing, really sing.

We did gigs all around small bars in America and I sang double-lead with Shaznay. On stage, as we started we said:

'Mel has just given birth and Nicole is ill.'

At one of our gigs, Britney Spears was supporting us. During the sound check, she noticed the new trainers I was wearing.

'I really like your sneakers,' she said.

I told her: 'I got them in the mall.'

Britney's Mum is full on; they are a double act. They went straight to the mall and bought a pair of identical trainers. As the warm-up act, she went on stage before we did – and she wore them – minutes before I did.

Later I complained to Nic.

'Britney Spears stole my shoes.'

Months later, when Donna Air reminded Britney that she had met me, she looked at her blankly.

'Who are All Saints?' she said.

It was a three-week tour. We did it. We were so proud of ourselves. We pulled it off. Shaznay and I really needed each other on that trip and we bonded. We ended up having a good time.

I came back to England feeling proud of myself. I had done it for the band, I had proven myself. Maybe now I would be allowed to take more of a role.

When I came back to England, I went straight to see a lawyer. I wanted to make my leaving legal. Shaznay was devastated by my decision. Mel, her sidekick, had just given birth and they were not on good terms. Shaznay did not even go the hospital to see Lillyella.

One afternoon, Shaznay rang our producer KG's house. He is my friend and I was there; I picked up the telephone.

'It's so good to speak to you,' Shaznay said. 'I really want you back in the band. Are you sure you want to leave?'

We talked and talked. The girls wanted me to stay. Deep in my heart it was what I wanted too. I had always believed passionately in All Saints – believed in our band even when Shaznay and Mel gave up. I loved our music, loved what we stood for. It was hard – so hard – to walk away.

As the girls persuaded me to stay, I began to feel valued, important. For the first time they were acknowledging that the band needed me, that I had a part to play. It was what I needed. After months of negotiation the band was still together, but John Benson was no longer our manager.

Nic was back in the band; the three of us carried on as before. Four weeks after America, we did the *MTV Music Awards*. Mel was still on sabbatical and I thought that, after our success in America, I would be taking more of a leading role, but Shaznay shoved me to the back again. Even though on tour we had shared the vocals on 'Lady Marmalade', for this show she claimed them all for herself.

The day before the show, Shaznay went into the studio and recorded herself singing the vocals so that, when it came to the show, she could both mime the vocals and rap. For me, this was a double slap in the face. Hadn't I just shown that I was capable of doing it? When she needed me, Shaznay was happy to make use of my skills but not to value me. Never that.

Nevertheless, despite all that Shaznay and Mel put me through, when we went up to accept our award for Best Breakthrough Artist my thoughts were of Mel. As soon as we got the award, I said into the microphone:

'This is for Mel who is watching at home.'

NATALIE NICOLE

Our performance at the awards show was one of our most powerful. The audience was so charged – twenty thousand people all loving what we were doing. The band vibed on that. We gave back as good as we got.

But the hassles with the band were taking their toll on Rob and me. I struggled to understand why, despite everything, Rob felt so utterly alone. More painful than anything else was the knowledge that I could not help him. I went with him to see a counsellor. I even went to Alcoholics Anonymous for him.

All Saints had just switched the Christmas lights on in Regent Street and were doing the *Pepsi Chart Show*, when, again, I had a premonition that my relationship with Rob was about to end. I was chatting with my friend Mark Wogan in the bar area, when my heart suddenly dropped to my stomach. My hands went cold. I was having a panic attack. I knew it was to do with Rob.

'How's Robbie?' Mark asked me.

'He's fine.'

But the feeling would not go away. As soon as I got outside I called Rob.

'I'm on my way home now. Is everything okay?'

'Yes,' Rob said, 'everything is fine.'

But I knew it was not. The feeling was so strong I did not want to go home. When I arrived, I said to Johnny Buckland:

'Will you do me a favour and wait downstairs? I've a feeling I'll be leaving again in a few minutes.'

I went upstairs to the house.

'How was your day?' Rob asked me.

'Great.'

'Nic, I need to tell you something.'

'What?'

'I think we should break up.'

I knew it. 'Why?'

'It's not your fault,' Rob said. 'It's mine.'

'This time I'm going,' I said, 'and I'm not coming back.'

Our relationship was under a lot of pressure. That is largely why it was so on and off. We got back together one last time. Robbie did a show in Amsterdam and I flew there to be with him. He bought me a thousand red roses and left them for me in my hotel room. Once more I thought we had a chance.

We had been back together for two weeks and we were all going to my parents' house for Christmas dinner. Rob had been partying hard the night before and was unable to eat. I covered up for him as best I could, eating some of the food off his plate.

After lunch, we all went to the pub round the corner in Belsize Park. Rob got really drunk. Back at my place, he had a panic attack and went wild.

'Stop it,' I said. 'You're scaring me. Stop it.'

'All right,' Rob said, 'I'll leave.'

It was Christmas night. It was snowing heavily outside. There were no taxis. I did not think he was serious.

'If you go out the door,' I said, 'don't come back.'

Rob left.

I did not hear from him. The next day there were pictures of him in the newspaper. He had passed out in the lobby of a hotel and some passers-by thought it would be funny to cover him with shaving foam and toothpaste and then call the press.

For me it was the final straw. Something about those photographs and the way he had been over Christmas made me realize my relationship with Rob was never going to get any better. Reality time. This was the end. I called his home.

'I'm coming to get my stuff,' I said. 'I don't want to see you any more. It has gone too far now.'

When I arrived at Rob's, he was still drinking – Guinness now. I took my things and left. This is how it is with me. I go back and go back too many times, then something in me snaps. It is my turn to say no and I always mean it.

This breakup felt different from the others. I was stronger. I was more used to the idea that we might not make it. I loved Rob, but our relationship was always on the verge of ending. It was always under attack. I could never relax into it. I missed him, but I also felt clear about my decision.

There was something I never understood about Rob – he would be in love with me one minute and the next we were over. I'm a sucker for people who need looking after and I felt motherly towards Rob, but life with Rob was a rollercoaster.

He always said: 'It's not your fault, I'm sorry to hurt you.'

But we never spoke about it. To this day, I still don't know why his love was so on and off – or the real reason why our relationship ended.

That New Year's Eve was set to be awful. Exactly a year previously, Rob and I were just beginning – and we spent New Year's Eve apart to hide our connection from the world. This was to be our first New Year's Eve together. I could not bear to be in England, so I went to see my old friends in New York. I was so upset, so fed up with my life that, for the first time ever, I flew without fear. I didn't care if the plane came down. Turbulence, so what?

When I got to New York, I headed straight for the apartment of my friend Allison Block. It was so cold the wind burned; it felt like stinging nettles in my face, but I wanted to go out that first night. I wanted to get drunk and party. So I hired a limousine to drive us around. I hired it again the next day and picked up Allison's sister Amanda and my friend Juliana.

We ate strawberries and drank champagne. Driving around singing and getting very drunk. We went shopping. In and out of department stores, trying on all the hats. I bought everyone a big party hat; mine was a white top hat and Allison had a cowboy hat. We tried on make-up and I bought a big snakeskin scarf to wrap around my hat. It trailed behind me. It was a great moment. For once, I felt like a rock star. And it was a comfort for me. I loved it.

Then back into the limousine with the music blaring. We went into a huge toy shop and played with all the toys. I bought Rachel a fairy outfit. It was fun and I felt confident again.

Drowning my sorrows, I got drunk every night. Allison was being paid fifty dollars a day at her work. I didn't want to be left alone with a hangover in her flat.

'I'll pay your wages,' I told her, 'if you don't go in tomorrow.'

For New Year's Eve, I hired a limousine again, only this time I wanted the best they had – a brand-new car with no miles on the clock. It was the most beautiful limousine I have ever been inside. It was festooned with balloons and streamers. We went to the flat of my friend Hughie Morgan of the Fun Loving Criminals and he introduced us to all of his friends. Then we went to a club, still wearing our outrageous hats and danced and danced.

What went on with me and Rob was very public and that was a strain. But when people ask me why was I so open about our relationship, I say, 'Why not? What's to hide?' The trouble was it became the only thing people ever talked about, wherever we were in the world. That was almost surreal, because it is not natural.

In the weeks following our breakup, I looked back at our relationship and realized clearly the part the abortion had played. I thought of the lyrics to Rob's song 'Grace'. He said by having the baby I was saving his life, in having the abortion I betrayed his trust. The fact that I was so easily manipulated and controlled by the record company must have been very off-putting for him. He would never speak about it and so I will never know.

13 - LIKE RAINDROPS

NATALIE NICOLE

Mel was back at work after the birth of Lillyella and we were preparing for our tour. We were rehearsing in a big warehouse – big enough to incorporate our whole stage set – which included four telephone boxes suspended from the ceiling and our dancers and crew. Twenty people in total.

Late in the afternoon, Nic came into the room beaming. She walked over to the stage and told us shyly: 'The record company just rang. They said they really like my song. Pete Tong wants to talk to Rob and get it recorded with everyone's vocals on it.'

I was thrilled for my sister, elated. But before I could say anything, Shaznay said: 'It's not going on the album.'

I watched Nic's face – watched the ebullience fade and a sharp hurt take its place.

'I'm not having Robbie Williams's name on an All Saints album,' Shaznay went on loudly.

I looked at Shaznay. She was wearing a long cardigan, and a black baseball cap. Her arms were crossed over her body.

'Why not?' I spoke for Nic.

'Our fans don't listen to Robbie Williams's music. He wasn't on the first album so why should he be on the second?'

'That's crazy logic,' I said.

'I'm right, Mel, aren't I?' Shaznay was canvassing support. 'Robbie Williams is using us to get his name on our album.'

Mel did not answer.

'She'll only be sorry when he breaks up with her,' Shaznay said. 'Having Robbie Williams's name on our album will be an embarrassment then.'

There were lots of people in the room – crew, dancers – they were shifting uncomfortably. Everybody was feeling embarrassed – everybody except Shaznay.

Shaznay was dating one of the dancers, Christian, and that gave her extra confidence. She felt the dancers were all behind her – sneering at my sister and her boyfriend. She was putting my sister down in front of everyone.

'Can we take this outside?' I hissed at Shaznay. 'Somewhere more private.'

Outside, Shaznay carried on repeating the same words and accusations. She was adamant that Robbie's name would not appear on the album. She calmed down outside, but her line remained the same.

'Why don't you pick out all the words Robbie wrote and then you can take him off the credit?' she said at last.

Nic looked miserable, utterly wretched.

'I don't remember who wrote which words,' she said.

NATALIE **NICOLE**

'Love Is Where I'm From' was the first song I had ever written – and, as Rob had encouraged, I had written it from my heart. It meant so much to me. I loved that song. It was the most personal, creative and real thing I had ever done. I so wanted to record it, to put it out in the world for people to hear, and maybe relate to.

In desperation I came up with the idea of asking Rob if he would mind using his initials instead of his name – that way Shaznay could not object to him being on the album. Rob did not like the idea. I understood that. The record company were on my side, they really wanted to record 'Love Is Where I'm From' as a single, but the more fuss Shaznay made, the more their enthusiasm was dented. Their calls to me became shorter and less frequent. Shaznay had won again.

NATALIE NICOLE

We first met Dave Stewart at Natalie Imbruglia's party. He is an amazing man; quiet, calm, spiritual. He has a really inventive mind. Crazy ideas. He is constantly looking for things to challenge himself. He has the maddest life. People are drawn to him. He brings the best out in everyone he meets.

We had heard he had written a film about sisters who turn outlaws.

'We're the girls,' we told him, 'the sisters for your film, *Honest*.'

'Okay,' Dave said. 'Come for a screen test.'

We knew straight away who would play each part: I would play the wild one, Mandy, while Nic would play the gentler one, Gerry – the street-smart ringleader. It was obvious.

NATALIE NICOLE

On the day of the screen test, the pressure of reading in front of people made me suddenly dyslexic. Dave filmed us doing a few scenes together. Then he disappeared for five minutes, came back and offered us the parts. He took us out to lunch but we were too excited to eat.

NATALIE NICOLE

We saw Dave Stewart again at the Brits. He was performing with Annie Lennox.

'Nat, Nat,' he said, running up to me in the corridor. 'You've got to meet Stevie Wonder.'

I followed Dave down the hall and into a room. Stevie Wonder was sitting there, surrounded by his keyboards. Just the three of us in a room.

'Hi,' I said shyly. 'It's nice to meet you.'

Stevie Wonder is a giant; really tall and he has massive hands.

'Stevie,' Dave said. 'Play that song for Nat – the new one.'

Stevie Wonder adjusted the knobs on his keyboards, picked up his hands and dropped them on to the keys. They fell like raindrops. I have never seen anything like it. He did not tap the keys, his fingers fell into them, knowing – feeling – exactly where everything was. Watching Stevie Wonder was even better than listening to him. I was stunned, overwhelmed.

'That's amazing,' I said when he stopped.

When I got back to the dressing room, the others were furious with me.

'Where were you?' they yelled. 'We're on in ten minutes.'

I had just watched Stevie Wonder play a song for me that no one else had heard. They could not take that away from me. No one could.

NATALIE NICOLE

At the Brits, we were asked to present an award to Natalie Imbruglia. A few days before, we went to Dolce and Gabbana to select our outfits. In the window, I saw a jewelled top. It cost £10,000.

'I'll have that,' I said.

We had been told that we could keep what we wore, but they drew the line at that top. I only got to wear it for the evening but it felt totally amazing.

We shared our dressing room with Kylie Minogue. She was tiny – and so quiet we barely realized she was there. I felt like an oaf compared to her, barging in and out of the room.

NATALIE NICOLE

Nic and I had landed parts in *Honest*, and so had Mel, so our stage agent, Tara Joseph, held a party at the Members Bar in Charing Cross to celebrate. When I arrived there was a list at the door and the names of those who had already arrived were highlighted. The actor Johnny Lee Miller was there. I made a bee-line for the toilet to check my hair. Walking into the room, I was really nervous. I held on to my mobile phone so I would look busy. I am very shy when it comes to someone I like.

I saw Nic at a table with Melanie and Tara and I went to sit with them.

'Johnny Lee Miller is over by the bar,' Nic said.

There he was. Suit trousers and a white shirt, open at the neck. He was smaller than I thought he would be. I looked away quickly before he saw me. People spoke to me and I listened and nodded, but I didn't hear what they were saying. All my interest and attention was focussed on Johnny, right up to the moment when Nic and Mel positioned themselves at his table and called me over.

'Natalie Jane Appleton,' they baited, 'come here and sit down.'

They were grinning like Cheshire cats. I went over.

'Hi,' I said, 'it's nice to meet you.'

'Hello.'

I was wearing white cropped trousers, a denim jacket and boots that laced up the back. And as we sat talking, he started playing with the buckle.

He said: 'Now that's one hell of a boot.'

I ordered us tequilas and shots. We both began to relax. We were laughing a lot and getting very drunk. Then we were kissing, in front of everyone. I remember coming up for air and people were staring.

At the end of the evening, he got in the cab with us and we dropped him off on the way home. I was very excited by Johnny, intrigued. He was funny, intelligent and sexy too. I wondered if I would hear from him again.

Tara rang the next morning. She said Johnny had called and asked for my telephone number. She told him she would ask me and that he should call back.

'What shall I tell him?'

She was teasing me.

'Give him my number,' I said. 'Tell him to call me.'

'I thought I'd better check.'

We were giggling. That moment – that first moment of a new relationship, when you know you are both interested but nothing has happened yet – is full of promise. Johnny called later that day and we arranged to go out for a meal the following night.

He was quiet and shy. He reminded me of a puppy. Over the next weeks, I began to feel close to him. I felt strangely motherly. I hugged him tenderly sometimes, like I was holding a child.

On my birthday, Johnny came to a family dinner in a restaurant. The normality of my family was a treat for Johnny, a new experience for him. I wanted him to be happy, to feel included.

Johnny was beautiful. Every time I looked at him, I thought wow. I loved the way he walked. He was sinewy, strong. He used to run every day – he was fit. And the way he spoke – even when he was moody, I loved the way his voice went down an octave and he touched his lips. I was transfixed by him. He looked even better on film. With his big puppy dog eyes.

After two months, Johnny moved into my house and All Saints started our British summer tour. It was a two-tier tour, starting in theatres around Britain and Ireland. For two months, I was on the road and Johnny often came with me.

NATALIE NICOLE

We designed the costumes for the show and it was fantastic to be on stage wearing our own creations – outfits we had visualized and drawn. We had a white leather look – hipster flares with little tops. A gangster look – pinstripe trousers with trilby hats and sexy tops. It was like being a kid and dressing up but glamorous, alluring. I loved our cowboy outfit: parachute trousers, leather tops and stetson hats.

Despite the conflicts, at that point, there were still moments when we had fun. We could be girls together and that is something I always valued. For costume changes, Shaznay and I shared a quick-change room. We used to race to see who could get into their outfit in the least time – the reward for this was a quick cigarette before we went back on. Mel was always the fastest, her desire for a fag being the strongest. Then we all puffed on her cigarette.

Travelling on the tour bus was a lot of fun. We used to joke about the bunk beds – they were like little coffins. I was so superstitious, I never used mine. Instead I used to sit up and watch videos. People used to let off wind, but no one would admit to it. Our musicians were blokes and all of them were health conscious. They ate organic food and drank fruit juices. Their healthy diet made them the culprits.

As a new mum, Mel would go to bed early and Shaznay rarely went out so, after the shows, Nat and I used to go to a bar with our head of security, tour manager and general nursemaid, Johnny Buckland. Johnny looks like Big Daddy with bleached cropped hair. Johnny loves to party; he is a lot of fun because he has no rules.

We also hung out with the hairstylists, Mel and Rochelle, and the dancers. We had a lot of fun, particularly with Jimmy (Hardcore) Barber and Kevin Methurin, who had been at the Sylvia Young Stage School with us.

We tried our best to get our musicians drunk; to tempt them from orange juice to tequila, but most of the time they could not be swayed. On the few occasions they came drinking, the next day they showed no signs of a hangover. They were so pure their bodies could handle it.

To celebrate our signing to star in *Honest*, Dave

Stewart invited me, Mel, Stuart and Lilly (who was five months old at the time) to his villa in the South of France for a five-day break. Word got out and the number increased: we were eventually accompanied by Mum, Rachel, Shiara, Dave and his girlfriend (now wife) Anoushka. Johnny Lee Miller came too, for the first two days.

We all flew to Cannes and were picked up by cars which drove us to Dave's beautiful house outside the city. We each had a suite of rooms to ourselves. Each morning we had breakfast together and then split up, some of us sitting by the pool, while others went to the beach.

We also did a photo shoot for *Marie Claire* while we were there. They sent a journalist, Kate Thornton, to interview us and we clicked with her. She was warm, witty, wise and fun to be around. Nat and I got in touch with Kate when we returned to England and she is now one of my closest and most trusted friends.

Fran Cutler, who belatedly joined the holiday party, was one half of Noel Gallagher's wife Meg Mathews's 2 Active PR company. On the second day, just before we started the photo shoot for *Marie Claire*, she told us:

'I've just spoken to Meg. She said the boys are recording in a studio five miles from here. Apparently the band are going to a party tonight and have asked if we want to go and join them.'

'Cool,' I said. 'I suppose that means tonight will be large.'

I was an Oasis fan. I used to read about them a lot in the newspapers. I was fascinated by their bad-boy brother image. I found it very appealing. In interviews, on stage and off, Liam and Noel Gallagher were just being themselves – brothers. I recognized the chemistry between them, the sibling thing, the fights that are always ongoing. It is part of the passion of people who love each other. Nat and I were always at each other's throats – still are. For years, I had admired the Gallagher brothers' closeness, honesty and utter lack of pretence.

'Wonderwall' was the first Oasis song I heard. I was twenty. After that, I loved everything of theirs that I heard. I think Oasis are better than the Beatles – they are more raw, they have an edge. I don't think they are given enough credit for their work.

I found Oasis fascinating; and I always wanted to meet Liam – but I never fancied him. I wondered what Liam was like, but my interest was in his music, his honesty and the fact that, like Nat and I, he was working and feuding with his brother in a band.

From all I had heard, Liam Gallagher was not a nice guy. But then a few months before Cannes Nat and Mel had been to the Steve Coogan show and Liam had been there at the after-show party. Nat rang me first thing the next day.

'Liam Gallagher bought us a drink last night,' she told me excitedly.

'What's he like?'

'Lovely.'

'Lovely?'

'Yeah, he walks like a monkey, but he's really sweet. He was there with his mum,' Nat said.

It was good to hear something positive about Liam for a change, instead of something nasty. Sitting in my lounge, I felt a stab of jealousy. For so long now, I had wondered what Liam was like.

That night, we started off with a meal at a beautiful

restaurant in Cannes. I got a bit drunk and as I sat there, thinking of the night ahead, meeting and partying with Oasis, I suddenly went off the idea. I felt reluctant to go all the way into town to meet the band. What was I, some kind of groupie? But Fran was full of enthusiasm and so I gave in.

On our way to the bar where Oasis were having a drink, our driver nearly knocked a cyclist off his bike. This near-miss fed our nervousness. The night was black through the car windows. Squashed together in the back of the car, Nat said: 'I'm scared.'

'I know,' I said. 'And we don't even know where we're going.'

All the bars in the square were busy. People spilled on to the streets, sitting at outdoor tables or lounging on mopeds. There was a party atmosphere in the streets.

'There's no way we are going to find them,' I said.

But we eventually found the bar and Fran led the way. She introduced us to Jason, Noel's guitar roadie, then the two girls who were doing the band's catering. They were warm and welcoming.

Then I saw Liam. He was wearing a black hat with a brim and round sunglasses. He looked like John Lennon. Taller than everyone else, he was standing on the edge of the pavement holding a drink to his chest.

Liam said hello to Nat because he had met her, but he did not look at me once. He stayed away, kept to himself and the people he knew. He was intimidating, impossible to approach. I thought: if he's not going to talk to me then I'm certainly not going to talk to him. I felt stubborn and was not sorry when the party came to an end.

We spent the next day sunbathing and getting drunk

on champagne. At midday Jason telephoned to say Liam and Oasis's drummer, Alan, wanted to come over to Dave's house that afternoon.

'Sounds great,' Fran said. 'Doesn't it, girls?'

'Fine by me,' Nat said.

'Me too.'

Liam, Alan and Jason arrived around 4 p.m. I felt less intimidated by Liam that afternoon. Perhaps it was seeing him in the daytime or perhaps it was just because this was our second meeting. I was able to say: 'Hello.'

Dave has six four-wheel motorcycles and Liam wanted to go for a ride.

'Take one of the bikes,' Dave said. 'It's beautiful up in the mountains.'

Liam said: 'I would, but I can't drive.'

'I'll take you,' I said.

Liam climbed on to the bike behind me and we set off up the rocky path. I could tell that he was nervous. For once he was not wearing glasses and a hat and I could see his face. He was cute, very cute in the daytime. Looking back, it was at this point I first felt drawn to Liam. He was shy. He was different, he was something new. The drive took twenty minutes and I swerved and braked and bumped purposely so that Liam had to hold on tight or fall.

I could not form a sentence or talk to Liam, but I wanted to be around him. Back at the pool, we joined the others and played a game of ping pong. Liam made me feel shy and out of my depth. We could not say a word to each other, but playing ping pong broke the ice.

Mum told Liam: 'I dream about John Lennon.'

Liam said: 'Me too.'

The three boys stayed for dinner that night and, the next day, we invited them back for a barbecue. We spent the day playing silly games. At one point we came up with the idea of sticking names on cigarette papers on each other's foreheads. I wrote Jesus on Liam and he put Hilda Ogden on me.

Now we had to guess by asking key questions. The other people could only answer yes or no. It took Liam all of three questions to guess his identity. He seemed quite taken by my choice.

'That's wicked,' he said.

The night wore on. I got more and more hammered. Liam is a very funny guy. There is something about him, in person, that is so utterly different from what you expect. He comes across at first as hostile and aloof, but he is a very easy guy to be around. His down-to-earthness is his magic. I could not know that before I met him. I could not know how much we would connect.

Once we started talking, it became easier to relax and be ourselves. Up until this point we had been very reserved but now, feeling strangely more comfortable with Liam than I had with a man in a long time, I got the giggles badly.

I ended up doing stupid dance routines for Liam and he loved it. I did not think: he is married. At that time I thought there was no way anything was going to happen. We were just having fun, enjoying each other as new mates.

At the end of the evening, Liam said: 'I'll see you soon, I'm sure.'

'Yeah, cool,' I said.

The next day, Dave announced that we were doing promotion for *Honest* at the film festival in Cannes.

'We're just talking about the concept,' he said, 'and you'll be introducing yourselves as characters.'

We had no idea how the film was going to turn out and certainly did not feel ready to answer questions about it.

'We are totally unprepared,' I protested, feeling overwhelmed.

'We'll have a good time,' Dave said, relaxed as ever. 'Just enjoy yourselves.'

The interest in *Honest*, and in members of All Saints starring in it, was huge – much bigger than we could have anticipated. We had not planned for a public appearance and had not brought anything special to wear. I borrowed a purple top and teamed it with my Levi 501s. We did lots of interviews and the next day the pictures were everywhere. Dave's instinct had been right – we were ourselves and it worked.

NATALIE NICOLE

Leaving Liam in Cannes was hard. He had made an impression on me. It is rare that I connect with a man like that, have such a laugh, feel so happy and so comfortable to be myself. But I had no idea if I would see him again.

A month later, I was in Safeway doing my shopping with Mum, when Nat called on my mobile.

'I am at Meg and Noel's house,' she said. 'You have to come over.'

'What are you doing?'

'Watching football and having drinks.'

'I've got all my shopping,' I said, 'and I'm with Mum.'

Nat can get me to go anywhere. She is so sure that her idea is the right, the only, thing to do.

'All right,' I said, 'I'll stop by for half an hour.'

It was around eight o'clock when I arrived. The front door to Noel's house was ajar. I walked in and all of a sudden, behind me, I heard: 'Boo.'

I whirled around and there was Liam. I had not anticipated seeing him. Jaundiced by the media's image of Liam and Noel, I did not expect them to be hanging out with each other. I felt a rush of happiness. It was a lovely surprise.

In the lounge, friends were watching the football. Rachel had a big bag of sweets and Liam was eating them with her. I wandered out into the kitchen and Liam joined me. Conversation was awkward, edgy.

'Our paths have never crossed before and now I have seen you twice in two months,' I said.

Liam laughed. We spoke about France and Liam told me Oasis were touring England.

'What's happening with the film?' he asked. 'After you left, there was lots about you in the French papers.'

A part of me wanted to explore our connection, but you never know where these things may lead. He was married and I did not want to be Nicole the home-wrecker. I decided to keep my feelings to myself.

The next day, I spoke to my mum.

'The feeling I have inside me is convincing,' I told her. 'There is something special between Liam and me.'

'He is a father and he is married,' Mum said. 'Move on, Nicole.'

And that is exactly what I did. I took my mum to Miami to celebrate Mother's Day. We spent an entire week lounging on the beach and eating ice cream. I thought a lot about my predicament: I could not get Liam out of my mind. I wanted to meet a man I connected with – what girl in her early twenties didn't? But in England, any man I went on a date with immediately became a subject for speculation and gossip in the papers. And me? I was seen as the full-time party girl flitting from one encounter to the next. It was wearing me down.

I longed to be anonymous, normal. In Miami I felt safe, shielded. One day on the beach, I met Travis – a blond, blue-eyed, totally gorgeous male model. If he could not take my mind off Liam, no one could. It was a fantastic feeling, to be in a relationship nobody knew about – nobody could judge or condemn us, it was fun, pure fun.

At the end of the holiday, I invited Travis to come back to England with me, but things were not the same. It was a holiday romance I tried to extend, but it didn't work out.

Then I met Gavin Rossdale, the lead singer with Bush, through a mutual friend. Determined to block Liam out of my mind, I used to go for walks in the park with Gavin and have dinner together; sometimes we watched movies. Gavin is really kind, calm and spiritual. He has Buddhas all over his house. I found him refreshing, a lovely companion. There was an attraction between us, but we always knew we would make better friends than lovers.

Around this time, Donatella Versace invited us to see one of her collections in Paris. She totally took care of us. First of all there were our rooms at the Ritz Hotel, then there was the convoy of police escorting us to the after-show party on the Champs Élysées. At one point I wound down the window of our limousine and waved at all the people lining the streets. Donatella Versace really knows how to make you feel like a star.

The Versace party was in a red room with a catwalk filled with plants. Boy George DJ-ed that night and everywhere you looked there were famous people – including Ralph Fiennes, Emma Bunton and Nick Rhodes. Donatella Versace is tiny and sporty. She was so excited to meet us.

'You guys have got such great figures,' she said. 'I want you to wear my clothes.'

So we were invited to go shopping at Versace in Milan. Donatella took us into her office where we were greeted by two tailors.

'Pick anything you like,' she said. 'Okay, darlings?'

We selected and discarded the most amazing outfits. Everything we liked was pinned and altered to our specifications.

'However you want it,' she said. 'You design it.'

I have never felt more like a princess.

NATALIE NICOLE

All Saints continued our UK tour, but now our shows were in massive arenas. I loved performing to big crowds. One night my friend Samantha Janus came to see me perform. Johnny was in the audience with her. After the show she pulled me to one side.

'Johnny did not take his eyes off you for the whole show,' she said. 'One hour and forty minutes and he never looked away.'

It was special for me to hear that. I could feel that he adored me.

NATALIE NICOLE

We each had a space in the show where we could talk directly to the audience. Mel would go on and say:

'Hello, everyone, I'm back. I've been away because I have had a baby.'

A huge cheer would rise from the crowd.

'Her name is Lillyella,' Mel would announce. 'And she's beautiful.'

It broke my heart.

Shaznay would be there beside her, clapping and cheering with the audience – all of them going wild. And I stood there, with the secret loss I still carried inside me. Mel's baby was now part of All Saints, celebrated in front of all our fans. But I had bowed to pressure and lost out. Every cheer cut me.

I never knew what to say to the audience but, by the end of the tour, I was more confident and felt I had things to communicate. I was no longer the quiet one at the back. It was our first night at Wembley Arena, our penultimate gig. As I spoke the introduction to 'Never Ever', I put my arms up in the air and started swaying.

'Come on, everybody,' I said. 'We're going to do a wave. We're going to start on the left and work ourselves all the way round to the right. Can we turn the lights up so we can see the audience?'

I was so nervous – what if it went wrong? What if people didn't know what to do – or would not join in? I counted to three. Then arms went up, up in the air, twenty thousand of them. Within moments, the whole auditorium were waving in unison.

It was a magical moment. I was being taken notice of. The audience were with me.

NATALIE NICOLE

Nic at Wembley was one of my all-time favourite moments. It was so effective, it was magical. Looking out into the crowd and seeing this immense wave of people – and thinking: my little sister did that.

14 - GO ON, LOUIS

NATALIE NICOLE

Honest took two months to shoot and I loved being part of the movie more than anything. For the first time, Nat and I did not feel like puppets. For me, the main thing about the film was that I was working independently and expressing myself creatively. I kept thinking to myself: I want to feel this way again – completely valued.

The whole time we were filming, I felt good about myself. I was praised for the things I did. Not to be scrutinized and judged made it a haven for me. No hostility, no childish secrecy, bitchiness or disrespect. Acting in *Honest* was the best thing I ever did because of the way it made me feel.

NATALIE NICOLE

What we enjoyed was the working environment. After all the miseries with All Saints, the family feeling on the set was a breath of fresh air. It was such a stark contrast to working with the band. Now I looked forward to going to work in the morning.

The actors, wardrobe and make-up people were treated with equal respect. There was no rank. It was a grown-up, professional environment and it made me want to work. It was a vindication for me. In the right environment I worked well and calmly. The experience showed me that, although they tried to blame me, the difficulties with the band were not my fault.

NATALIE NICOLE

In the film the sisters disguise themselves as men. As soon as we put on men's clothes, we felt male. How strange that clothes can do that. I did all my own stunts – even climbing the fountain in Trafalgar Square. It was an accomplishment for us – no matter what the press said.

The film hit the headlines for our nude scenes. I did a sex scene with Peter Facinelli, who played the American journalist, but it was a closed set – just a couple of cameramen. Peter tried to coach me through it, but still I needed a shot of tequila.

It was so quiet. All you could hear was him kissing my neck. I thought I would be able to handle it because being topless on the beach is no big deal, but at one point I just wanted him to get off me. I felt sick. I cannot bring myself to watch it. It is only snogging, but the audience thinks we are having sex.

You do not get a director like Dave very often. He is a guardian angel, friend, family. Honest and wise. He is also very easy-going – he would call 'action' and then he would be round the corner playing his guitar. He plays guitar all the time. He took us under his wing. His house in the country is like a health farm, a sanctuary, and we often hung out there with him and his fiancée Anoushka.

When Dave Stewart came to see us, Shaznay blanked Dave so badly he commented on her rudeness.

'So, what's wrong with Shaznay?' he asked.

How could we tell him that any friend of ours was automatically not a friend of hers?

After *Honest* was finished, we were never allowed to talk about it. Shaznay had not been part of the movie and so she made it taboo. It was not a major success so Mel, who had played the sweet and naive sister, Jo, dismissed the film and that enabled her to regain her partnership with Shaznay.

When the press gave us a hard time over *Honest*, I rang Rob. I turned to him instinctively, as a friend. He was kind, consoling. He knew what bad press felt like and his attitude was philosophical and very calming. It felt good to talk to him, to hear his voice. He was someone I deeply, truly valued.

I did not see Liam again until I was invited to the party to launch Paul Weller's tribute album. Liam rarely went to parties, but Noel's wife was putting the party on so I knew there was a possibility he would be there. The party was in a huge warehouse. The long entrance was lined with Minis, all shining their lights on to the arriving guests. The Bootleg Beatles were playing and around three thousand people were standing around and dancing in the different rooms.

I was standing by the door with Shiara when Liam

walked in with his entourage. I felt nervous. People turned to look at him. He walked in with a serious face, but he noticed me straight away and when he looked at me he smiled. I felt embarrassed. I pretended I had not seen him.

Liam came over and said hello. Instantly, I knew there was something there for me. A definite attraction. It was fierce. I am not usually easily drawn to men – let alone married men. I was frightened by my feelings.

'Hello.'

'Hi.'

'I like what you're wearing,' he said.

I was wearing a black skull T-shirt, Vivienne West-wood jeans and black boots with little red kitten heels. I was also wearing an Elvis Presley belt with a lion on it.

'I've got that belt,' he added.

'Do you want a drink?' I asked him.

'Yes,' he said. 'Sure.'

We went to the bar together. It was the first time we had seen each other in a public place and it was filled with people who knew Liam's wife – hangers-on and people who loved nothing more than to stir up trouble.

Liam spent most of the evening at the door, having an argument with people who had been spreading rumours about him. I got very drunk. I wanted to talk to Liam, but I was worried people might pick up on my feelings for him, they might jump to conclusions.

I had to do something before I left. It had been five months since Cannes and I was frightened I might not see Liam again – I might not get another chance. And then I would never know what his feelings were, if he felt the same way about me. I looked around the room. I needed something to write on. I walked to the bar at the back and found a cardboard box. I ripped off a flap and asked a waitress for a pen.

Usually I think of consequences, it is something Mum has taught me – think before you act and make an informed choice. I can talk myself out of most things. But that night all there was in my head was a voice saying: do it, do it. Liam Gallagher was not happy. He and Patsy were not in a supportive relationship. I did not feel I was intruding and I didn't feel guilty.

Liam and I had fun together – we laughed together as friends. If there was more between us than that, I had to know. It was the first time in my life I had ever acted like this – laid myself so on the line. Alcohol helped. Alcohol and the hugest feelings. It was dangerous for Liam and me to be seen there together, dangerous to flirt. That is why I did it, that night. I had a different – a rare – head on me. The more we saw each other, the more something was starting to happen. It was a mad high.

'Here's my number,' I wrote, 'call me.'

It was a big piece of card – the size of a shin pad. As I left, I touched Liam's arm and gave it to him.

'That's subtle,' he whispered, but he was smiling. 'Looks like half a tree.'

A few days later the papers reported that Liam and Patsy had split up. I did not hear from Liam but, a month after the Paul Weller party, the record company told us All Saints were invited to the Oasis gig at Wembley. I was very excited and wondered whether I would see Liam and, if I did, whether it would be different now.

I went to the gig with Nat, Shaznay and her boyfriend Christian. Mel wanted to stay at home with Lillyella so

240

we invited our choreographer, Paul Househam, to use the extra ticket. I wore blue jeans and a red tank top.

People imagine pop stars are always given VIP treatment at gigs. Not true. Our seats were right up at the back amidst – so it seemed to me – the most mad hooligan Oasis fans. It was virtually impossible to see the stage. But the concert was good – really good – exciting and raw. Liam's stage presence was compelling.

After the gig, we made our way to the hospitality room. There was a disco and around four hundred people were dancing and drinking, showing off the passes around their necks. Half an hour passed, an hour. I was very drunk and convinced I was not going to see Liam, when four huge bouncers approached me.

'Are you Nicki?'

'Yes.'

'Liam wants to know if you want to come backstage.'

My heart was pounding. Everyone was looking at me. One of the big guys was Steve Allen, Liam's security guard. It was clear to anyone who knew him that Liam had sent his bodyguard to get me.

'I'll come back for you in half an hour,' Steve said.

When the bouncers had left, I started shaking. Fear, excitement and adrenalin. I felt I was going to burst.

'You've got to come with me,' I said to Nat and Shaznay. 'I don't want to go by myself.'

'Why not?' Nat was teasing.

'It will be embarrassing,' I said. 'I might be in the way. I think it's better if we all go backstage, like it's a band thing.'

'Okay,' Natalie said. 'We'll come with you.'

Around 1 a.m. the bouncers came back and led us through a series of corridors to Liam and Noel's dressing room. There were about twenty people there – wives, girlfriends and close friends. Liam was right by the door. The smile on his face was so big; he was happy to see me.

I walked towards him, really nervous.

'Nicole,' he said.

And then he kissed me – really full on in front of everybody.

I was a bit shocked, embarrassed. I didn't want to look like 'the other woman' to the band's wives. I felt happy for Liam, I cared about him, I wanted him to be happy. But I also felt none of it was to do with me. I was not the reason he and Patsy split up. Their relationship was doomed a long time before Liam met me. I never felt like I came between them. As powerful as my feelings were for Liam, I stayed away from him for a long time.

'When you walked through the door you were like a princess,' he said.

I was so happy to be there. Liam introduced me to everyone. We were both very drunk. I briefly met the other band members. Noel was very sweet.

I said: 'What are you doing now?'

'Going home,' Liam said. 'Come in my car with me.'

I looked at him, at his face, his eyes. He knew what he was saying, he had obviously thought about it. There were photographers outside, they were waiting – waiting for a scoop such as this. If we left together, it would be in all the papers that we were an item. So soon after the breakup of his marriage. Was he sure, really sure?

'Oh my God,' I whispered to Nat. 'We're leaving on our own, Liam and I.'

Liam and I left Wembley together. Lights clicked and flashed in our faces as we made our way to his Range

Rover. The driver was waiting and Liam gave him my address. We were together.

On the way back to my house in Hampstead we stopped off and bought beers. It was there my mobile rang. It was Nat.

'You just left me at Wembley,' she hissed. 'Where's the car to take me home?'

'I don't know, Nat, I'm sorry,' I said.

I felt bad about leaving her, but I was with Liam. In the morning she would understand. In the back of the car, Liam kissed me again. Once we started kissing we could not stop.

We got back to my house at around 4 a.m. and sat up together getting very drunk.

'I'm going to take you on a magic carpet ride,' Liam said. 'Hold tight.'

It sounded exciting. Where was I going to go?

We got up at about ten the next day and went to Nat's house. Spice Girl Mel C was there. Nat had befriended Mel C a couple of years earlier when they did the television show *Never Mind the Buzzcocks* together. When they met, it was an instant connection. The record companies wanted to play up the rivalry between the two bands, but to Nat and me the Spice Girls were individuals and we liked them as people.

We all went to a pub near the hotel where Liam was staying in Maida Vale. The press got photographs of Liam and me together that day, outside the pub. We had a wonderful day. My feelings for Liam were no longer wrong. That was marvellous, heady. Liam was a free man; we were not doing anything bad. It was a relief. Finally we could start to see where this thing between us was going to go.

'You have to come to the gig tonight,' Liam said.

It was the second night of the Oasis tour and he really wanted me to be there, but I was exhausted from the night before and I had my own work to do.

'No,' I said. 'I'm due at the studio with Shaznay and Nat.'

We said goodbye outside the pub. Liam said he would be in touch soon. I thought I would hear from him the next day, but he did not get in touch again for three days. I tried not to feel upset. I rang his mobile. He did not answer. What was I doing getting involved with someone in the music business again? I felt such an idiot.

'What do you think has happened?' I asked Nat.

'He's gone on a bender,' she replied. 'Don't worry. He'll be back in touch when he's ready to.'

'He's just split from his wife,' Mum said. 'Don't expect too much from him. He married too young and it all went wrong for him. Give him his freedom.'

'I just want a phone call.'

I knew Liam used to go missing for days at a time but wherever he was, and however wasted, he could have called me. I just wanted a phone call. I thought back to our first night together, after the gig, when Liam said he was going to take me on a magic carpet ride. He advised me to hold tight. In the midst of it all, I remembered that. Perhaps this was part of the holding tight.

On the third day a front-page article in the *Sun* told the nation I was 'smitten with Oasis wildman Liam Gallagher'. Worse, the writer Dominic Mohan made it look as if I had given him an exclusive interview.

The headline was: 'My love for Liam by Nicole Appleton'. And went on to quote me as saying: 'I am really into this relationship. He's knocked me out and

I'm very keen – he's a very special guy and it's a very special relationship.'

It was lies. I had not said one word about Liam to Dominic Mohan. Additionally, a so-called friend of mine apparently told the *Sun* that I could not stop talking about Liam and that we could not keep our hands off each other.

'She's not viewing it as a casual thing and thinks there is a real future for them. We haven't seen her like this for a long, long time.'

I cringed. Now Liam would think that I had gone to the papers. He would have no respect for me, no interest. He would never call now. I burst into tears.

Then I called Dominic Mohan.

'You're going to ruin something so great,' I yelled at him.

'But you are together,' he said.

'I never came to you with this story. And you have quoted things I never said. I did not come to you with an exclusive. I did not tell you about my feelings for Liam.'

'But you are together, aren't you?'

I ended up screaming at him.

'Don't get involved. It is a complete invasion of privacy. You don't know me. You don't know what's going on in my life.'

I slammed the telephone down on him. Burst into tears all over again and then the phone rang. When I picked it up, my hands were shaking.

'Hi.'

'Hi.'

It was Liam. When I most needed him to, he was calling me.

'What's wrong?'

There was concern in his voice.

'The papers,' I said. 'Have you seen them?'

'Yeah.'

'Yeah?'

'It's bollocks.'

He wrote it off so simply – I should have known he would.

'I don't want you to think I went to the papers,' I said.

'Don't worry about it.'

'I do worry about it,' I said. 'It's lies. They say it is an exclusive and there are quotes from me, but I never spoke to them.'

'Do you want me to call Dominic?' Liam offered.

'No,' I said. 'I've already done that. It's what he wants. More quotes.'

'Come to the hotel,' Liam said, 'and pick me up.'

I put the phone down, but I could not stop crying. Unless it has happened to you, I don't think you can realize how violated, vulnerable and utterly exposed you can feel when lies are broadcast about you. The people close to me knew, of course, who I was, what type of person, what mattered to me. The Nicole Appleton the papers shoved at the nation was not me – and there was nothing I could do about it.

I was too upset to drive, so Mum drove me to Liam's hotel. It was a big white house with ten rooms. Liam had been living there for six months; in one big room with very floral wallpaper. There were clothes everywhere. His whole life in a hotel room.

When we got back to my house, I finally asked Liam. 'Where the fuck have you been? I was annoyed

Feeling very separated in France. (Can't you tell?)

With our great friend, Dave Stewart, in Cannes

Me Tarzan

Florida holiday

My man smiling

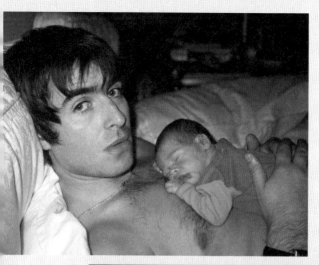

My two boys, Liam and Gene

With Liam in
Disney World

My favourite place

Liam lying next to our sand pictures in Florida

At Dave Stewart and Anoushka's wedding

Liam practising his skills

A typical night out with all four of us

because I didn't know what was happening. I really felt left hanging.'

'I ended up at Johnny Marr's [guitarist with the Smiths],' he said. 'I ate sunflower seeds and played my guitar.'

'All you needed to do was call me,' I said.

It never happened again.

Liam looked ill. He was really skinny and his hair was ratty and greasy. He looked like he needed a good wash. I didn't know what to make him for dinner – what he liked, what he was used to. In panic I called Tara.

'Can you run to Marks and Spencer's and pick up something to make for dinner for Liam?'

'What sort of thing?'

'God, Tara,' I said, 'I don't know. Whatever you think.'

'Okay,' Tara said.

She turned up with chicken breasts, salad and crisps. A really healthy meal. I prepared it for him and he ate it. It was only much later I realized how much he – like me – prefers junk food: chips and burgers and ice cream.

We hung out at my house for days. We would get up, go out for a drink and go to bed. The more I got to know Liam the more I liked him – and the more the similarities between us became apparent. Liam is the youngest of three brothers I am the youngest of four sisters.

Liam, like me, is very, very close to his mum, Peggy, and would do anything for her. He speaks to her five or six times every day – either to wind her up or just to touch base. We both have a morning ritual of calling our mums. Liam understands my closeness with my family. Like me he puts his family first – before every-thing. The differences are in our fathers. Liam's dad came and went and was not really in the picture of Liam's childhood.

The first time we ventured out together, it was a Saturday night three weeks after the gig at Wembley.

'Let's go to a pub,' Liam said.

'Where?' I said, instantly nervous at the thought of the furore it would cause with photographers. 'Not far,' I said. 'Somewhere close by, in Hampstead.'

Liam agreed. We walked out of my front door and to the end of the road. We looked both ways.

'Here we go,' Liam said.

We walked out on to the street and across the road to the pub. I kept expecting something awful to happen. But nothing did. We went to the House on the Hill and, after that, it became our favourite pub. We would sit there all day, drinking vodka and Red Bull. We talked and talked.

One day Liam and I sat outside the House on the Hill from midday until eleven at night. We started with Pimms and lemonade then moved, quickly, to vodka and Red Bull. We ended up taking Red Bulls home with us so we could carry on.

That day I drank the most I have ever drunk. When we woke the next morning, we both went downstairs and had a can of beer for breakfast. Then we went for a walk on the Heath, still drunk from the day before.

I felt and smelt like a wino, but it was such good fun. Liam made it fun; he made it okay. With Liam, there are no rules. His whole attitude is one of – fuck it, who gives a shit, let's just have a great time. Being that drunk with Liam was a lovely floaty feeling; it was exciting too.

Often, hungover, we would go for a walk on Hampstead Heath. It was the summer. Hot. So hot I wanted the skies to open and rain to pour down on us. We walked on the wet days too.

We used to sit on a bench by the lake on Hampstead Heath and watch the ducks for an hour or more. One time we saw a brother and sister fishing. They were totally absorbed in what they were doing.

'How long have you been fishing?' Liam asked them.

He always talks to children. They love him; he's like a big and funny teddy bear. But these children were so engrossed in their task they totally ignored him. They didn't want to have to talk to adults – they were busy.

It was so satisfying watching them. Liam and I sat in silence with them for three hours. When they moved down the lake, we moved with them. We were utterly content.

We used to sit in and watch movies and talk shows, one after another. Nat and I are huge fans of American talk shows, and people who come into our lives usually end up sharing this passion. Talk shows are totally addictive.

We rarely went into town; avoided parties and trendy bars. That was something we had in common. We had done it, done it all to death. I was fed up with the fact that, every time I went out, it was seen as an opportunity to rail against 'party animal Nicole Appleton'.

What Liam and I wanted most was harmony; just to be around each other in the easiest of settings and in the most normal way. I think Liam craved it – the normality with which I surround myself. The domesticity, the homeliness. It is not what the papers wrote about us, but it is the truth.

Liam lived at my house; occasionally he went back to the hotel to get some stuff. I cooked a big dinner every night. Liam helped – he always chopped the onions and it was funny watching him tear. He enjoyed being in my kitchen. We used to blast the music on the radio and dance around the kitchen. It was good fun.

NATALIE NICOLE

My relationship with Johnny was going badly. In the beginning he was something different, something special, but after eight months our time together, instead of being passionate and exciting, became routine: we would go out, party, get pissed, come back home and go to bed. Then as soon as Johnny woke up he would go for a two-hour run because he felt bad for partying the night before. We were drawn together by fun and excitement, but now found we had nothing in common.

Johnny got very close to me at one point and yet he was very self-contained. The whole time I was with him, I felt there was something not right, something that made him unhappy but he couldn't talk about it. He was looking for something, but he didn't seem to know what it was and he wouldn't tell me. Every time I tried to find out what was going on inside him, he panicked and steered the conversation around to something else.

When it came to trouble, he would switch off. Then I didn't know who he was. He was a complete stranger to me. I was working a lot and he was absent inside himself.

I went round to see my friend Donna Air. We sat at her kitchen table, lighting cigarette after cigarette.

'I'm not happy,' I told her. 'I'm letting my relationship with Johnny drag on.'

Donna usually advised me to stick with Johnny; she knew the chemistry of our attraction – and the importance of it in keeping a relationship exciting and alive. But this time she was less certain.

'Why don't you walk out?'

Why didn't I? Johnny was cute. The word does not convey what I felt and yet, when I think of Johnny, that is still the word that comes to mind. He had the most beautiful face. I found myself staring at it. I never got tired of it. His exquisite bones, his beautiful blue eyes. The animation in his face. When he smiled it was sunshine beaming at me.

But by Christmas, Johnny and I were fighting a lot and – always a bad sign for me – I was losing weight.

'What's wrong with you, Nat? You're so thin.'

Shaznay was staring at me. I usually wear baggy clothes but that night, hanging out at Shaznay's flat, I was wearing a tight outfit – grey jeans, skin-tight sleeveless T-shirt, cowboy boots.

'Your boots look bigger than your legs,' Shaznay said.

I looked down; she was right.

'You look concave.'

'I know,' I said.

Stress, misery, lack of self confidence – I can never stomach those feelings and food. When I am unhappy my appetite goes.

Too much partying left Johnny anxious and depleted. On top of that, he was getting scripts through the post, but he could not find a film he liked. Johnny was miserable, but he would not talk. I tried to be warm towards him, to love him out of it, but he pulled away from me.

That is when my pride kicked in. I pulled away from him, just as hard, harder. Distant and uncommunicative. We were going nowhere.

Eventually I asked Johnny to move out of my house. It was Christmas. For the Millennium Eve celebrations I went to Nic's and met up with Mum, Dad, Lee, and Tara Joseph, who by then was our manager. We decided to go to see the fireworks and all walked from Nic's house to Primrose Hill.

It was a long walk. I had a magnum of champagne in my hands. It was really heavy. The hill was packed but our Great Dane, Sadie, helped clear a path as people backed away from her. As I stood watching the fireworks light up the sky, I missed Johnny, but I knew it was time to move on.

A few days into 2000, we went to Norfolk to film the video for the first single from our new album, 'Pure Shores', the theme song to the movie, *The Beach*. A few weeks earlier, with Johnny, I had dyed my hair black. The night before the photo shoot, I told my on-site hairdresser, Alex Price:

'I want to go back to being blonde again. I want to go back to being the old Nat.'

'But your hair is so brittle from the black dye and peroxide. Just the front then,' she suggested, 'dye the front so that you look blonde.'

With trepidation, Alex bleached my fringe and the sides of my hair. Then she piled loads of conditioning treatments into it. I sat up for a while, nervously playing with my hair, as strand after strand snapped off in my hand. We went to bed. Alex did not sleep for fear she would wake up and find me bald.

When I saw blonde me in the mirror, I felt relieved. Hair colour greatly alters your appearance. With blonde hair lightening my face I no longer looked so hollow-eyed and sad. Alex blow-dried my hair.

'I was worried I was going to have to find you a wig,' she confided.

I managed a smile.

'Thank you. You have no idea how much I needed to see the old Nat again.'

Shaznay walked into the room and saw me.

'Your hair looks wicked,' she said.

I was looking better. A compliment from Shaznay was rare.

Three wet days shooting the video for 'Pure Shores'. We were freezing cold and wet but it was good to be focussed on work again. To put my mind where it was meant to be.

NATALIE NICOLE

This was the first video we had made in a year and, hierarchy-wise, things had gone from bad to worse. The cameras were always on Mel, who was the main singer, or Shaznay who wrote the lyrics. Singing only on the chorus and harmonies, it was hard to feel part of the song – now Nat and I were being pushed right out of the video too; we felt like extras.

We decided to make a stand, to fight to make our mark.

'We are a four-part band,' we told the director, Vaughan Arnell. 'We need to be more visible in the video.'

He was great. He listened to us and began to include us more. Shaznay was furious; she felt the camera was not on her sufficiently. She burst into tears. She said she did not want to do the video with him any more. We were all embarrassed and upset. The truth was, Shaznay did not like anyone who gave Nat and me attention. She always had to be the important one.

NATALIE NICOLE

At that time, our shows were being booked by the agent, Louis Parker. It was a huge shock to us when he died suddenly. Louis's funeral was in Wales and the four of us went there together. I had never been to a funeral before and was unsure what to wear – especially as Louis had specified that he did not want anybody to wear black. I wore a blue Adidas tracksuit and put my hair in a ponytail. I felt uncomfortable wearing make-up.

In Louis's home town, everyone knew him. Police were patrolling the area; there was a megaphone on top of the church. Leroy Thornhill from the Prodigy sat in the pew beside me. I listened to the speeches thinking: this is what happens, we die. I felt such sadness.

As the coffin went by, I saw Shaznay's body crumple. Leroy pulled out a roll of toilet paper and we passed it around. We were all united in our grief for Louis. That day changed me for ever. I realized – with a clarity that has never left me – that it is a mistake to take things for granted. A lot of things which worry me are not important. It put my daily concerns into context.

After the funeral, there was a party. One hundred and fifty people having farewell drinks and watching fireworks. They were spectacular. We all looked to the sky. Go on, Louis. Everyone was crying.

At that party, Liam Howlett of the Prodigy saw me. Months later he told me that, as our eyes met, he made a deep connection. Caught up in my grief, I have no memory of that moment. I think sometimes that I would like to see a hypnotherapist to try to recall it – the moment that catalysed the most significant relationship of my life.

A few days later, we attended the premiere of the movie, *The Beach*. Shaznay had written the movie's theme song, 'Pure Shores'. We all wore glitzy Dolce and Gabanna clothes. I wore new PVC Versace boots with the thinnest of heels. I felt very glamorous.

It was the first time I had seen the film and I was riveted. Afterwards, we all decided to go to the after-show party. Jamie Theakston was there. We had seen each other a few time since we split up and we were friends. Not for the first time, I thought how we would always have made better friends than we did lovers. Johnny was there too. It was the first time I had seen him since we parted. I gave him a hug. It felt good to know that, even after breaking up, the warmth between ex-lovers can endure.

We released 'Pure Shores' five days later, on Valentine's Day. Mel's pregnancy, the film, our tour – we had been off the scene for a year. 'Pure Shores' was our comeback single and we were excited and nervous to see how it would be received.

The first time it was played on the radio was on Zoe Ball's Radio 1 *Breakfast Show*. I cried. Would the public still want to know us? I so wanted everyone to like it. It was released at the same time as Christina Aguilera brought out 'What A Girl Wants' so we knew we had huge competition. When the midweek sales figures came in, we were told we were number one.

'Pure Shores' was top of the charts – would it stay there? I had a gut feeling that it would – inside myself I knew – but listening to the *Pepsi Chart Show* countdown that second week, I was very jittery. Nic was with me – and Mum and Dad, writing down the title and position of every song in the top forty.

When it got to the song that was at number two, we all got into a circle and screamed. I cried with happiness.

'We did it, we did it, number one for the second week.'

We had never been at number one for more than a week. Nic and I were dancing around the kitchen. Kate Thornton and Samantha Janus called to say congratulations but, apart from that, this was a family moment. We enjoyed it on our own.

'Pure Shores' went on to become the second biggest-selling single of the year. It was a huge accomplishment. Shaznay wrote the lyrics and I was proud of her. It was a strong song and it was an honour to be part of it. In the beginning I wanted to be in All Saints because I loved the music. That was still true. Every time we performed 'Pure Shores', the crowd loved it. As soon as the music started, they went crazy. It was the best response we had had since we released 'Never Ever'.

We started work on our second single from *Saints and Sinners*, 'Black Coffee'. A song we all liked, it was not written by Shaznay, so I thought Nic and I might finally get a chance to sing something more than backing vocals. But when we arrived in the studio Shaznay was already there, staking her claim. Mel had sung our last single, 'Pure Shores', so Shaznay obviously wanted to be the star on 'Black Coffee'.

'Don't you think we should all get a chance to have a try at this song?' I said.

There was silence in the room.

'It's not worth it, Nat,' Nic said.

'Yes it is,' I said. 'We all vibe with this song. We all deserve the right to have a chance.'

Management relented. I went into the booth and sang 'Black Coffee', but I was nervous. I knew I was being tested and judged. Without support, it is hard to do your best. When Shaznay was chosen to sing 'Black Coffee' no one was surprised. I had been allowed a chance at a solo only to placate me.

I began to feel used and I slacked off. I did not care any more. Being on tour is very intimate, the lack of friendship highlighted my loneliness. I felt isolated. I missed Rachel, my home and my parents. Nic was my only consolation, the only friendly face. I drew strength and comfort from her, but it was not enough.

For years I drank for enjoyment, now I was drinking to escape. Drinking because I was unhappy. If there was alcohol around, I was the first to open it. On the plane I would drink wine, then I would come off the plane with bottles and carry on drinking as we got our suit-cases. Then I would go into a hotel room and have a drink.

I was an insomniac and, when I was away from home, alcohol helped me sleep – it knocked me out. But I had restless nights because of it. Dehydration and exhaustion.

I did not want to be with anyone. I wanted to be alone with my drink. Alcohol numbed things.

Nic would call me to watch movies with the others in one of their rooms, but I preferred to drink myself to sleep in my room. Drinking and smoking cigarettes until I passed out. Alcohol was my only comfort. My friend. When I went to work the next day, people said I stank of alcohol, but I didn't care. I didn't drink during the day when I was working. I looked forward to going back to my room so I could drink to shut off.

I spent a lot of time with Mel C. She was someone I could talk to. She understood. She knew what it was like to feel your creativity was being trampled – and all for the image of the band.

One night we got drunk together and I stayed over at her house. The next day I felt too ill to go to work. Management called and said they were going to fine me £10,000 for not showing up. I was horrified. It was a rule that had been bandied about – fining us – but why was I the first person they enforced it with?

I started crying. Mel C felt dreadful for me.

'I'll pay your fine for you,' she said.

I would never have accepted, but it meant a lot to know she cared that much. Mel C has a generous heart.

NATALIE NICOLE

When I turned up for work that day, I discovered that Melanie had left the country.

'Melanie can't take your sister any more,' Shaznay said. 'She's gone to France.'

'France? What are you saying? Is Mel going to be

fined for not turning up or does that rule just apply to my sister?' I asked.

NATALIE NICOLE

In the end the fine was waived but the situation added to my feeling of disappointment and lethargy. We were trained singers, but we were never allowed to sing. Nic and I wrote songs, but they were never released. I felt our role in the band had shrunk; all we were doing now was promoting Shaznay and Mel.

15 - JUMPING BEAN

NATALIE NICOLE

It was August. We had just done our show at the V2000 concert in Cheltenham and the band was ready to go home. Usually I leave with them, but my friend Donna Air was there, interviewing bands for the *Big Breakfast*.

'Why don't you stay?' she asked. 'We can hang out.'

I had never stayed behind at a festival before – usually we did our thing and then piled into the van to leave. Nic was staying on for a while with Liam. All around me people were having a good time.

'We can go watch some bands and have fun,' Donna said.

I suddenly felt excited.

'I would like to stay,' I told Johnny Buckland, our tour manager. 'I want to enjoy myself with my friend Donna.'

When the rest of the band left I had a sense of freedom. I felt freer than I had in months. I could do whatever I wanted to. I grabbed a beer from the backstage bar. I felt so happy. I was Natalie – not Natalie of All Saints – just Natalie, out for the evening with a girlfriend.

There were three tents, each with a stage. We had a couple of shots of Jägermeister with the Blood Hound Gang and then watched their gig from the side of the stage. It was one of the happiest days of my life. I was on such a high, so happy and filled with life, I rushed on to the stage and danced with them. A photograph appeared in the paper the next day. I love that photo – it is a memory of a day when I really loved my life.

It began to get dark. I was standing outside one of the tents with Nic, Liam and Amanda Ghost, when I saw a guy wearing purple sunglasses. The glasses were low on his face and they made his eyebrows look high. He had a blond mohican haircut and a pierced nose.

He was wearing baggy parachute trousers and a punk jacket with badges. I liked the way his clothes hung on him. He wore them with style. He looked funky. He smiled and it was the smile that hooked me. He smiled like Gizmo from *The Gremlins*.

It was towards the end of the night. We were watching Supergrass play. I was standing with Keith Flint from the Prodigy and four other people. I pointed to the guy with the sunglasses and the smile and I asked:

'Keith, who is that?'

'That's Liam,' he said. 'He's in my band.'

'Really?'

I was surprised. I thought I had never seen him before and yet I had seen Keith's band at parties.

Keith asked: 'Why?'

'Just wondering,' I said. 'He's cute. Will you put in a good word for me?'

'Certainly,' said Keith.

Apparently, when Keith told Liam that I was interested in him, he didn't believe him. They had a long-standing game between them where they used to lie about such things to wind each other up.

I told my friend Amanda Ghost I was interested in Liam and she laughed her Marge Simpson laugh and wandered over to him too. Ten minutes later, she came back.

'He likes you.'

I screamed and jumped around. I felt like a jumping bean.

Fifteen minutes went past. Liam was talking with Keith and watching the band play. I was also aware of him watching me, checking me out. Growing impatient, I went up behind him and banged his knees with my own. It was a silly, childish thing to do. He laughed and carried on talking to Keith. I felt stupid. I knew he could not make me out.

Keith introduced us. I was so excited I kept jumping around.

'Why don't you all come back to my place?' Keith said, as the band finished and the field started clearing.

I looked at Liam. 'Are you going?'

'Yes. Are you?'

My heart was hammering. 'Yes.'

There were three cars, including the All Saints' car which was waiting for me. As we started walking towards the cars, a huge hand grabbed me and held me back.

'Are you leaving?'

It was Gerard, the bass player with the Blood Hound Gang.

'Yes,' I said.

'Stay,' he said.

'Get off me,' I said. 'I've got to go.'

I didn't want to be separated from Liam. Liam tried to get into my car, but there was a jumble of people and I ended up driving with Keith and Donna. Meanwhile, Liam was quizzing my friend Amanda all the way to the house – to check I really did like him, to ensure it was not a wind-up.

The first thing I noticed when I arrived at Keith's was the dogs. Fifteen of them in the hallway – Weimaraner puppies, running around and collapsing all over each other. They were so sweet. An instant and welcome diversion, something to do with my hands and eyes. I felt nervous, now, to see Liam again. We were in a different environment, with a different atmosphere. I didn't want to look stupid. I didn't want to mess up.

I stayed in the hallway playing with the puppies. Liam hadn't arrived yet and, as the minutes went by, I began to think that maybe he wasn't coming. Disappointment. Men are a diversion, a distraction – I began to go along that path and then the doorbell rang and, of course, it was him.

Liam went into the kitchen and, after a while, I felt confident enough to go in there too. There were about fifteen people in there including Donna, Amanda, the other members of Liam's band, Keith and Leroy, and a couple of people Leroy had brought back.

I drank a beer and talked to Donna and Amanda. Liam and I skipped around each other for a quarter of an hour, totally aware of the other person, but pretending not to be. I don't think either of us knew how to start the whole thing between us again.

I found myself out on the patio, embarrassed, nervous. Liam joined me. I had never met anyone I liked so much at first sight. We stood silently. The energy was crackling between us, but neither of us knew what to say, how to start the whole thing rolling. The sky was dark and seemed near.

Liam was distant and cool. I know now that he was

protecting himself. But that night it was easy to read his reticence as lack of interest. I was scared to look at him, I kept looking out into the garden.

We talked about music and about the gigs we had seen, giggling a lot. He was quirky, sharp, interesting. I liked the way he talked, the words he used. I liked the things he said. And his smile. Still like Gizmo, still crooked. It was the only part of his face I could see, dark sunglasses still covered his eyes.

'So,' I said, taking my courage into both hands and blurting the words out before I could stop myself, 'are you seeing anybody at the moment?'

I was looking at the ground between us, I did and did not want to know. It seemed so important, even then. I knew that I was drawn to him.

'Yes.'

'Have you been seeing her long?' I asked.

'Yes,' Liam said. 'Ten years.'

'I'm barking up the wrong tree here, then.'

'No,' Liam said, 'you're not.'

He pulled me forward and kissed me. And once we started kissing we could not stop.

This party of fifteen or so people hung out together for the next five hours. Sometimes in the garden, moving then to the jacuzzi. We all sat around drinking and smoking. I found a pen and started drawing on Liam's arms: 'N&L TLA' (Nat and Liam, true love always).

Then he took the pen and drew a hinge in my elbow socket. It was realistic, detailed. I loved it.

We started playing games around the house. Hide and seek, chasing each other. I felt wild, outrageous, caught up in something magical. I ran out from behind a wall, flashed my boobs at Liam and ran away.

It was 3 a.m.

'I have to go,' I said. 'I have a show to do tomorrow.'

'Stay another half an hour,' he said.

I did. And another hour. I was wide awake. I felt as if an electric light bulb had been switched on in my head. I did not want the evening to end. I did not want to be separated from Liam. I feared that when we parted we would never see each other again. The evening was so magical, the energy between us was so special. So pure, somehow. The finest quality. I did not know when I would ever feel this good again.

It was 5 a.m. It had not quite got light. We sat by a window in the lounge, looking out. We both had drivers waiting outside.

'I have to go,' I said.

'I know.'

I wrote my telephone number on a piece of cigarette packet.

'Call me.'

'Tomorrow.'

Liam called the next day. It was his birthday. His girl-friend had arranged a small party for him. We chatted comfortably, happily.

'So,' he said. 'Do you want to meet up?'

'Yes.' I was certain. 'I do.'

'When?'

'Soon,' I said.

'Tomorrow?'

'Fine.'

'Shall I pick you up at your place?'

'Yes – around four o'clock.'

'See you then.'

I couldn't sleep that night, laying awake in the dark, thinking about spending time again with Liam. The time between now and then was just time to be endured. I had never felt so drawn to anybody. There was a sense of rightness, of familiarity, of inevitability about our connection. The thirteenth-century Persian Sufi poet Rumi said: 'Lovers do not find each other, they are in each other all along.' This was how I felt about Liam, from the beginning. It was as if I had always known him.

The intensity of my feelings was frightening. I could not eat before he arrived, or sit or do anything, except pace up and down, drinking wine and looking in the mirror. My heart was racing. The waiting was so unbearable I almost wanted to cancel the whole thing.

When the doorbell rang, I felt nauseous. The moment I had been waiting for, he was here, and I had no idea how to act. The house was a mess, totally chaotic. Tissues, clothes, ashtrays and glasses all over the floor. There was no way I could let him see this, see me.

I pressed the button on the intercom.

'I'm on my way down.'

Liam was leaning against the wall sipping a beer.

'Hi.'

'Hi. How are you?'

Liam had been at a friend's house, having a few drinks for confidence. He was quite drunk.

It was a hot day. We walked through Hampstead, past the shops in the high street, talking as we walked. Our bodies colliding on the pavement. Walking side by side. We had a beer in the House on the Hill, walked on and had a second in the King of Bohemia.

I had a permanent grin on my face. I couldn't get rid

of it. I knew I looked goofy, but there was nothing I could do about it. I couldn't hide the fact that I wanted to be with him.

'Do you want to eat something?' Liam asked.

'Could be a good idea.'

We started walking up the hill. The sun was hot in our faces, there was a fluid feeling in my body. One of those moments in life when it feels so very good to be alive – when you are right where you want to be with who you want to be with. I did not see the man walking towards us, or the camera he pointed at us until the blur of the flash.

'What the – ?'

'Thanks,' the photographer said. 'Do you have any-thing to say to our readers? I'm from the *Mirror*.'

'Come on, Nat.' Liam steered us away from the photographer and up a side street. He was visibly ruffled. I felt bad – bad for him and his girlfriend. This was a part of my life – I was used to it; being snapped at no matter what mood I was in, no matter how private the moment.

'I'm so sorry,' I said. 'I totally understand if this is too much for you – if you don't want to see me.'

There was a silence.

'It's fine,' Liam said. 'Really.'

'What about when your girlfriend sees us in the paper?'

'It will bring things to a head,' Liam said. 'But things are already going that way.'

The House on the Hill restaurant was empty. We sat inside and looked at the menus. As I scoured the possi-bilities, all I was really thinking was: what would be the easiest thing to eat – something that would not dribble or get caught in my teeth. I settled on Pasta Arrabbiata – small pasta pieces.

I was chattering away, embarrassed and nervous. Liam sat sideways on to the table, still wearing his sunglasses. His barriers were up and, clearly, he was not about to let them down. I know now that he was playing it cool to protect himself, but that afternoon, to me, he looked arrogant and carefree.

'It's weird,' I said, 'we move in similar circles and yet I never saw you before the V2000 concert.'

'I saw you about six months ago,' Liam said. 'At the funeral of Louis Parker.'

'You were there?'

'I was at the bar and I saw you,' Liam told me. 'You looked at me for a moment.'

'I don't remember,' I said, scanning my memory.

'I remember what you were wearing,' Liam said. 'An electric blue Adidas top.'

I was totally amazed.

The alcohol helped. Three beers and two bottles of wine later, we left the restaurant.

'Where now?'

We needed something to do, somewhere to go.

'My sister Nic's place is near here,' I said. 'Do you want to meet her?'

'Sure.'

'Liam Gallagher will be there.'

'I've met Liam.'

Nic opened the door to us in baggy tracksuit bottoms. She took one look at Liam H and paled. Embarrassed that Liam H should see her in a scruffy moment, she ran back into the lounge before he was even inside the door. When Liam H and I walked into the lounge it was empty. Nic and Liam G had obviously been chilling out on the sofa, but now they were both upstairs fixing their hair in the bathroom mirror.

Then they came back downstairs again as if nothing had happened.

'Right, Liam, nice one, mate.'

We stayed with Nic and Liam G for a couple of hours. Then we went to the Light Bar at the St Martin's Lane Hotel. By this time, we were hammered to the point of illness. Liam lives in Essex so he booked a hotel room. We went upstairs. We felt awkward. I went on the jogging machine. Liam laid on the bed. It was morning, the room was filled with light. We kissed. Liam fell asleep and, in time, I did too.

I woke around 6 a.m. and realized Liam was in the bathroom. He was in there an hour. Clearly I could handle my drink better than he could. I lay there with my eyes wide open.

When Liam came back into the room, he looked awful. I was exhausted, I didn't want to get up yet, but I felt very uncomfortable. He was embarrassed and I was embarrassed for him. He was so ill he could barely communicate.

I could see all he wanted to do was be left alone with his hangover misery. My presence was making it worse for him. I knew he didn't want me there.

'I'm going,' I said. 'I'll go down first and you can follow me – in case of reporters.'

I got out of bed and began gathering my things together. It was a horrible, awkward moment.

'I'll call you,' Liam said.

'Yeah, okay.'

I didn't think I would hear from Liam again.

★

The next night I saw Amanda Ghost in a restaurant.

'Amanda,' I said, 'have you spoken to Liam?'

'Yes, he called me.'

'What did he say? *Exactly*,' I insisted, 'including the "ands" and "thes". Start at the beginning, don't leave out any details.'

'He said the night went well, but that he drank too much to overcome nerves and fucked it up. He said he got ill and you left. He's annoyed with himself. He said he didn't like parting from you on a bad vibe.'

'I didn't like it either.'

'He asked me to ring you and see if you still like him.'

We were like teenagers, unable to talk to each other, liaising through a friend.

'Does he want to see me again?'

'If you want to see him.'

I was not sure why, not after the awkwardness and the downer of the end of the evening, but I was still so drawn to him, to something in him. Of course I still liked him. I was relieved we would see each other again.

A week later, Liam and Keith picked me up and we drove to Reading Festival to hear Oasis play. Keith sat in front with the driver, while Liam and I sat on the back seat. It was a long drive and we were both really shy. We could not talk. I kept looking at Keith's bare feet positioned on the dashboard. I telephoned Nic from my mobile. She was in a car with Liam G about half an hour ahead.

Suddenly Liam's phone rang. I could hear by the way he was talking that it was not good news. He put the phone down and was silent.

'That photo the photographer took of you and me,

Nat,' he said. 'It will be in the *Sunday Mirror* tomorrow.'

'I'm sorry.'

'It doesn't matter.'

The picture was something Liam could not escape from – something he could not bullshit his way out of. And he did not want to. Whether his girlfriend saw the photo or not, he said, their relationship had been over for a while.

It was a relief when we arrived. In the VIP area, we parted to talk to other people. That was easier, less awkward. We were on a date, but we were not quite a couple. We were both playing it too cool for our own good. As Oasis came on stage, Liam H came and stood with me and put his arms around me. That was how we stayed throughout the gig.

At the end of the festival, there was talk of a party.

'I'm going to go back to Essex,' Liam said.

I knew he had to sort his life out.

'That's fine,' I said.

We climbed into separate cars but, after a few miles, Liam H's car pulled over and we all moved around so that Liam and I could travel together.

Liam went home and told his girlfriend it was over. She moved out the same day. This and more I discovered from Amanda. Over the next days, Liam and I communicated through her. It was so hard for us to relax with each other; we were both analysing everything, wanting to know how the other person felt but not having the guts to ask.

'Amanda, what does he say? Does he like me?'

'Yes, I've never known Liam to be like this.'

He was not gambling his relationship on me; he was making changes to be on his own. Nevertheless, the fact

271

that he was single moved our relationship into a new dimension. We no longer had to hide.

For the first few weeks we kept going out, having a laugh and getting really drunk. Liam started staying over at my house. Falling in love is the scariest thing. Scary and exciting. The newness is full of possibilities, but you do not dare to speak them – do not even dare to really feel them.

We did the lottery show with 'Pure Shores'. I was on stage, singing – which is the thing I love most in the world. I came off stage and there was a message on my mobile from our press officer.

'There is going to be something in the paper tomorrow about your ex. Natalie, please call the press office.'

I called them instantly.

'What's going on?'

'Natalie, I am really sorry to have to tell you this.' The press officer's voice was shaky.

'What is it?'

'Carl has sold a story to the *News of the World*.'

Having been absent for three years, years when I needed his support, Carl had called a few weeks earlier out of the blue. I was clear-sighted about his materialistic motives for getting back in touch. But for Rachel's sake I decided to give him another chance – a chance to be a father to Rachel. Rachel was seven and I did not want her to be denied her father. I wanted him to make her feel special, to let her know she was wanted.

'He has sold pictures too,' my press officer continued. 'I have the text in front of me. I got an advance copy.'

'What does it say?' I could not get the words out quickly enough. 'Read it to me.'

'Now?'

'Yes now, now –'

I was screaming. I could feel my whole life disintegrating in front of me. And Rachel. What about Rachel? How could he do this to us? How could he do this to her? Money. I knew the answer even as I was asking the question. He did not care about Rachel – it had all been about trying to make money out of me, to cash in on our past together. I wanted to kill him. I did not know how I would face the world.

I listened to my press officer's voice, telling me as calmly as he could what the next day's papers would be peddling. Carl had given them a minute by minute account of our relationship including 'jealous rages' which were just marital scraps, and 'three in a bed romps' which were really just three people in a bed.

It was grotesque. Carl had sold stories about me before – initially they were about me and Samantha Janus because she was famous and I was not. Now they were printing sleazy and explicit details of our sex life. Things I have never done with him – or anyone. Stories that made him appear larger than life. I was so furious, so helpless, so angry. He was the father of my child. How could he do this?

I put the phone down and immediately rang Carl.

'How could you do this to your own daughter?'

'How do you know about it?'

Carl was perplexed – he did not know the way the media works. That when you are a public figure you sometimes hear about things before they are printed, but you have no power to do anything about them.

'My press officer,' I said. 'You're only just back in Rachel's life and you're letting her down again. How much did you get?' I spat the words at him.

'Not enough.'

Then he started screaming at me again, that high-pitched scream and it all came rushing back, all the years of being beaten down and diminished by him. Always my fault. I was always to blame. Somehow, even now, he had total justification inside his own head for why he had betrayed his former wife and daughter.

I began to shake. I was sobbing. When I saw the paper the next day, I was horrified anew. Nothing could have prepared me for the pictures and the details splashed across the front page and four inside pages. One of the stories reported what, he claimed, I did with a banana. Lies, all lies. I felt like I had nothing left that was my own – not my reputation, not my privacy, not my own skin. He had taken it all from me and made it public property. I felt naked, more naked than naked. Utterly exposed.

I had to face people in shops, at work, people in the press and, worst of all, the other parents at Rachel's school. I wept and wept and then I set my face. I had to deal with it. I had no choice. I had to be bigger than this for Rachel's sake. The story ran for three weeks. The final week, Carl advertised his new stripping troupe.

I tried to keep it from her, but one week Rachel saw me on the cover of a newspaper. When she asked about it, I told her: 'Don't mention his name. He's not your daddy. A daddy is someone who takes care of you.'

I had never put Carl down to her before, but now he was out of our lives, totally out. There was nothing good that he could possibly offer to Rachel. She had a hard time at school after this. She felt humiliated. She told lies – said she did not like the truth because it was boring. The truth was she missed having a dad. It goes against the grain for a child to discover her father is the bogeyman.

NATALIE NICOLE

We were in a restaurant having a family meal, when Rachel followed me into a cubicle in the toilet and locked the door.

'I know Carl has written something bad about Mummy again,' she said.

I was stunned – and trapped – not at all prepared for this. But I knew Rachel needed to talk to someone who was not directly involved, someone who would be totally honest with her.

'Okay, Rachel,' I said. 'What do you want to know?'

'Do you like Carl?'

I hesitated only a fraction of a second.

'No, Rachel, I don't.'

'Okay,' she said. 'I'm going to go and give my mum a big hug.'

NATALIE NICOLE

Dave Stewart and Anoushka invited us to their place in the South of France. I was in desperate need of a holiday.

'Why don't you invite Liam to go with you?' Mum suggested one afternoon.

We were sitting in the house, drinking tea, and Rachel was upstairs playing. I had been seeing Liam for five weeks. I knew that I was falling in love with him and it was like standing on the edge of a cliff. I tried to look away.

'It will be an opportunity for you to spend quality time together,' Mum said.

I knew it was a good idea. You find out so much about a person when you actually live with them, as you do on holiday. Lots of little things come out. It speeds up the process – you can know very quickly how you feel about a person sharing the same roof with them.

'I'm not sure –' I said.

'It's up to you of course,' she said, 'but it seems like a gift to me.'

She left it at that. She never pushes or coerces me. Mum is always just there when I need her, saying the right thing, letting me know that I am loved no matter what. It is this that has helped me keep going so much of the time. The connection between my mum and myself is the strongest, most life-supporting thing in my life – like air, an invisible thread that keeps me up and stops me going under. There is nothing about me that she does not know.

And so her words stayed with me. The idea would not go away. I ran it past Nic and she liked it too.

'It will be fun, Nat,' she said. 'You, me and two Liams.'

We laughed at the prospect of having two Liams in one house. She knew that I was scared, she also knew how much I already felt for the new man in my life.

'Go on, do it, Nat,' she said.

'I have to,' I told her. 'But what if it all goes horribly wrong?'

That night, in a restaurant with Liam, the words were bubbling in my mouth: do you want to come on holiday with me? I bit them back so many times. We had finished eating pasta and we were waiting for dessert – I always love to eat dessert, the favourite part of any meal – sweet things.

'Liam, I want to ask you something.'

'What?'

Whenever I looked at him, my stomach lurched. It was hard not to touch him, to be always touching him, some part of my body in contact with his. There was a feeling that this was meant to be and the more I felt that, the more I wanted to run away from what I was going to say. People think that falling in love is delicious – and it is – but they forget the angst. The scale of which matches the passion exactly.

'Nic and Liam are going to Dave Stewart's place in the South of France next week. And I was wondering –'

I began to fiddle with the tablecloth, plaiting its fringes between my fingers, making a concertina to take my mind away from what we were in.

'Would you like to go with them . . . ?' There, I had said it, I had blurted the words out. 'With me,' I added, uncomfortable in the silence that was now between us. 'Do you want to go?'

'Okay,' Liam said.

It was a brave thing for him to do; it was early in our relationship and he was going on holiday with people he didn't know. Both terrified of being hurt, there were still silences between us, and so many barriers. Liam was so shy and reserved, it made it hard for me to relax. Potentially three full days together could be awkward – but there was such a pull to be with each other. I could feel my heart beating. No going back now, this was going to happen. Liam and I were going on holiday – I began to glow inside at the thought.

Dave Stewart's house in the South of France is built into the side of a rock face. It spills down the rocks and has four floors. The views out across the sea are spectacular and wild. A private terrace leads out on to the sea.

The first morning when I woke up there next to Liam, I looked across at this sleeping man and thought: what does he eat for breakfast? I had no idea. He was so familiar to me, so utterly known and yet it was very early days – I did not know any of the simple everyday things about him. I got out of bed as quietly as I could.

I went to Nic and Liam's bedroom and tapped on the door. They were asleep, the shutters were closed and I could see their heads leaning in towards each other. Nic stirred as I came in.

'What is it, Nat?'

'Do you want scrambled eggs and bacon?' I asked.

'Yes and tea.'

'Come on then, get up,' I said.

I needed someone downstairs in the kitchen with me. Liam's awkwardness was making me feel shy. Nic threw on a pair of shorts and a T-shirt. I was wearing baggy pyjama bottoms and a vest.

'Come on then,' Nic said.

Dave's kitchen is little and bright white with stainless-steel cabinets. While I cracked eggs into a bowl and scrambled them, Nic started cutting bread. We had a large crusty loaf Dave had left us.

'I feel torn,' I told Nic. 'I'm on holiday so I want to relax, but I'm also here with Liam so that means half of me is worried about the way I look, my hair and not wearing any make-up.'

Nic laughed. 'I know what you mean. Half of you wants to chill,' she said, 'and the other half of you wants to make an effort.'

'Exactly.'

Liam H came downstairs in his khaki shorts and black T-shirt. He looked rumpled and nervous and gorgeous.

'We've made eggs and bacon,' I said, feeling more confident with Nic in the room.

'I'll go get Liam,' Nic said and she left us on our own.

There was a moment of tension. The two of us together and on our own in the kitchen. I busied myself with the pan and then he came towards me and he kissed me. That always dispelled any tension, anything we could not put words to.

I think I knew in that moment it would all be all right, but I am a worrier. I cannot help it. Negative scenarios run through my mind. It is self-protection. If I can possibly avoid it – I do not want to get hurt. Anticipating difficulties makes me feel I can outsmart them. I know that is not necessarily the case.

There was a radio at the house, but we could not tune it, so we played the one CD we had with us – 'Black Coffee' – over and over all day. Lying on the sun lounger by the pool, I found it difficult to stay still. It was impossible to just lie there and sunbathe when Liam was lying beside me. I was so aware of him the whole time. I constantly wanted to be talking to him and touching him. I knew he felt awkward because this was my environment – I had been here before. He did not say anything, but I knew that he thought about it.

I used to look at couples who had love, respect and

trust between them and I used to wonder how they got there. How did that happen? On that holiday I began to see it is about the right person – and a feeling of completeness. Two beings who make each other brighter.

NATALIE **NICOLE**

The night before we left France, we went for dinner with Dave and Anoushka to an exclusive restaurant in the hills. We drove up a long windy road to the most beautiful and romantic of settings. Huddled amongst ruined old buildings, a church lit up and majestic under a dark and starry sky. We got out of the car and went towards the door. A doorman dressed in a white shirt and wine-coloured trousers.

'We have a reservation,' Dave said.

We walked inside. The restaurant was tiny, twelve tables each covered with a glass top spaced out on a verandah. The glasses and cutlery shone. A string quartet in the centre of the room. The walls of the restaurant were covered with Picasso paintings – originals. I stood in awe. My mouth open.

Nat told me: 'Liz Taylor comes here all the time.'

'I can imagine.'

We were taken to a table. A few moments later, Dave's friend Quincey Jones, the producer, arrived. Nat and I looked at him with the utmost respect. He had worked with incredible people including the Jackson Five and Stevie Wonder. He was very down to earth and wise. He told us loads of stories. He was in his seventies and looked great.

I asked him: 'Did you ever meet Marilyn Monroe?'

'Yes.'

'Frank Sinatra?'

'Yes.'

I told Quincey Jones that I had seen a documentary on the Kennedys and it portrayed Frank Sinatra as a mobster.

'Everybody's got a good guy and a bad guy in them,' he said.

16 - SAINTS AND SINNERS

NATALIE NICOLE

We were halfway through working on the second album. It was being produced by Madonna collaborator William Orbit. It was taking a long time because we had written forty songs; also we had to work around William Orbit's schedule and he was all over the place.

The sense of being sidelined increased. Listening to the tracks, Nat and I were hardly there at all. We were backing voices; our position could not have been more clear. Recording our third single from *Saints and Sinners*, 'All Hooked Up', frustrated and disappointed, Nat and I called a meeting with our new manager, Steve Finan, at his house.

'Why is it that Mel and Shaznay sing the leads on every song?' I asked.

Shaznay was wearing a cream sheepskin coat, her hair was scraped into a ponytail.

'It's because Melanie calls and asks me beforehand,' she said, not even looking at me.

'What are you talking about?' I was outraged. 'We've done two albums together and this is the first time you've told me I have to call you to ask for a solo.'

'I don't need to hear this,' Shaznay said, dismissing me.

Singing solos has always meant more to Nat than me. I wanted her to have what she deserved, what she had a right to.

282

'The second album is all Shaznay's and Mel's tracks,'
I said. 'At least let Nat have one of the songs – let her
sing just one.'

Nat spent the next hour pleading her case.

Shaznay and Mel had switched off. They were looking
out of the window. We were getting nowhere.

I looked at Steve.

'I want it to work between you,' he said. 'You are a
brilliant band.'

Mel sat there, picking at her thumbnail. Finally, she
looked up.

'I just want you to know,' she said. 'I am leaving the
band.'

Nat and I had spent the last hour and a half begging
for a bigger part in the band and, all the time, Mel was
planning to leave. If anyone had reason to walk out, it
was me. I could not believe it. Why hadn't she said
something earlier?

'Oh, Mel,' Shaznay said. 'Don't leave. I need you.'

I felt humiliated.

'When I joined this band I was confident and bubbly,'
I said. 'Now look at me – I am portrayed as a blonde tart
of a backing singer.'

I could not hold myself back. All my rage and pain
about the abortion in New York welled up. For the first
time, I accused Shaznay.

'You think you have the right to control me, to
control my body. I'll never forgive you for that.'

I stood up and Shaznay did too. We were ready to hit
each other, but Steve held me back and Nat held Shaznay
back.

I walked out. I felt sick to my stomach. This was the
worst row we had ever had.

I felt grateful to Nic for sticking up for me. After that meeting the record company gave me a chance to be part of the single; they said I could sing the first verse on 'All Hooked Up'.

The finished verse sounded great – so close to Mel's voice that no one could tell the difference. Nevertheless, when it came to the video, Mel mimed along to my line – she put her face to my voice.

My period was late. I needed to take a test. I knew if I went to a chemist and bought a pregnancy test, the speculation would make front-page headlines, so I asked my sister Lee to get the test for me.

Before I did the test, I sat on the side of the bath and considered what I was about to do. I knew I was pregnant. A month earlier I had thought I was pregnant, but it had been in my head; this time the feeling was in my gut.

The packet said to wait two minutes for the result, but a blue line appeared on the paper straight away. There it was. Positive. Time was suspended. I thought: I am going to be a mother. Having given up that chance before, my heart opened. I wanted this baby so much.

'I'm having it,' I said to Liam.

'Give me a hug,' he said.

I was amazed at how instantly supportive Liam was – especially as he already had Lennon with Patsy. We were both shocked. But we shouldn't have been. Getting drunk all the time, we had been careless. I had come off the pill because it made my body retain water and I needed to look trim for work. Liam knew I had no form of protection. We both knew the score.

For two weeks, I was happy to be pregnant. In the third week, the doubts began. We had only been together for three months. We were still getting to know each other, lazy days and unhurried time. It was special – this connection we had between us. A baby might ruin it. Liam did not say so, but I felt it, within myself. We would be stopping something – this joyful exclusive lovers' bubble we were living in – for ever.

Liam is a wild man. I knew his media reputation – and even though that was a far cry from the Liam I knew, I was acutely aware of how much he rates his freedom. What if Liam got bored? I wanted to be associated with fun in Liam's life, with excitement and passion and good times. We had not had enough of that.

NATALIE NICOLE

Despite her threat, Mel stayed in the band. A week later, we were doing a sound check for *The One and Only*, a Sky Special to be taped later that day. We were singing six songs live in front of an audience of All Saints fans. It was going to be an intimate show.

It was the last hour of the sound check and we were singing a new song, 'Whooping Over You'. Nic had one small part to sing on her own, but Mel was singing over her. I could not hear Nic's vocals because Mel's vocals were turned up so loud. I was fighting just to hear Nic's voice. I was sick and tired of it.

'For fuck's sake, there are four people in this band,' I

said angrily. 'Can you turn Mel's vocals off and let Nic sing the line by herself?'

Mel was furious.

'Fuck you,' she said.

She grabbed her bag and walked out of the auditorium. Ten minutes went by, fifteen, twenty.

'How long does it take to cool down?' Shaznay was agitated. 'Where is she?'

We waited. The tension was unbearable.

'I spotted her leaving the building,' one of the sound-check guys eventually volunteered.

'Where did she go?'

'To the cab office.'

'Is she there now?'

Our manager Steven Finan ran out of the building and across the road to the cab office. He called Shaznay on her mobile phone.

'Melanie has hailed a cab and gone home,' he said incredulously.

We knew it would take Melanie forty minutes to get from the studio to her house in Wandsworth. We waited for her to get home and then Shaznay called Mel.

'We're on stage in less than two hours,' she said. 'What on earth do you think you're doing? What are you playing at? You can't leave the three of us here. You've got to come back.'

When Shaznay got off the telephone she was in tears.

'Mel wants to leave the band,' she said. 'This time she means it. She said she's had enough. Nat having a go at her was the final straw.'

Once again, I was being scapegoated. My one comment about Nic's voice could hardly have been the cause of such a momentous decision. Mel was looking for an excuse to walk out and, unwittingly, I had provided it.

Nic telephoned Melanie and then I spoke.

'I'm sorry,' I said. 'Please come back.'

Melanie was silent.

'Put Shaznay on,' was all she said.

We were all crying.

'We will be sued,' Shaznay said. 'How dare you put us in this position? You owe it to the band to come back. You owe it to the fans.'

'It's over,' Mel told her. 'I want to stay home with my child.'

The minutes were ticking by. The fans were arriving. How could she be so unprofessional?

'I'm going to her house,' Steven Finan said. 'I'll do my best to bring her back.'

We sat in the dressing room, Nic, Shaznay and myself. We were all in shock. At a loss to know what to do. Downstairs the fans were arriving – one thousand of them, coming to see us. We could hear them. It was 7.30 p.m. – the time we were due on stage and still no sign of Melanie – or Steve.

'Someone will have to go on stage and tell the fans we're running late,' I said.

One of the organizers was dispatched. From our waiting place, we could hear her.

'All Saints ask you to be patient and bear with them.'

I felt sick. Shamed in front of our fans – many of whom, we knew, would have travelled hours to get here. It was getting late and some of them were really young. They were expectant, excited, and we were letting them down.

And the whole time I was sitting there thinking: things are worse, Shaznay, worse even than you think. I am pregnant.

When Steve finally walked into the changing room with Melanie, we were all too tense to be relieved. It had taken him two hours to convince her to return and do the show – and even then, on the way back, she made him stop so she could buy cigarettes.

'I got out with her,' he told me afterwards, 'in case she did a runner.'

We went on stage at 10 p.m. The fans had been waiting for two and a half hours. How dare we do that to them? It looked so arrogant.

'A big sorry to all our fans and thank you,' Shaznay said, 'thank you for being patient and waiting for us.'

A cheer went up.

'We'd like to start with "I Know Where It's At".'

We were awkward with each other on stage. At the end of the show when we all walked back into the changing room, Melanie walked past me as if I wasn't there.

'I want to speak to Shaznay alone,' she said.

She walked into one of the changing rooms and locked the door.

'As long as she explains to Shaznay she thinks it's okay,' I told Nic angrily. 'But all our reputations are on the line.'

Shaznay and Mel were in the room for ages. They

would not open the door, so Nic and I got into our car and went home. I do not know what they said to each other in the room that night, but I do know at the end of it they were firm allies against Nic and myself. Slagging us off always bonded them. It was the perfect way for them to make up.

The next day, the papers were filled with stories about Melanie leaving the band. If she was really leaving, then we needed to decide our futures, make plans, look ahead. I rang Shaznay. She was crying.

'What are we going to do?' she asked.

'If Mel doesn't want to be in the band, we have a choice,' I said. 'We can carry on without her as a three piece or we can get someone to replace her. There's no reason why All Saints should stop because one of us has had enough. We're good,' I said. 'Bloody good. Our careers do not depend on Melanie Blatt.'

NATALIE **NICOLE**

Once again Mel came back to the band – no excuses, no apologies – as if nothing had happened. I told her I was pregnant and she said she was happy for me, but I had lost respect for her. She was not the Mel she used to be – she was no longer my great mate.

A week after she had walked out on us at the Sky Special, we went to Sweden for the MTV Music Awards. At the rehearsal I had a cough and a sore throat. A doctor was called. As he wrote out a prescription for antibiotics, he looked up from his pad and said:

'I just need to ask you a routine question before I give you these – you're not pregnant, are you?'

I could not take this medication if I was pregnant and I needed something in order to perform. I had to tell the truth.

'I am pregnant,' I said. 'I've just found out.'

Our tour manager, Johnny Buckland, was in the room and his face lit up.

'Are you really?'

'Yes,' I said.

'Hurrah,' he said.

Liam had told his band about the pregnancy; it was a matter of time before word got out. It was time to tell Shaznay. As I walked towards her, my head was filled with images of the way she had reacted when Nat was pregnant. I was scared.

'I've got something to tell you, Shaznay,' I said, and I told her.

'Pregnant?' She looked at me and lifted one eyebrow. Her composure was flawless. 'Congratulations,' she said, but her smile was frozen.

She left the room quickly – no doubt to slag me off behind my back. I don't care, I told myself. But I did. Stupidly, I wanted her to be happy for me – we were in the same band, we were supposed to be friends.

At the MTV Awards, Shaznay ignored me the entire time. I would walk into the room and she would pretend I was not there. It was horrible, painful. Her boyfriend Christian and the other dancers formed a gang with Shaznay and Mel. That meant Nat and I were on our own, again.

One evening I got into the small hotel lift. Shaznay was in there with Mel and the dancers. Shaznay turned her back on me and said to everyone:

'Do you want to go to the bar?'

She then said all of their names individually – leaving mine out. I hated her in that moment – and the rest of them, all of them, for letting it happen. They were frightened of her, that is why no one spoke out against her cruelty. I felt hot tears at the back of my eyes.

The day after the awards, we flew back to London for the Children in Need charity show. I tried to tell Liam how I was being ignored and how painful it was, but it sounded so ugly, so petty.

'I want you to see it,' I told him, 'see it for yourself.'

'Do you want me to come with you to Children in Need?'

'Would you?'

'Of course,' Liam said, 'if you think it will help.'

The programme was being filmed at the BBC and Nat's friend Mel C was in another studio recording *Never Mind the Buzzcocks*. She came to visit us in our dressing room.

'What the fuck's going on in here?' she said. 'It's icy.'

Liam nodded.

'Nic and Nat are working really hard, but it doesn't matter what they do – the other two have got it in for them,' Liam said. 'You don't treat people like that,' he continued, 'trying to control their lives.'

My friend Kate Thornton was in one of the other studios, guest presenting a live TV show called *Liquid News*. She arrived soon after.

'Thank God you're here,' I told her, almost in tears.

Shaznay continued to blank me. It was blatant.

'How can they treat you like this?' Kate was incredulous.

'I'm so relieved you can see it,' I told Kate. 'It's not in my head.'

I was sitting with Kate, when I got a telephone call from my publicist.

'I'm sorry to have to tell you this, Nicole,' he said, 'but the papers know you're pregnant.'

It was Saturday night. The Sunday papers were going to print it the next day.

'I've only known for a week that I'm pregnant, now the whole world is going to know,' I told Kate.

Kate was amazed.

'It's such a well-kept secret,' she said. She had not even told her boyfriend.

'It must have been leaked by the doctor I saw in Sweden,' I said. 'Tomorrow it will be broadcast to the world. I'm not ready for that. After what I've been through and the state of my health, there's a real risk that, physically, I might not be able to carry this child.'

'It's irresponsible of the papers to flag up a pregnancy at this early stage.' As my friend, Kate was angry for me.

'What if I have a miscarriage?' I said. 'It will be misconstrued as abortion. This isn't fair. What am I going to do?'

At that moment, my mobile rang.

'Don't pick it up,' said Kate.

When I played the message back, it was Dominic Mohan from the *Sun*.

'I heard the good news,' he said. 'Call me. I want to know where to send flowers.'

'They want me to confirm it,' I told Kate.

'We have to think about the best way to handle it.' Kate tried to be calming. 'If you don't confirm it, how will they know it's true?'

We were in a busy dressing room. There were BBC production crew around, dancers trying on clothes and having their hair and make-up done. Nat had gone off with Mel C. I didn't know what to do.

'Let's call your press officer and find out what they know,' Kate suggested.

Liam had left and I didn't know how to get hold of him. As Kate and I discussed what to do, I felt a sense of relief in my body: once the world knew I was pregnant, there would be no way Shaznay could force me into doing anything. At least this would mean I could not be bullied.

When Shaznay realized what was going on she was annoyed.

'Why didn't you come to me?' she asked. 'It's wrong that Kate knew about the papers before me.'

Shaznay had been blanking me for days, but she still expected me to go to her for advice about my problems.

'Kate understood,' was all I said.

A week later, we had a photo shoot and interview with the *Big Issue*. I woke that morning and something was very wrong with Kid, the cat that Rob and I had bought together. She was limp and the sides of her mouth were bright pink and foamy. She was hiding under the stairs and gagging.

I thought maybe Kid had a fur ball in her throat. I grabbed her and squeezed her to try to make her throw up, but it seemed to make her worse. She was bleeding from the mouth. Panic stricken, I put her in the car and drove like mad to the vets. I thought she was going to die. At the vets, I burst into tears.

'Something's wrong with her,' I sobbed. 'Please help me.'

The vet felt her head and throat.

'I need to take an X-ray,' she said.

All I wanted was to stay there with my cat. Being separated from her was an agony. But I was due at the photo shoot.

'Call me as soon as you know anything,' I said.

I drove to the photo shoot. When I was nineteen a friend's puppy died in my arms, and that was all I could think about.

NATALIE NICOLE

When Nic turned up for the photo shoot she was crying.

'Kid is bleeding from her mouth,' she told me. 'I don't know what's wrong. She might be poisoned. She might die.'

Anyone who knows Nic, knows how close she is to her three cats. They are people to her, her loves. She was totally distraught. She kept checking her mobile. She could think of nothing else. My heart ached.

The telephone rang. The vet had taken an X-ray and discovered Kid had swallowed a needle. It was lodged in her throat. The vet was going to have to operate to get it out.

'I made it worse.' Nic was distraught. 'I kept trying to make Kid be sick and all the time the needle was puncturing her throat.'

Shaznay walked into the room and, although Nic was crying, she walked straight past her. I could not believe it. No matter what was going on between them, Shaznay knew how Nic felt about Kid.

We did the shoot, and then it was time for the interview. Nic was too upset and Mel did not want to take part, so Shaznay and I did the interview. We were miserable and fed up. It came across. Shaznay said, 'Natalie's really vile when she's angry. Nic can be the same . . . They've always been good-time girls.'

You could tell how bad things were from the pictures and the body language. Shaznay and Mel kept hugging and touching each other to prove a point to Nic and me, alienating us. Nic and I were sick of trying to prove ourselves. One headline said we were the world's most hated women. I wanted to say: is doing charity work hateful?

I wanted to tell them how, a couple of years ago, Nic spent £1,500 on children's toys and took them anonymously to a hospital. There was no press there and all the kids were sleeping. She did it because she wanted to. The media image was so wrong.

Two days later, we did the Smash Hits shows at Earl's Court. When we walked into the rehearsal, Mel was vomiting.

Nic was concerned.

She asked: 'Is there anything I can do for you? Do you want anything from the canteen?'

Mel ignored Nic. Then Shaznay walked into the room and Melanie called out: 'Girlfriend.'

It was as if Nic and I were not there. There was so much tension. By this time we no longer shared hairdressers and make-up artists. We each had our own. Our hairdresser, Alex, and our make-up artist, Sarah, were also being ignored.

From the other side of the room, I could hear Shaznay inviting the security guard to her Christmas party. Nic and I were clearly being excluded from that too.

A few days later, 7 December, was Nic's birthday.

Shaznay and Mel didn't call or send a card. Nic was having a dinner party at Gaucho in Hampstead, so I rang to invite Shaznay and Mel.

'I have other plans,' Shaznay said, 'but I'll see what I can do.'

She rang back half an hour later and left a message on Nic's machine.

'I can't make it,' she said, 'it's a bit late notice. Mel says happy birthday.'

Mel did not call.

Later that week, we were rehearsing for the Capital Radio Awards and I threw myself into my work. Clothes are important to me; always have been. I love the process of putting unusual items together, creating an individual look. Money made it easier to achieve what I was after, but I had always had a firm idea of what I liked, of what worked.

I asked our stylist, Neil Mortan, to get me a mod coat. On the day of the show Nic and I turned up early and he had two for us to choose from. They were great, exactly what I had imagined in my mind.

Nic put one of the coats on. She looked at herself in the mirror and instantly liked it. I tried the other one on. The hood was missing but, apart from that, it looked great.

'Will you sew the hood on for me?' I asked Neil.

'Sure,' he said.

I knew I was going to wear the coat but, while Neil worked on the hood, I tried on other bits and pieces that he had brought in for us: army trousers and little vests.

I was called into the bathroom to have my hair and

make-up done. When I went back into the changing room, Shaznay was sitting on the sofa reading a magazine and wearing my mod coat.

'I'm wearing that coat, Shaznay,' I said.

She looked up from the magazine. She looked at me, but through me at the same time, as if I was nothing – not worthy of attention.

'No, you're not,' she said, 'I am.'

'I asked Neil to get me that coat,' I said.

I took a step towards her, towards the coat.

'I just tried it on,' I said. 'Neil was sewing the hood on for me.'

That should have been the end of it. Shaznay should have just taken the coat off and given it to me, but there was too much history between us. Shaznay was pulling rank.

'No,' Shaznay said. 'I'm wearing it.'

She pulled the coat tighter around her. The coat was not that great, in truth, certainly not worth a battle, but there was no way Shaznay was going to relent. She was making a point. She was restating her power and, in so doing, grinding me into the ground.

Three years of put-downs, of being made to feel inadequate, disposable. The unfairness and pettiness choked me. Not this time, no way. I had proof that the coat was mine to wear – I had Neil.

'Neil,' I called to him, 'can you come over here?'

As Neil came towards us, I could see from the way he walked, from his whole demeanour that he was scared.

'Neil,' I said, 'I asked you to get me a mod coat three weeks ago, didn't I?'

'Yes,' he said.

'You said it was okay for me to wear it, Neil,' Shaznay said.

The silence was long and loud.

'I didn't think you were going to wear the coat, Natalie,' Neil said at last. 'You walked out of the room.'

'To have my hair and make-up done –' I began to protest.

'I'm wearing the coat,' Shaznay said.

Neil was lying because he was scared of Shaznay – the most influential member of the band. It was always the way – people sided with Shaznay because she had the seat of power. I felt sick with impotence. This was wrong and there was nothing I could do about it.

'Neil, I asked you to sew the hood on for me,' I said, but he would not look at me. 'You're lying,' I said to him. 'You know that coat is mine.'

He was looking at the ground.

'Why haven't you got the guts to tell the truth, why won't you support me?'

'I didn't know for sure, Natalie,' he said again.

'For sure?' I was shouting now. 'I asked you to sew the hood on for me.'

I had truth and right on my side.

'It doesn't matter what Neil says,' I said to Shaznay. 'I'm telling you it's my coat and I'm in your band. Do you believe Neil over me?'

'Yes,' she said, 'I do.'

There were so many messages in this situation. It was a reenactment of all the issues that were between us, all encapsulated and laid out before me. I looked at Mel. She knew I was not lying.

'I'm not getting involved,' she said tartly. 'You were quick enough to tell Shaznay you wanted to replace me.'

I was dumbstruck. Shaznay had told her. I had only suggested replacing Mel because I wanted the band to continue. I had not wanted Mel to leave. I did not want to replace her. I did not want All Saints to end. I felt embarrassed and angry. How could Shaznay do that? Our band was being ripped apart.

It all came out then, all the things I had been feeling and sitting on, the slights and humiliations aimed at Nic and myself. The words came from my heart.

'You've been so mean to my sister. You walked past her when her cat was dying and you didn't even call her on her birthday!' I yelled at Mel. 'And you, Shaznay,' I continued, 'you've been going around inviting everyone to your Christmas party except me and Nic. You're a bitch,' I said.

'You better go home and pray to God,' Shaznay said.

'You made me this way,' I retorted. 'I was never like this before I met you.'

Shaznay glared at me and then turned away.

'I don't care if you don't speak to me. But Nic was crying over her cat and you ignored her,' I said. 'Nic never did anything wrong.'

I wanted to hit Shaznay. She knew it. She wanted to hit me too. We came very close, but we had a show to do. I knew I had to hold it.

That night, Shaznay and Mel played up the separation on stage. To get at us, throughout the entire performance Shaznay went to Mel and interacted only with her, singing only to her. As the lead singers, they thrived on it. They overdid the whole thing – over-performing, over-hugging each other, grabbing all the attention. Nic and I were not on lead vocals so this made it harder for us. We looked at each other. It was so juvenile. It made us all look stupid. We felt embarrassed and wondered what the fans thought.

Singing the backing vocals and harmonies on 'Pure Shores' and 'Black Coffee', my head and stomach were churning. Shaznay got all the credit, all the good press and, now, my coat. What more did she want from me? Every shred of my dignity and pride?

When we came off stage, Nic and I were so stressed out we needed to unwind. We went to a bar with Shiara and Alex. They felt bad for us. They saw it all. Because we spent so much time together with a punishing and relentless schedule, relationships between the band had become too strained. The record company worked us so hard, none of us felt nurtured, so any tension between us was amplified.

Unlike the manufactured pop acts that dominated the market, we were four very single-minded people who gelled on one level, but also wanted to pursue radically different agendas. We were a band of two halves – Nic and I were never taken seriously as musicians and our lifestyles were interpreted as vacuous.

Our second album was called *Saints and Sinners* because of the way we had been perceived. The saints were Shaznay and Mel – the sinners were Nat and I. It was not real but, by this time, we had got used to it. No matter what we said and no matter how hard the others partied, Nat and I carried the label for the band. Enough was enough. We had to leave with something intact.

'It's like chronic toothache,' Nic said. 'It hurts and the pain gets worse and worse, but you keep putting off the visit to the dentist, all the time knowing, eventually, you will have to go. And when you do, the tooth is removed and you feel better. It also leaves you with a big space.'

We talked about calling our lawyers. Our eleven-date nationwide tour was sold out. With a new single, relatively new album and a tour at stake, splitting up would cost millions in cancelled dates and appearances.

'Shaznay really wants to do this tour – and I do too,' I said. 'But we can't go on tour with them, it will be hell.'

Nic agreed. 'It will be total alienation on the road.'

We had come close to breaking up so many times and, at the final moment, come back together. This time was different. The pile of hurts had got too big. We had no choice.

The next day Nic and I contacted our lawyers and said we wanted out. Nic and I were not going to subject ourselves to this any more.

'But you are under contract to do the World Sports Awards in two weeks' time,' they said. 'If you don't honour your commitment to that you will be sued.'

Two weeks later we went to the Royal Albert Hall for the sound check for the World Sports Awards. It was the first time we had seen Mel and Shaznay in two weeks. We stayed at opposite ends of the room.

We were singing live with a pianist. On stage we looked at each other and managed professional talk, but that was it. Our performance at that sound check was amazing. For once you could hear all our voices, Nic and I were not drowned out.

Afterwards, Jimmy, one of the dancers, told me: 'Everyone in the audience had chills – goose bumps.'

I was sad. I knew we were the best. None of the other

girl bands could touch us. There was no one like us. That was the shame of it, the waste. We were the best.

When we went on stage that night, for our final performance, I wore a T-shirt saying: 'I love Liam.' I knew Shaznay would cuss if she saw it, so I kept my denim jacket on and then whipped it off at the last minute, to reveal the words on my chest. My final public act of defiance.

The performance was broadcast live on television. The tension between us was so bad I started to shake. The whole place was silent. You could hear a pin drop. The last thing I remember is looking at Mel and agreeing a note in the harmony.

This was the last commitment we had to All Saints. When we came off stage, we went straight to our cars. I did not want to hang around. All I wanted to do was get home and call Liam.

When Mel looked at me on stage, it was as if nothing had happened. It would have been easy to just go back to work – I had done it for years. But not any more. Deep inside me, something had changed.

In the car, I said to myself: my life is going to change now. I had cried enough. No more tears. When I got back to the house, Mum and Dad were there.

'The performance was great,' they told me.

Mum hugged me.

'It's time to let go,' she said. 'Your happiness is all that matters. No matter what, we are here.'

I felt disappointed. I was so proud of All Saints and we had worked so hard. But in the end it was not about what was best for the band or best for the album, what matters was who got to do what – who got to star. Nic and I did not ruin the band – Mel and Shaznay did. I felt ashamed. Ashamed of myself. How could we talk about being one of the best bands in England and then just be walked all over? I felt stupid, a fool.

We were told if we pulled out of the tour we would be sued, so Nic and I got our own independent lawyers. No more handing over control. We took our futures into our own hands. I think Mel and Shaznay were shocked. They always thought: Nat will never leave. They were relying on me to hang in there.

NATALIE **NICOLE**

The band was over. Nat needed reassurance, to know that we were going to be okay, that we could carry on working. Nat was worried about Rachel and being able to support her. Once you have been a single parent, that fear never leaves you. Nat remembered the hard days, where she had come from. She did not want to go back to that. Who would?

I knew my life was not All Saints. My life was not over. I was matter of fact and really together.

'We can do it again,' I told Nat.

It was a feeling I did not sway from.

'I was the one that made All Saints happen in the first place – it was me who pressed our demo tape into people's hands. When the band was on stage, it was us all eyes were drawn to. We are watchable. I know we have got something, Nat, star quality – a quality that can't be manufactured. We have got it and they haven't. People will want more of it – more of us.'

Here then, at the end of the band, my confidence was returning to me – my instincts, my sense of myself. Nat holed herself away with Liam H at his place in Essex. I got on with making it happen – seeking opinions, meetings with lawyers and managers. Cutting ourselves off from the past so we could be ready for the future.

It was almost a relief for me. I was sick of fighting. I was glad to be out of it. I felt so tired. It was like coming out of a bad relationship. You wait so long that when you finally leave, you do not go back. Time passes and, with distance, you realize you are better off without it.

Being pregnant gave me a good and wide perspective. It was over. That is what Mel and Shaznay had decided – had made inevitable. Nat and I had walked away but only because they left us with no alternative. No tears. I had expended all the emotions I was prepared to.

I had a child to think about. My child came first. Before Gene was even born, then, I felt I was required to be a mum. I had a baby in my body – a body that was not as strong as I would like it to be – and so I could not allow stress. Nothing was going to harm my child.

17 - ABOUT LOVE

NATALIE NICOLE

Being pregnant calmed me down. I wanted my body to be as healthy as possible, so I cut down drinking alcohol. Liam cut down with me. We had been on a roll of drinking – drinking for breakfast, lunch and dinner. It was a lot of fun but, without a drinking partner, suddenly a couple of beers were enough for Liam.

On the rare occasions we went out drinking, I would have one glass of wine so I could feel involved and I would hold it all night; sipping at it even when it was warm. I never had the feeling that I was missing out on anything, because I was so excited knowing I had a baby in my stomach. When I was two months pregnant, I had a scan. Our first sighting of our baby. It was wondrous.

A lot of people – the press included – expected Liam and me to fall out. The last thing Liam wants is another child – so the speculation went – and Liam and Nicole have not been dating that long. But the closeness between Liam and me grew and grew.

The Liam I live with is so different from the Liam the press love to write about. He is passionate about his work; he gets stressed and he has a drink and then his tensions come out. But the next day he is totally sweet again. He is very honest and people push his buttons because they love his reactions. Sometimes he gets annoyed and sometimes it is very inappropriate, but he has his reasons.

Liam is like a really good movie – intense and unpredictable. He has a big heart – a clumsy heart. Every morning before eight o'clock, Liam calls his mum Peggy. Then he passes the phone to me and I call mine.

'What's going on in the Appleton camp?' he asks when I get off the telephone.

He loves to know what's happening in my family. He loves my mum, but he loves my dad more. My dad is a role model in his life; someone he can call to talk to about football. He is always excited to speak to my dad; he likes having him around and going for a beer with him.

NATALIE NICOLE

I have a love-hate relationship with Nicole's Liam. We have the worst fights but we love each other to death. We are like brother and sister. When I am upset, he listens to me – really listens. When I am sad, he cries with me. We have similar personalities. We are both very intense.

NATALIE NICOLE

Liam is very stubborn and when he and Nat fight, I feel torn. I am always in the middle. I cope by thinking: fuck them both. Liam H never gets involved; he is very neutral. Like me, he stays calm. In a way, Nat has chosen a partner who is like me, and I have chosen one who is like her. Sometimes when I'm with Liam he reminds me so much of Nat.

I had a great pregnancy. It was very satisfying, very domestic. And Liam and I got stronger and stronger. A week before our first Christmas, Liam made cup cakes. His task was to make parcels to adorn the Christmas stocking cake I was making. He was wearing an apron. I loved him for wearing that apron.

'I can really get into cooking,' he said.

Liam is a continual source of surprise. We went to buy Christmas cards. I went for trendy white cards – symbols more than anything else. When I looked around for Liam, I found him buying the most traditional of cards – with families, fireplaces, Christmas trees and stockings.

Liam is a real homebody. He likes to come home, put his tracksuit bottoms on, lie on the couch, hug me and watch TV. He likes to eat too – sandwich spread is his favourite thing; also roast dinners, bangers and mash, eggs on toast. He makes a great cheese sandwich.

NATALIE NICOLE

Freed from working with Shaznay and Mel, Nic and I set about creating new songs. The record company wanted to keep us on as a duo but we did not know which way we wanted to go musically. Back to square one. I spoke to Tara and said we needed to be sent backing tracks. This was the way we had always worked with All Saints.

Nic and I were open-minded; there were no rules this time and that gave us freedom to do what came naturally. All we knew was that we wanted to create music we enjoyed. Initially, out of all the music we were sent, I found myself attracted to songs that were big on bass beats. I found an up and coming producer, Gareth Young, and we put together songs that were a mixture of rock and pop – songs with a sense of power and fun. At first I was scared of failing, but the feedback from Nic and the rest of my family was so good that my confidence grew.

Two months after the break-up of the band, I went to Cornwall to record our first three tracks, two of which I co-wrote. When I had been in the studio with All Saints, I always felt either daunted or bored. Here, then, for the first time, I began to feel like a singer – a singer with ideas. It was tremendously exciting.

Nic was busy with her pregnancy so, when I came back from Cornwall, I looked around for a different challenge; a sound that would bring variety to our album. Marius de Vries, who used to work with William Orbit, sent us songs that were electronic. I never would have imagined I would have been attracted to writing to electronic music, but Liam and I used to wake up in his house in Essex and listen to Marius's tracks. We liked their moodiness.

Marius's music took Nic and me on a completely different vibe and I started to write soft songs on top of electronic sounds. It was a happy combination. I was excited – also frightened – I did not know what the future held.

NATALIE NICOLE

Liam loved the music Nat and I were creating so much it made me love it more. When I got home from the studio, he always wanted to listen straight away to what I had done. He played my music when he was getting ready to go out and in the car – he knew the words.

NATALIE NICOLE

Liam and I went to Disneyland. It was one of the best times of our lives. The whole place was magical for Liam. He is very romantic; he loves trees and landscapes and he has a thing about birds'-eye views. When he is on an aircraft, he always sits by the window. He loves to see things from above.

Liam is totally obsessed with ostriches – their bizarreness, inquisitiveness and eyelashes. He is such a special person. Very creative. He is intense about his music and does not compromise on anything to do with his work. He is also drop-dead sexy. His only fault is that he leaves the margarine and milk out of the fridge – that and the fact he always sticks his used chewing gum on the side of the bed.

When we had been together for eight months, I proposed to him. We were in the foyer of the theatre where my sister Lee was appearing in *Popcorn*. I turned to Liam, put my hands on his shoulders and said:

'Babe, will you marry me?'

And he said: 'Yes.'

We were really excited. We did not watch the play; we spent the entire two hours holding hands and feeling like schoolkids. When we came out of the theatre, I told Lee and she screamed.

I had not planned to propose to Liam, it just seemed like the natural thing to do. With Liam I had had the best eight months – he made me feel full of life. I had never been happier. I wanted to share every experience with him. He even loved the nerd in me. I had found my soulmate and my partner in crime. With him I was complete.

And he loves my family, which is so important, and they love him.

Rachel loves him to pieces and he is perfect with her. We took her out to dinner to tell her we were getting married and she cried because she was so happy, which made me cry. Then Liam cried.

My bond with Rachel is so strong now, but she hates the fact that her family are famous. One day Nic and Liam G took her to school in Liam's Cherokee. Gary Numan came on the radio and the two of them were singing at the top of their voices. As they got closer to the school, Rachel kept telling them to shut up. When they dropped her off, they called, 'Bye, Rachel,' out of the window. A group of her friends gathered and thought it was so cool, but Rachel was just furious and embarrassed.

'I hate you, Liam,' she shouted.

Rachel is still angry about All Saints. It will take time for her to forgive me for not being there for her. She is entitled to her feelings. All I can do is give her as much love as I possibly can. I question myself – did I do the right thing? But then I tell myself no one's childhood is perfect – mine wasn't and I turned out okay. Rachel is a beautiful and heart-full child. She is bright and very lovely in spite of it all.

When I was seven months pregnant, Liam and I found a house. Looking round it, I told him:

'I can visualize a lot of noise in this house because it will be filled with a family. It won't be quiet. In every room there will be pictures, and our kids' work on the fridge.'

Liam said: 'Carry on, don't stop. Tell me what else you see.'

He is very much into the whole family thing.

I used to grab Liam's hand and put it on my jumping belly. He would freak out.

'Leave the baby alone, you'll hurt him. I don't like touching their heads,' he said. 'In case something happens.'

'I bet you're jealous that I can have a baby growing in my body.'

'Yes,' Liam admitted, 'jealous of the good feeling.'

Around this time Oasis went on tour to America. Liam and I were separated for five weeks. He rang every day, five or six times, from the moment he woke in the morning. We missed each other terribly, but I had a baby inside me and so I never felt alone. The baby would kick and I would talk to him.

The last two months of pregnancy took so much out of me. I could not sleep comfortably and felt very frustrated. By the time Liam got back from America, sleeping was virtually impossible. Sometimes I cried at night, because the only way I could sleep was on my back and all that weight on my spine was painful. Liam would build me a pillow nest and try to make me comfortable.

'I don't know what else to do, Nic,' he would say.

And we would cuddle, but it was like cuddling around

a basket ball. I felt so ugly. My boobs rested on my stomach. It looked like one large mass. I felt really fat and wondered if Liam was going off me. I only put on about two stone in weight, but my hormones were raging and they made me paranoid and jealous.

'I can't wear this,' I would say tearing off a favourite pair of trousers. Then, trying something else. 'Do I look fat in this?'

Liam was scared to say anything – if he was honest and said, yes, I would bite his head off. If he said no, I would call him a liar.

But I loved having a baby in my stomach. I knew when he hiccuped, jumped, moved. Whenever I felt upset, I touched my stomach and instantly felt soothed. I used to put my arms around my stomach, hugging my unborn child and myself. My pregnancy was a happy time. I felt content.

A few days before I was due to give birth I went for a check-up.

'The baby is right down there,' my health worker told me. 'It could happen any time.'

I asked if I could be brought on before my due date. Liam and I were being hounded by paparazzi and it had got to a stage where a combination of nerves and hormones were making me afraid to go out. The press panicked me – their interference was more intrusive than usual. I felt vulnerable and wanted to hide.

We arrived at the hospital at 7 a.m. Liam ordered an English breakfast and sat there eating it and showing off in front of me.

'Are you hungry, Nic?'

'Yes, I'm starving.'

'But you're not allowed anything.'

'I know, I know.'

I was nervous. Scared and excited. It was a challenge. I had friends who had had caesarian deliveries, but I wanted my baby's birth to be as natural as possible. I wanted to be present, fully present. And I wanted to be able to hold my child afterwards and walk out of the room with him – not lie flat on my back.

In the delivery room, the doctor examined me and said: 'His head is so nearly there, it's quite shocking. I'm amazed you haven't gone into labour.'

'I can feel the pressure,' I said, 'but it's not painful.'

The doctor applied a gel to dissolve the wall and the moment she did my waters broke. I felt the sensation of warm tea tipping down my legs, and she said she could feel the baby's head.

'Do you want an epidural?'

'Half,' I said, 'I want to feel the contractions so I know when to push.'

I started to cry with fear and excitement. Mum was there, the nurse and the doctor. I had an overwhelming feeling: this is it. There was no pain at all. *Richard and Judy* were on the television. As I was told to push, Liam was watching *Mid Day Money*.

Then he was by my side like a football coach:

'Come on, Nic, come on, Nic.'

Liam thought I would be in more pain and was waiting for me to scream, but I had an easy labour. As Gene's head came out, I said:

'Look down, Liam, look down.'

When Liam saw Gene's head, he cried. When I saw Liam crying, I cried.

Then I saw Gene's head. It was amazing, incredible.

He had loads of hair. Gene came out perfect, beautiful. The doctor gave him to me. I was in love with Gene straight away.

I said: 'Look, Liam, he's got hair like you.'

Giving birth is the most amazing feeling in the world. It is something you have to feel for yourself to know, really know. It is a miracle, magic, the most unbelievable and yet the most natural thing ever. I am still amazed by the fact Gene lived and grew inside me – Gene was born from my body. It changed me for ever.

Afterwards Liam said: 'Watching your child being born is the most amazing thing ever. Better than my football team winning or playing music – and they're pretty amazing things, so it's got to be good.'

Gene weighed 6 lb 13 oz. Liam ordered lots of champagne. Nat arrived, and Rachel, Dad and my sister Lori. Then Liam's mum Peggy, my agent Tara, my sister Lee and her boyfriend Guy. I ate a tuna sandwich with crisps inside. It tasted so good, so delicious. And that first cup of tea.

People kept handing me champagne, but I could not handle it yet. Through my pregnancy I had said, as soon as I could I would get drunk and smoke. But, as so many mothers find, it was not the case.

In the afternoon, Liam's brother, Noel, and his girl-friend, Sarah, came. I felt overwhelmed. There were so many flowers – the room was filled with the scent of lilies. Liam has bad hayfever so we moved them all into the lounge. Every time Liam went in there he returned red-eyed and sneezing.

Towards the end of the day, the mad rush of visitors died down. It was good to have the room clear. Liam and I were left alone with our mums. Together, we bathed Gene and he fell asleep in the water. He had a slight tan colour. I could not stop staring at him. I dressed him in a white towelling Babygro. He smelt yummy, of baby shampoo.

I put Gene in the plastic cot the hospital provided but, every few minutes, I kept jumping up. I could not leave him alone. Looking and looking. When Liam went to wet the baby's head at the pub with Nat and my dad, I was glad to have some space and peace.

I lay back in my bed with Gene in my arms. I knew there were press outside the hospital. I thought: I hope everything goes okay out there. Liam is very protective of his family and private life. I hoped the press would be kind to him.

NATALIE NICOLE

Outside the hospital, the press took pictures of Liam. They asked him questions.

'How does it feel to be a new dad?'

Liam said: 'I'm like the cow who jumped over the moon.'

I went with Liam and Dad to a pub around the corner. The press were waiting outside. A photographer walked into the pub; he said he did not know Liam was in there. He went into the toilet with his camera around his neck and when he saw Liam, he shoved the camera in Liam's face.

Liam said: 'Get away from me.'

The photographer took another picture and Liam pushed the camera away with his hand. He was having his privacy invaded; it was rude, wrong. Liam left the pub and walked back to the Portland Hospital. Across the street there is a clinic for the blind. Running backwards in front of Liam, trying to take as many snaps as possible, one of the photographers collided with a blind man and his dog and knocked him into the wall. He carried on snapping at Liam regardless.

Liam was furious. So was I, running up the street behind him.

'The poor man. He has no idea what is going on. And you just knocked him over and frightened the dog,' I was screaming at them.

NATALIE NICOLE

It was Nat who told me about it. She came into the room first. Liam was waiting outside.

'Liam got into a row with a photographer,' she said.

On the day of my son's birth; I felt nauseous.

'All they care about is money – and publicity for themselves. I wanted to punch them all,' she said.

'It feels like a circus,' I said.

'The press started with me,' Liam told me. 'It got overheated.'

'I knew something was going to happen,' I said. 'I had a gut feeling.'

I could not even have my baby in peace. Later that day, we found out the photographer in the pub had decided to say Liam hit him and he was suing him. After that, I had Gene in bed with me all the time. I was terrified someone might come into the room and take him. Gene had a big alarm stuck to his heel. He was my baby – but he was a famous baby – someone might want to harm him.

★

When Gene was born, I thought Rob might call or send flowers, but I did not hear anything from him. I know the thought of Gene and me must hurt him. Sometimes I wish I could speak to Rob. We shared so much. We don't have any contact now, but I would like to think that if he ever needed to talk, he would call me. I am Rob's friend. I will always be.

Gene was two days old when I got a call from reception.

'You have a visitor.'

'Who is it?'

'She says her name is Melanie.'

'Melanie who?'

I thought maybe it was Mel C from the Spice Girls. The receptionist checked.

'She's from your band.'

'Are you sure?'

'Yes. She's here to see you.'

My heart started pounding. I had not seen or heard from Mel in eight months, now she was downstairs, wanting to see me. I had just woken up. I needed to change.

'Tell her to give me ten minutes,' I said.

NATALIE NICOLE

Two days after Gene was born, Nic called me.

'Guess what,' she said. 'Guess who's here.'

'Who?'

'Melanie Blatt.'

I was shocked. But only for a moment; I knew, for her own conscience, Mel had to go. Nic was there through everything for Mel – she was always good to her. Mel could not live with herself if she did not visit Nic now she was a mum. She would have felt too guilty.

'Where is she?' I asked.

'She was on her way, but she must have panicked,' Nic said. 'She called from the front desk. I told her to wait ten minutes.'

'You don't have to see her, Nic. Not after what she's done to you.'

'I know,' Nic said. 'But it's too late now. She's on her way up.'

'Okay,' I said. 'Call me as soon as she's gone.'

While I waited for Nic to call me back, I thought a lot about Mel – more than I had in a long time. Mel had problems with me because I was outspoken. She wanted me to do things her way and be quiet about it. That was impossible for me. It was not in my nature. But Nic kept her mouth shut. And she loved Mel and Lilly. Nic still had a picture of Mel and Lilly on the wall in her bedroom. That made me feel so sad. I could not understand how Mel could turn on Nic the way she had. How could anyone let a friend like Nic go?

NATALIE NICOLE

Melanie walked in with Lillyella. She put her arms around me straight away.

'I'm really sorry I was a bitch,' she said. 'I don't want to lose you as a friend.'

Mel looked tearful. I said nothing. I was warm, but together. I just listened warily as she apologized and told me how she felt. Liam was there throughout.

'I heard about your pregnancy on the radio,' Mel told me. 'I went into a shop to buy a bar of chocolate and I

318

heard that you had had a baby boy. I burst into tears and ran out of the shop. Your baby is so beautiful,' Mel said.

Then she filled me in on the details of her life. She, Stuart and Lilly were moving to France. She was doing a single with Artful Dodger – singing on someone else's track. All I did was stare at Lilly. I was shocked by how much she had grown, saddened by how much of her life I had missed. Mel said she was sorry.

'I had to call you – I used to cry every night,' Mel said. 'At one point, Stuart was going to phone for me.'

The old Melanie was back – the one I grew up with, the one who had been my closest friend for more than a decade. But all I could think was: why did it take Gene's birth for her to say sorry?

I thought of all the times during my pregnancy when I would have relished contact with Melanie – someone to discuss pregnancy with, childbirth. My best friend – but when I really needed her she had turned her back. I could not forgive her for not getting in touch with me when I was pregnant. It was too late now. Nine months too late.

Showing up without warning, she expected me to be fine. Mel knew me – what a softie, what a pushover I am. She knew I hated conflict. After all that had happened, all the bitterness and horror, she thought she could show up two days after my son's birth and just reinstate herself in my life. She was utterly convinced I would just accept her apology and go back to being her friend.

I was calm, coolly friendly – I did not want to confront the issues. Melanie was talking about our early days together in the band. But I did not want to talk to her about All Saints – this meeting was not about that. Not about Melanie and her life and her feelings. She was here to visit my child and I wanted that to be the focus. I felt uncomfortable, awkward, trapped. And strangely unemotional. It was like meeting up with an ex — you're reminded of all the good things you had but, at the same time, you know you could never get back together.

The best thing about the visit was seeing Lillyella and I focussed my attention on her. She was eighteen months old. She had grown so much. I felt sad that I was no longer in Lilly's life. My body tensed as I thought again: Lilly is the age my child would have been.

Mel stayed about half an hour.

'Can we meet up?' she asked as she left. 'I'll call you during the week.'

She hugged me again. Tight, warm.

'We can go shopping and have tea. I've really missed you, Nic.'

She looked lighter than when she had come in, happier, more at ease. I hugged Lilly.

When they left, I sighed with relief.

'How was that?' Liam asked me.

'Odd.'

It was all I could think of to say. I sat there in the hospital room with my lover and my new baby boy — this was my life now, the centre of my life. I felt a long way from Mel. A long way from All Saints.

'Mel's apology has come too late,' I told Liam. 'And yet it doesn't matter as much as it did. Not at all.'

'Why's that?' Liam asked me.

'Because Gene is here.'

I had Liam, Gene and a new career to look forward to, I felt complete. And in that moment I hoped that Mel — and Shaznay too — found that completeness within themselves. I wished for them to be happy – as happy as I was.

NATALIE NICOLE

Nic called me straight after Mel left.

'How was it?' I asked.

'I think it helped Mel,' Nic said.

When Mel chose Shaznay over Nicole, she lost someone really special – the person who brought out the humour in her life. She let her best friend go.

'You weren't holding out for Mel to call you – you're happy with your life,' I said. 'It is Mel that is suffering, not you, Nic. This meeting was closure.'

As I said it, I realized I no longer felt any bitterness.

Before we signed our record deal, the four of us were strong both as a group and as friends, but business really did get in the way of our friendships. We were a great band. On stage it really worked; off stage it fell apart. But there is a lot of love there. We went through a lot together.

NATALIE NICOLE

I was booked into the hospital for a week, but I was desperate to take Gene home. At the hospital people were in and out of the room all the time and I hated it. Every time flowers arrived a different nurse would appear – no doubt to take her peek at the famous baby. It made me feel exposed. Also I was certain I could do everything for Gene quite naturally; I hated being told what to do.

After two nights we left. I knew the press were still camped outside and this made me afraid. I felt vulnerable and cumbersome – I could not run from them with a baby in my arms and I had a fear they would overpower me. They are bullies; I am frightened of them – I was afraid something might happen. Once the paparazzi tried to run me off the road and almost caused an accident. My head was filled with fear for my baby.

Liam was protective.

'We'll get you both out safely,' he promised.

The press expected me to stay for a week, so they were not prepared for my early exit. Two cars waited around the back of the hospital with two big security guards. They got me, Gene and Liam into one car and the other followed. I kept Gene covered the whole time until we were inside the flat Liam had rented for us while our house was being renovated.

Home. This was what I wanted. In my own bed with Gene. Our own kitchen, making our own food. I looked at Gene and he looked straight back at me. I had the strangest sensation: it was like he had been here before.

Before my eldest sister Lee was born, Mum and Dad had a son, Nicholas. He died when he was one week old and, since I had been a child, I had felt linked to him. He was the first child born to my parents, I was the last. It was a strange bond. Throughout childhood, whenever we drove past the place where Nicholas was buried, my feet got cold.

I had the sense that spiritually Gene might be Nicholas. Gene might be a reincarnation of my brother who died – a sense that has stayed quietly with me. A life coming through another life.

I breastfed Gene. It was tiring – and hugely painful. On the third day I felt as if someone had stuck a cigarette on my nipples. After the fourth day it got easier and, after that, it was the easiest thing in the world.

I loved waking up in the morning and seeing Gene there. It was such a pleasure.

'Why don't we take Gene out?' Liam suggested. 'We can take him for a walk in the push chair.'

Panic flooded me. It is hard for any new mother – feeling she is being scrutinized in public, losing points for all her mistakes. But being recognized and having people gawp at you just makes it all so much worse. I did not know what to do with a baby in public. I could not bear the thought of being stared at.

'No,' I said. 'Not yet.'

Liam didn't push it. Two days later, Mum got involved.

'There's a barbecue at Rachel's school today,' she told me. 'Why don't you come with Liam and Gene?'

'It will do you good to be out with people,' Liam coaxed.

So, when Gene was four days old, I took him out in public for the first time. I lacked confidence in everything: how to strap Gene into his car seat, driving with him, taking him out. The more I thought about it, the more I was convinced I could not do it. The mind is so powerful – if you feed it negative messages it laps them up. I was freaking myself out.

As we walked into the school I had a panic attack. For the briefest moment I thought: I cannot do this. Then we were bombarded by Rachel's friends – and the whole school.

'He's so beautiful . . . how old is he?'

Surrounded, I worried Gene might not be able to breathe. It took all I had not to scream at them to get away. When Gene needed to be fed, I took him to the car and fed him on the back seat. I felt strained and exhausted after that first trip, but it was useful, necessary.

When I was in hospital, Shaznay's assistant had telephoned to arrange for Shaznay to visit me at home. Shaznay came that afternoon. We talked about Gene, but it felt unnatural, uncomfortable. We were like strangers.

When she left, she said: 'Let's call each other.'

But I knew we never would.

The next day I took Gene for a walk up and down the street. This was to become a daily activity – I was training myself to be out in the world.

When Gene was two weeks old, I took him to Brent Cross shopping centre. People kept coming up to us all the time.

'Is this Gene?'

Everybody knew his name. So much had been written about him in the press and he was still only two weeks old. I took Gene into the baby-changing room at Fenwick's and all the mothers there knew who he was. New mothers bond with each other. We could relate to each other. I felt safe with them. They were not judging me.

It was around then that Liam and I decided to go out for the first time and get drunk together. We went to a restaurant in Hampstead with Kate Thornton, her boyfriend Ritchie, Liam's guitarist, Andy Bell, and his wife, Eda. This was my turn to wet my baby's head. I went for it with tequila.

The next day I woke up with the worst hangover. I could not look after Gene the way I wanted to. It upset me. Liam had a hangover too, but he was happy to sleep

324

it off. Mothers cannot do that. Throughout my fairly saintly pregnancy, I had been looking forward to a time when I could just go wild again. But that first bout of drinking took the edge off me wanting to do it. Hang-overs and caring for a baby are not compatible. I had to make a choice.

I always knew Liam was going to be a good dad. So many men have an attitude around kids of 'Leave me alone, I'm a grown-up'. But I had seen him with Rachel and his other son, Lennon. Even strangers' kids are attracted to Liam. It is as if he has 'child friendly' printed on his forehead.

'You can't be cool around kids,' Liam said. 'Kids make you look uncool.'

Nevertheless, two weeks after Gene was born Liam confessed to me that he had been frightened he might not know how to bond with Gene. He never mentioned it to me while I was pregnant, he kept it to himself, but he was frightened that he might not get on with the new baby.

I was glad Liam told me. I knew it must have been hard for him. My body had nine months to prepare itself for Gene's arrival, but for Liam the connection inevitably came only after Gene was born – after he could see and touch him. I understood that.

'I was scared too,' I told him. 'Would I love my baby?'

'And we both do,' Liam said. 'Big time.'

Liam is besotted with Gene – and with Lennon – and really hands on. He likes being part of a family and helping out. He brings me tea and toast in bed every morning. We are a good team. We are ourselves with each other. We have a very honest relationship and we talk a lot.

When Gene was a month old, I left him with my parents and went with Liam to Japan. Oasis were doing a week of concerts in Japan and Thailand, and Liam and I had arranged this trip while I was pregnant. It seemed a good idea at the time – a precious opportunity for Liam and I to refind the wonder of the connection we had before I fell pregnant. I did not want us to lose that – we had had so little time alone together.

Also, some men can feel pushed out when a baby is born. The mother's attention, naturally, is so pulled towards her new charge that the father may feel redundant, unloved. I knew I talked about Gene twenty-four hours a day, seven days a week. I did not want Liam to feel he was not important to me. Liam is a sensitive person. He likes attention, he likes to be the centre. That was why, hard as it was to leave Gene, I decided I had to go.

I made a video for Gene before I left, and asked Mum to play it to him every day. Making it brought me to tears. I had no such visual record; all the photographs I had of Gene were being developed and all I had was his passport photo. I took that with me, in my purse.

On the way to the airport, I started missing Gene – terribly. I began to think leaving him was not such a good idea. Maybe I should just turn around and go back. Liam could go to Japan on his own. I did not have to go. My mind went to and fro – I did not know what decision to make. Part of me thought I might lose Liam. Liam needed me too.

It will be fine, I told myself. This was just anxiety at parting from Gene. It would all be fine. It was only for a few days and I could not have left him with better people – my mum, my dad and my sisters.

On the aeroplane I was in tears.

'I don't think I made the right decision,' I told Liam, 'leaving Gene.'

'We couldn't have brought him with us, it's too far,' Liam reasoned. 'And we had to make way for our thing. We left Gene with his grandparents,' Liam said. 'Not axe murderers. He's fine.'

Liam's words made sense to my head, but my heart was breaking. As I sat on the plane I began to think that I had all the time in the world to be with Liam but now, when our son was helpless and needing to bond with his mother, was not the right time. I should not have left him. But it was too late to go back.

We made the most of our time in Japan. I had only seen Liam perform a couple of times so it was wonderful to watch him, to see him in action, in his element. The magic that had been between us in the beginning was still there – the total delight in being around each other.

I looked at Gene's photo every day. I called Mum several times every day too.

'How's Gene?'

'He's fine.'

'Is he eating okay?'

'Yes.'

'What about sleeping?'

'That too. He's really fine, Nicole. Don't worry about Gene. Enjoy yourself – have a break.'

But, back in England, the papers were having a field day. I knew what they were saying was right – hadn't I felt it all, every barbed and difficult word of it, moments after I said goodbye to my son? I had made a mistake, a big mistake, but to have it made so public cut deep.

I kept it all in – I did not want to be a drag on Liam. But one night we got drunk together and then I let rip. I did not know what to do with my pain, with the anguish, so I took it out on Liam. I blamed him.

'The press are making me look like a bad mother.' I burst into tears. 'You're not involved with Gene the way I am,' I said. 'It's me who's responsible for him – not you. They don't know how I'm feeling or why I left Gene. It's your fault. If not for you I would never have left him.'

'I didn't make you – it was your idea. It's crazy to feel guilty. Gene is fine. Stop worrying about him.'

'That's easy for you to say,' I retorted. 'I know how I feel. I came out here to be with you and now I've been branded a bad mother.'

'You're not a bad mother,' Liam said. 'You've done nothing wrong.'

I felt so confused and exposed. Public judgement and hatred are hard things to live with – even if your self-esteem is good.

'They say you abandoned Gene, but you left him with his grandmother and aunts,' Liam said. 'They have no right to criticize you.'

Liam hugged me.

'If you make a mistake, you learn from it,' he said, 'and you don't do it again. In future, we will take Gene everywhere with us. End of story.'

We wanted to know whether we could still be Liam and Nic, as we had been before. The thing was, we were no longer Liam and Nic – we were Liam, Nic and Gene. That is what I realized when I left Gene behind. There was no going back, there was no other way. We were a family now. And that was wonderful.

The plane journey back took too long for me. I couldn't wait to be with Gene. I prayed for a safe landing. All I wanted was to be back with him. We arrived home at 5.30 a.m. I telephoned Mum and she brought Gene straight round. When she arrived, I flew down the stairs. In the kitchen, I hugged Gene like I would never let him go.

Two days later, Liam, Gene and I flew to Cannes for Dave Stewart and Anoushka's wedding. Managing the push chair and the other baby paraphernalia was hard work.

Relaxing at last in our seats, we were both grinning.

'It was so nice doing it on our own,' I said.

Liam agreed. We loved it – the feeling of being a young couple just getting on with being a family. We had such fun at the wedding. I am convinced it helped Liam and Gene to bond – the fact that there was not always someone there to take Gene out of his arms and do it 'properly'.

This was our first time away as a family and it pulled us all together – that and being around all the people we loved most.

NATALIE NICOLE

Dave is one of my most favourite people. He has kept a calmness, a beautiful air. Anoushka, too, is remarkable. To be invited to celebrate two fabulous people getting married – and in a place that held such very happy memories for Liam and myself – felt like a gift.

The wedding took place on the beach. As I looked around, I saw the most amazing people: the Rolling

Stones, Dennis Hopper, Belinda Carlisle, Jon Bon Jovi, Natalie Imbruglia, Bono.

We all gathered outside the beach bar – barefoot, as per the invitation's dress code. We had flowers around our necks; we were drinking rum cocktails.

Ten metres into the Mediterranean, there was a canopy on stilts. There were two thrones and Anoushka sat on one. We gathered at the edge of the sea and Dave arrived on a speed boat. He was wearing a white suit and had a crown of flowers.

He joined Anoushka under the canopy and the Indian writer and philosopher Deepak Chopra recited their vows. Dave and Anoushka vowed they would always be free – but connected. It was the most spiritual wedding I had ever been to. It was about love.

Liam stood behind me, his arms around my arms. I could not have felt more content. As I heard the vows, I pretended I was saying them to him – and him to me. You will always be free – and loved.

I wanted to do my Christmas shopping early, so a few weeks later Mum and I went to Brent Cross shopping centre together. It was there we saw the new Mini. It was parked in the middle of the mall as part of an advertising promotion.

'Isn't that cute?' I said, stopping to admire it.

'I'd love one of those,' Mum replied.

'Sit in it,' I encouraged her.

So she did.

It was a mad idea – exciting and wild and utterly mad. The sort of thing you can only do when you have had the success that our band had – the whole point of all that hard work and chaos and messed-up life.

'I want to buy you one,' I said.

'Don't be stupid, Nat.' Mum was appalled. She hates the thought of us spending money on her, but I took the salesman's card.

As soon as I got home, I telephoned Nic.

'She loves it,' I said. 'You should have seen her face. Shall we get Mum and Dad the new Mini for Christmas?'

Nic was as thrilled with the idea as I had been. 'We'll go halves,' she said immediately.

'Yes – and keep it a secret until Christmas Day.'

That set the tone then, for Christmas. A bubbling excitement. Freed from the band and all the put downs and arguments, it was possible to harness all my energies for my family. Present buying was a total joy – and every time Mum and Dad discussed the idea of maybe buying themselves a Mini, Nic and I could barely contain ourselves (but had to run out of the room to scream).

The car was delivered two weeks before Christmas. Black with tinted windows and a sunroof, we stored it in the garage at Liam's house in Essex. When I woke at Liam's house on Christmas morning, I was so excited I felt I might burst. At 9 a.m. Liam, Rachel and I went downstairs to the Christmas tree and opened our presents to each other. Liam had painted me a picture of the rock band Kiss. He is a brilliant artist and a total perfectionist. His present was so beautiful I cried.

It was lovely spending Christmas morning at Liam's. He has designed the interior of the house himself and it is minimal and restful. If Liam had not been a musician, he would have been an architect. He has a real flair for design.

We opened our gifts slowly, savouring them. I had bought Liam a big remote-controlled Cherokee, which

he loved. We had also bought each other lots of senti-
mental additional gifts. Liam's present to Rachel was a
small four-wheeled motorbike. We had hidden it in the
garage so it was a surprise. We took her outside and she
drove round and round in circles. I remembered how,
as a child, I used to love sitting on the lawnmower
because it was the closest I got to having something to
drive. Rachel's present was what I would have loved
most when I was her age.

NATALIE NICOLE

I was also totally excited about Christmas. Liam and I
had moved into our new house only a few weeks before.
After being cramped in a rented flat for six months, it
was great fun to lay out all our things, hang our favourite
pictures on the walls and then decorate like crazy. We
went for a traditional look. Just the way Liam likes it.

Everything we had in our box, we threw on to
our Christmas tree – it was multi-coloured and utterly
uncoordinated. We had lights coming down the staircase
interwoven with bits of fir tree and pine cones. In the
fireplace, we hung three huge stockings.

It was our first Christmas with Gene. After all I had
been through that meant the world to me. The week
before Christmas I started counting down the days and,
on Christmas Eve, I was filled with an excitement I had
not experienced since my teens. Gene slept in-between
Liam and me that night, but I was buzzing so much I
could not sleep. We watched television in bed until
midnight, then Liam and I hugged each other.

'Merry Christmas,' he said.

'Merry Christmas.'

Then we both stared at Gene who was fast asleep.

Gene woke as usual at 6 a.m. All the family were coming to our house for dinner and we had a long day ahead, so I wanted to take it easy. Liam's mum, Peggy, was with us and she started busying herself in the kitchen while we contemplated our stack of presents.

Liam gave me a computer, something I had always wanted, and I got him a black corduroy Burberry coat. We had bought each other loads and loads of knick-knacks – underwear and socks and odd gifts like mugs with funny faces. We bought Gene so many things, all of them wrapped up and laid out around him. We got him a little steering wheel which vibrated and made cute car noises. We also got him chew toys and lots of clothes, but he enjoyed the wrapping paper most of all – it was bright and colourful and he held on to it and got very excited.

Mum and Dad arrived at midday and, while Mum helped Peggy prepare the food, we watched TV. Liam's brother, Noel, arrived soon after and we all watched football and danced around to Christmas songs in the kitchen.

We had the traditional Christmas lunch and pulled crackers. The whole time I was thinking about Mum's face – what it would be like when she saw the gift Nat and I had bought her. Every ten minutes I rang Nat on her mobile.

'Where are you?'

'We're on our way.'

I was so anxious and excited that, in the early afternoon, I put on old skool house music to match my mood. I kept darting to the door, peering out for Nat and the new Mini. As soon as Nat and Liam H pulled up, I ran out of the house to help them bring in their presents while Liam G did his utmost to keep my parents in the house and out of sight. We tied a bow around the car and then I grabbed Mum's hand.

'Come outside,' I said.

When Mum saw the car she didn't say a word. We were all outside, standing on the freezing ground in our socks.

'Mum,' I said. 'It's for you. From me and Nat.'

Mum started crying. She doesn't like us to buy her big things and worries that we might be silly with our money but, for once, we had bought her something that she could not take back or say didn't fit. Dad was hiding his feelings, but I could tell that he was totally chuffed. He took the keys and sat in the driving seat.

'Come on,' he said to Mum. 'Let's go for a ride.'

My sister Lee arrived with her boyfriend, Guy, then Lori with her husband, David, and their son, Frankie. The rest of the afternoon was spent opening presents. There was a toy mound for the children and loads of clothes. I bought Nat tracksuit bottoms and a cashmere top. She got me an anorak with a fur hood and pom poms.

Dad loves smoked salmon so Lori and David had bought him some in weird and expensive packaging. Liam took one look at it and was amazed.

'Who bought your dad pink tights?' he asked.

I couldn't stop laughing.

By eight o'clock I was totally exhausted. Everyone was drunk on B52s. Dad was playing the piano really loudly, so I went to bed and crashed out. But, about an hour later, Liam came to get me, insisting that I come back downstairs to play *The Weakest Link*.

Quite quickly, it became apparent that Liam was the weakest link. Secretly, we all voted him off – and it was hilarious listening to him trying to defend himself. Liam was showing his rough side but nobody minded – we all knew each other so well. We were a family. I looked around; it was the one time in the year when we were all in one room and the sight filled me with joy. Another year and we were all here – healthy and happy. Together.